Development, Security, and Aid

E S T. 75 1938
YEARS
THE UNIVERSITY OF GEORGIA PRESS 2013

GEOGRAPHIES OF JUSTICE AND SOCIAL TRANSFORMATION

SERIES EDITORS

Deborah Cowen, University of Toronto
Nik Heynen, University of Georgia
Melissa W. Wright, Pennsylvania State University

ADVISORY BOARD

Sharad Chari, London School of Economics
Bradon Ellem, University of Sydney
Gillian Hart, University of California, Berkeley
Andrew Herod, University of Georgia
Jennifer Hyndman, York University
Larry Knopp, University of Washington, Tacoma
Heidi Nast, DePaul University
Jamie Peck, University of British Columbia
Frances Fox Piven, City University of New York
Laura Pulido, University of Southern California
Paul Routledge, University of Glasgow
Bobby Wilson, University of Alabama

Development, Security, and Aid

GEOPOLITICS AND GEOECONOMICS AT THE U.S.
AGENCY FOR INTERNATIONAL DEVELOPMENT

JAMEY ESSEX

THE UNIVERSITY OF GEORGIA PRESS
Athens and London

© 2013 by the University of Georgia Press
Athens, Georgia 30602
www.ugapress.org
All rights reserved
Designed by Walton Harris
Set in Minion Pro by Graphic Composition, Inc., Bogart, Georgia
Printed and bound by Thomson-Shore
The paper in this book meets the guidelines for
permanence and durability of the Committee on
Production Guidelines for Book Longevity of the
Council on Library Resources.

Printed in the United States of America
17 16 15 14 13 P 5 4 3 2 1

Library of Congress Cataloging-in-Publication Data

Essex, Jamey, 1977–
    Development, security, and aid : geopolitics and geoeconomics
at the U.S. Agency for International Development / Jamey Essex.
        p. cm. — (Geographies of justice and social transformation)
    Includes bibliographical references and index.
    ISBN-13: 978-0-8203-4247-4 (hbk. : alk. paper)
    ISBN-10: 0-8203-4247-5 (hbk. : alk. paper)
    ISBN-13: 978-0-8203-4454-6 (pbk. : alk. paper)
    ISBN-10: 0-8203-4454-0 (pbk. : alk. paper)
    1. United States. Agency for International Development. 2. Economic
assistance, American. 3. Geopolitics. 4. Economic geography.
5. United States—Foreign economic relations. 6. United States—Foreign
relations. I. Title.
    HC60.E736 2013
    338.91'73—dc23

                                                    2012024591

British Library Cataloging-in-Publication Data available

CONTENTS

ABBREVIATIONS

CBO	Congressional Budget Office
CRS	Congressional Research Service
DCHA	Bureau for Democracy, Conflict, and Humanitarian Assistance
DEC	Development Experience Clearinghouse
DFA	Director of Foreign Assistance
DLF	Development Loan Fund
DoD	United States Department of Defense
DRI	Diplomatic Readiness Initiative
ECA	Economic Cooperation Agency
EGAT	Bureau for Economic Growth, Agriculture, and Trade
ESF	Economic Support Funds
FAA	Foreign Assistance Act (of 1961, amended)
FAS	Foreign Agricultural Service
FTF	Feed the Future
GAO	General Accounting Office/Government Accountability Office (after 2004)
GATT	General Agreement on Tariffs and Trade
GH	Bureau for Global Health
ICA	International Cooperation Agency
IDCA	International Development Cooperation Agency
IMF	International Monetary Fund
LDC	least developed country
MCC	Millennium Challenge Corporation
MDG	Millennium Development Goals
NGO	nongovernmental organization
NSS	National Security Strategy of the United States
OCO	Overseas Contingency Operations
ODA	official development assistance
OPIC	Overseas Private Investment Corporation
OSS	Office of Strategic Services
PL 480	Public Law 480 (U.S. food aid program)
PPD	Presidential Policy Directive
PPDA	Peace, Prosperity, and Democracy Act of 1994
PVO	private voluntary organization

QDDR	Quadrennial Diplomacy and Development Review
RIF	reduction in force
TCB	trade capacity building
USAID	United States Agency for International Development
USDA	United States Department of Agriculture
USTR	Office of the United States Trade Representative
WFP	World Food Programme
WTO	World Trade Organization

ACKNOWLEDGMENTS

In the sabbatical application I submitted to my department and dean in August 2010, I stated that my primary sabbatical project for the 2011–2012 academic year, when I could put aside teaching duties and departmental meetings for several months to write uninterrupted, would be to complete a book on the U.S. Agency for International Development. Rather than waiting for my sabbatical to start, I actually began work on it in late 2010, in order to submit the manuscript proposal in early 2011. While I had initially envisioned myself sitting down, starting on page 1, and ending on page whatever, in a discrete linear process with a clear beginning and a definitive end, I quickly realized it wasn't going to work that way. While I did do the bulk of the writing in summer and fall 2011, I realized then that the writing process actually began long ago, and that no work is ever totally and finally "finished." I revisited, repurposed, or revised pieces I wrote several years prior, including not only previously published articles that had appeared in *Geoforum* and *Antipode*, but also portions of my PhD dissertation, which I completed in 2005 in Syracuse University's Department of Geography. I even found myself digging out notebooks from my dissertation research, full of quotations copied from microfiche that I had spent hours staring at in the Science, Industry, and Business Library branch of the New York Public Library. I returned to government documents and reports, congressional hearings, and interview transcripts that I had already read numerous times before, and I found silences, gaps, and missing pieces that I had overlooked or not uncovered in past research. I also discovered, somewhat to my astonishment, that I actually enjoy reading grainy, decades-old government reports with handwritten notes scrawled across their margins and scanned so that they appear on the computer screen at a slightly oblique angle.

Having now more or less completed the book, I am reminded of all those who assisted and supported me in past research and writing that made its way into this volume, and I am thankful to all who helped me as I worked out new ideas, arguments, and written material. First, I am grateful to my institution, the University of Windsor, and my faculty union, the Windsor University Faculty Association, for the opportunity provided by the sabbatical I enjoyed during the 2011–2012 academic year. Without the time away from teaching and service work this sabbatical provided, I could not have contributed the kind of focused time and energy it took to write this book. The university also provided support in the form of a Humanities and Social Sciences Research Grant in 2006, which funded research that went into the previously published pieces incorporated into this book, and managed the Standard Research Grant I received in 2010 from the Social Sciences and Humanities Research Council of Canada (SSHRC) for research related to material in chapters 2, 3, and 5.

As noted, this book contains material previously published in articles in *Antipode* ("The Neoliberalization of Development: Trade Capacity Building and Security at the U.S. Agency for International Development," appearing in vol. 40, no. 2, in 2008) and *Geoforum* ("Deservedness, Development, and the State: Geographic Categorization in the U.S. Agency for International Development's Foreign Assistance Framework," appearing in vol. 39, no. 4, also in 2008). These are both incorporated into chapter 4, though a short section of the *Antipode* article also appears in chapter 2. I am grateful to Wiley-Blackwell and Elsevier, respectively, for granting permission to republish these works in adapted, updated form here. Short sections of my PhD dissertation, titled *The State as Site and Strategy: Neoliberalization, Internationalization, and the Foreign Agricultural Service*, appear in an adapted format in chapters 2 and 3. I reiterate my thanks to all those who provided support and feedback on those articles in their original formats, and to the members of my dissertation committee: Gavin Bridge, Noel Castree, Jim Glassman, Scott Kirsch, Don Mitchell, Beverley Mullings, Tom Perreault, Scott Prudham, Katharine Rankin, Susan Roberts, Mark Rupert, and Tod Rutherford; several anonymous reviewers; and my research assistant Brian Fox. Thanks also should be extended to those anonymous USAID staff who allowed me to interview them for the research that went into the two articles noted above, as well as to those devoted staff who help make the agency remarkably open to public scrutiny and the kind of critical analysis I attempt in this book.

Many others are in line for my thanks and gratitude for their support and feedback during the research and writing for this book over the last two years. My departmental and institutional colleagues at the University of Windsor (as well as those who have moved on to other universities in recent years) have been supportive in numerous different ways, providing sounding boards, ideas, and, at times, much-needed coffee breaks. The administrative staff in the Department of Political Science office and the university's Office of Research Services have been indispensable. Uri Marantz, who served as my research assistant in fall 2010, also deserves thanks for his assistance on this project, as do those numerous master's and undergraduate students in my courses who have prompted me to think not only about the arguments I make in this book but also why they matter.

A shorter version of chapter 5 was first presented as a conference paper at the 2011 annual meeting of the Association of American Geographers, held in Seattle, Washington. I received valuable feedback from and had an excellent and lively discussion with the other participants during and following our paper session—Ed Carr, Lucy Jarosz, Emma Mawdsley, and Susan Roberts—and benefited from conversations before, during, and after that conference with Lisa Bhungalia.

I am also exceedingly grateful for the hospitality and support I received from friends in the Washington, D.C., area who hosted me during research trips to the capital region in 2006, 2008, and 2010. Jim Ketchum and Melissa Hamby, Susan Austin, and Aman Luthra opened their homes to me, while Carolyn Gallaher and Katie Wells also helped make my time in Washington much more enjoyable and productive. Numerous other friends and colleagues have shaped my thinking on the ideas and arguments presented in this book, and on writing and career development more generally, and helped me maintain my roots in geography as I entrenched myself in a political science department. Matt Farish, Laam Hae, Matt Huber, Clayton Rosati, Bob Ross, and Patrick Vitale, among many others, have contributed to that project.

Derek Krissof and the editorial board and production staff at the University of Georgia Press have been extremely helpful and reliable in helping me move this book along smoothly and at a brisk pace, and I am grateful to the support they have provided. I also thank the press's anonymous reviewers for their comments and suggestions on the manuscript.

Last but of course not least, I thank my family for their unending support and love. My parents, Tommy and Flo, and my sister and brother-in-law, Heather and Tyler, have provided encouragement and lots of questions, as well as welcome respites from work during visits home in Kentucky. While a good deal of this book was written while sitting at my kitchen table, I actually completed most of it during an extended stay in Berlin, Germany. This was possible not only because I was on sabbatical but also thanks to the hospitality and kindness of family and friends in Berlin, where Regine, Christian, Geli, Renate, Josephine, and many others made our time there thoroughly enjoyable, even if it was far too brief. Most importantly, my partner Janina has endured my writing process with amazing patience and humor and helped me keep an even keel throughout, dragging me away from the computer and into the outdoors when necessary, and providing me always with love, kindness, laughs, and a wide assortment of baked goods. My greatest thanks are reserved for her.

Development, Security, and Aid

CHAPTER ONE

"One-Half of 1%"

Geopolitics, Geoeconomics, and USAID

VISITORS TO THE PUBLIC INFORMATION CENTER of the U.S. Agency for International Development (USAID), in downtown Washington's Ronald Reagan Building, are greeted by the words "one-half of 1%," bolted to the lobby wall in letters fashioned out of wood from official aid shipment crates (see figure 1). The small sign in front of this somewhat strange message indicates that "one-half of 1%" represents USAID's share of the federal budget, a rather paltry sum dwarfed by the amount of federal money budgeted annually for military expenditures and servicing the national debt. The return on this minuscule budgetary outlay, the sign states, "is one of the best values for [the] U.S. taxpayer's dollar." I first encountered this display in July 2006, when visiting the Public Information Center while doing research on USAID; it still adorned the lobby wall when I arrived for a second visit in August 2008. When I returned for a third time in July 2010, the wall featured instead a large poster detailing USAID emergency aid programs in Haiti following the devastating earthquake in that country several months prior. When I asked the receptionist whether the "one-half of 1%" lettering had been removed, she laughed and said no, it remained intact under the Haiti poster.

The relative permanence of this budget line at (more or less) one-half of 1 percent of federal government spending, and its announcement as the first message encountered on entering the information center, speaks to USAID's position within the U.S. state and the agency's confidence in its mandate, mission, and standing.[1] The defensiveness with which the agency declares both its relatively minuscule budget and its broad impact, and the juxtaposition of these against one another, offers a glimpse into the deeper and more complex web of inter- and intrastate relations that have shaped USAID's institutional and political evolution across a wide range of geographic locales and strategic activities. The agency itself is an important global actor in the political economy of development, and a critical geographical and historical examination of the agency highlights the uncertain and winding path of official development practices and discourses, strategic decision making within the state, and the sociopolitical

1

FIGURE 1. One-half of 1%. The phrase "one-half of 1%" is bolted to the lobby wall in USAID's Public Information Center in Washington, D.C.'s Ronald Reagan Building. (Photo by author.)

and economic forces that align themselves with particular political, state, and hegemonic projects. This work focuses on the tangled web of relations, projects, and practices shaped by USAID and which in turn shape the agency. My analysis builds from two conceptual frameworks, one regarding the structure of the capitalist state, the other dealing with intertwined but distinct, sometimes complementary, sometimes competing "geostrategic discourses" of geopolitics and geoeconomics.

It is important to note the active work geostrategic discourses perform, and the work of "geo-graphing" that goes into making and reproducing them in a world of ever-shifting contexts (Sparke 2005). Discourses do not, of course, drop from the sky fully formed, and they are useful and powerful to the extent that they circulate and shape how political, economic, and other social agents see and make the world and their place within it. As Lawson (2007, 40) summarizes in her examination of the making and remaking of development geographies, "Discourses are both socially produced and socially producing—bound up in intimate power relations with the institutions and societies that they describe." Geopolitics and geoeconomics comprise two distinct but interrelated discourses guiding state strategies and policies, and they provide powerful frameworks for shaping how development-oriented actors such as USAID, as well as the objects of its development strategies and programs, view the world and act upon it.

Most crucial for my examination are the distinctions between and intersections of geopolitics and geoeconomics as forms of geostrategic discourse and how these shape state- and scale-making practices. The demarcation and strategic positioning of territorial states within an international state system girded by capitalist economic relations has long formed the corpus of geopolitics. Geopolitical logic has served as the basis not only for statecraft, military strategy, and development intervention (Slater 1993) but also for popular geographical imaginations and views of world order; a deconstructive analysis of this logic grounds the contemporary subfield of critical geopolitics (for overviews and representative discussions, see Dalby 2008; Ingram and Dodds 2009; Ó Tuathail 1996). The term *geoeconomics*, on the other hand, stems initially from the work of security consultant Edward Luttwak (1990), who coined it in response to an emergent post–Cold War order in which, he argued, national economic position in a brutally efficient world economy would trump military strength as the primary ordering mechanism for the state system. As a set of discursive constructs and a platform for devising political and economic strategies and policy, geoeconomics concentrates on "building international partnerships that advance 'harmonization,' 'efficiency,' 'economic leverage' and 'growth' against the supposed threats of political 'radicalism,' 'anachronism' and 'anarchy'" (Sparke and Lawson 2007, 316). Although Luttwak's usage of the term continues to circulate in official policy, pundit, and defense circles (see Barnett 2004, 2006, 2009), the underlying concept now not only functions to inform the exclusive and narrow realm of national and global security strategy formation, especially where making "better" U.S. policy is concerned, but also serves as a broad descriptor of a distinct vision of international relations, social and spatial order, and political economic connectivity.

My emphasis on geostrategic discourses, and especially on geopolitics and geoeconomics, follows from a growing body of critical work that interrogates how discourses produce, reproduce, and frame connections, processes, and flows between places and across scales and how such framings circulate and shape strategic decision making, not just by powerful actors and institutions but also by those challenging dominant power relations and working toward oppositional and alternative projects (Cowen and Smith 2009; Gregory 2004; Power 2003; Roberts, Secor, and Sparke 2003; Sparke 2005; Sparke and Lawson 2007). In addition, Matthew Sparke's (2007b, 338) work detailing geographers' responsibility to engage in critical analysis of how geographical relationships and understandings are made "by multiple, often unnoticed space-making processes and space-framing assumptions" also underlies the approach I take (see also Jackson, Ward, and Russell 2008; Massey 2004; Sparke 2007a).

Despite USAID's importance as a global development actor and a major component of U.S. foreign policy strategies since the early Cold War era, geographers have not carried out a sustained and focused examination of the organization's inner workings and external relations. The agency is one of the most deeply internationalized institutions within the U.S. state, with staff stationed at field sites and embassies around the world and in Washington and a mandate to promote economic and political development in developing states in line with U.S. foreign policy objectives. The agency therefore provides a window into geostrategic thinking and action from within the heart of the American state. The tensions, compromises, and contradictions driving the development and deployment of geostrategic discourses are written into the very structure and character of USAID. This likewise demonstrates the constrained evolution of mainstream postwar development theory and practice and the creation and reproduction of the Third World/Global South as a geographic space in need of development intervention.

Attention to how USAID works from, reproduces, and is limited by its geostrategic assumptions and framings, and what this has meant for theorizations and practices of development more broadly, is crucial in the context of global interdependence and crisis. On one hand, USAID views recent global economic, financial, and food crises as evidence of the need for further development intervention, largely under the geoeconomic rubric of neoliberal globalization and geopolitical considerations linked to the "global war on terror" framing underdevelopment as a breeding ground for state failure, international crime, and terrorism. On the other hand, the lack of development progress and the geoeconomic push for further global integration and openness has meant prolonged crisis and reform within USAID itself, as it works to reposition itself alongside other U.S. state institutions with a stake in development aid and programming and within the expanding nexus of civil society and private channels of development and humanitarian assistance that make up the "global aid architecture."

A critical geographical analysis of geostrategic discourses thus comprises an effort to understand how this architecture is structured and structuring and how powerful, even hegemonic, forms of discourse shape and are shaped by the institutions composing it. The path of geopolitical and geoeconomic discourses as they relate to development assistance and institutions such as USAID, however, should not be understood as a crude chronological progression from the geopolitics of Cold War developmentalism to the geoeconomic rhetoric of "borderlessness" that marks contemporary neoliberal globalization. Indeed, as Neil Smith (2003, 457) demonstrates in his analysis of twentieth-century American imperialism, "the transition to a 'geo-economic globalism' was not initiated at the end of the American [twentieth] Century but marks the crucial break with territorial expansionism at its beginning." The considerable historical and geographical overlap between these two broad geostrategic discourses and the imperial practices they inform and underwrite stands as much more prevalent than any temporal or spatial disconnect between them. While the remainder of this work illustrates that the temporary dominance of one discourse and associated institutional configurations over the other can be periodized to some degree, the historical trajectory remains rooted in a complex intertwining and in the institutional materiality of USAID and the American state.

In pursuing my examination in this way, I intend, as Cowen and Smith (2009, 24–25, emphasis in original) do, to "trace the emergence of a political-geographic logic of economy, security and power somewhat at variance with that proposed by geopolitics," and which *"recasts rather than simply replaces geopolitical calculation."* Most importantly, Cowen and Smith (2009, 25) emphasize consideration of the "geopolitical social" and "geoeconomic social," or the ways in which the ordered logic of strategic discourses and their attendant practices and institutions are central to both the creation and defense of a clearly bounded national territory, and "the making of national social order." In their view, the geopolitical social has dissolved and been reconfigured in favor of a new geoeconomic social and spatial logic, such that geopolitics is "dead but dominant" as a mode of explanation and sociospatial ordering; I will return to this point in the concluding chapter, but for now the (attempted) totalizing, ordering logics that animate geopolitics and geoeconomics deserve further attention (Cowen and Smith 2009, 23).

As discursive formations and platforms for articulating and enacting political economic strategies, geoeconomics differs from but meshes with geopolitics. Each emphasizes specific but related aspects of the many geographic, social, political, and economic relationships that form between places, across scales, and through extensive formal and informal networks and institutions. While *geoeconomics* itself is a relatively new term, the recognition that a deterritorializing logic of economic connection exists alongside and, at turns, intertwines with and contradicts a territorializing logic of political control and closure is not confined to Luttwak and his critics (see Arrighi 1994; Glassman 2005a; Harvey 2003) and can be studied across multiple historical and institutional contexts. Agnew (1994, 2005a, 2005b) and Agnew and Corbridge (1995), for example, provide a theorization of territoriality and sovereignty that highlights the historical development of state sovereignty on the basis of territorial control as well as the specific conditions of American hegemony in the context of globalization and what they term the global *geopolitical economy*. While I return to the question of American hegemony and imperialism more fully in later chapters, it suffices to note here that the state, or at least the legitimate exercise of state power, and the scalar and spatial foundations of the state and statecraft are shifting terms of debate and analysis in contemporary geopolitical practice. This is in large part due to the incompleteness and contingency of territorial control and the inability of discursive framings linking globalization, state power, and political economic change to keep pace with the social and geographical realities of these processes.

Roberts, Secor, and Sparke (2003) have argued that the period just prior to and following the terrorist attacks of September 11, 2001, are defined by the emergence of "neoliberal geopolitics." They use this term to refer to a system of discourse and practice in which an overriding geopolitical concern with security, couched especially in terms of the global war on terror and enacted through new forms of managing global-local connectivity, has coalesced (steadily but uneasily) with a geoeconomic emphasis on unfettered flows of trade and investment in a liberalized world market system. Mitchell (2010, 289), meanwhile, emphasizes the geostrategic power of enframing language, noting that the "imaginative geopolitical scripting of the neoliberal era . . . has moved from a Cold War conceptualization of security attained through effective spatial containment, to an idea of security won through effective spatial administration." Again, however, the problem of temporal and geographical reductionism must be avoided, as these discourses of security do not simply supplant one another over time or space in a linear fashion. To return once more to Cowen and Smith (2009, 24), we must be careful not to frame geopolitics and geoeconomics as entirely distinct from one another in their historical evolution or in their spatial and geographical exercise; they thus argue that the emphasis on geostrategic discourses in Sparke's work, and in much critical geopolitics, "begs rather than answers the question of the historically and geographically specific life of geopolitics as practice and discourse."

Examining the discursive making of worlds through the production, reproduction, and deployment of geostrategic discourses is therefore necessary but insufficient for adequately capturing how USAID operates with respect specifically to the political economy of development. The tensions between coeval but competing geostrategic understandings of the world, and how they are integral to the making and remaking of USAID's institutional structure, strategic decision making, and political and economic position, are the primary focus of this work, which attempts to reconcile the multiple threads outlined above with respect to geopolitical and geoeconomic discourse and practice. To accomplish this, I also employ a second framework, which places state institutions and their chosen strategies within the larger nexus of a global capitalist political economy, without treating particular institutional actors' decision making in a deterministic manner or assuming all strategies or decisions are made according to either endogenous institutional interests or exogenous rules and interests dictated from the towering heights of economic control. This is important so as not to lose sight of development as understood and practiced by USAID, and indeed by the global development industry that includes state agencies like USAID as well as international and intergovernmental bodies, NGOs, private charities, and capitalist firms working simultaneously across several scales and in a multitude of sites. Using this framework, which stems from a Marxian political economy perspective on the contemporary state, and especially the "strategic relational approach" as outlined by Jessop (1990, 2000, 2001a, 2001b, 2002a, 2002b, 2008), I examine USAID in its "triple identity": as one particularly important *site* among many within the U.S. state for articulating relations with and within the Global South, the global aid architecture, and the United States itself; as a *product of strategies* used by social forces intertwined with the agencies and functions of the state; and finally as a *generator of strategies*, albeit in constrained and sometimes contradictory ways (Glassman 1999; Glassman and Samatar 1997).

This approach has the benefit of focusing analysis on the *strategic selectivity* of political economic actors, which Jessop (2002a, 40) defines as the "ways in which the state considered as a social ensemble has a specific, differential impact on the ability of various political forces to pursue particular interests and strategies in specific spatio-temporal contexts through their access to and/or control over given state capacities." The strength and ability to exercise these capacities are neither inherent nor completely endogenous to the state or its institutional components, as they "always depend for their effectiveness on links to forces and powers that exist and operate beyond the state's formal boundaries" (Jessop 2002a, 40). In other words, I examine the production, reproduction, and use of geostrategic discourses within and through USAID not just by focusing on the content of the discourses themselves and how they frame the geography of development intervention but also by concentrating on how the agency selects strategies and policies from the options ostensibly available to it. As I demonstrate in subsequent chapters, USAID has been prone to shifting political and economic winds since its establishment in 1961, and the meaning and practice of development interventions the agency has undertaken have changed accordingly. This has not been a simple one-way causal relationship, however, and this approach to understanding state institutions also ensures that the analysis of USAID remains reflexive, highlighting the dynamic, mutually constitutive relationship between geostrategic discourses and the institutions using them. The overlaps and tensions between geopolitics and geoeconomics stand not only as abstract framings and conceptions of global relations and the conundrums of development relative to world order but also as the ideological and material underpinnings of USAID's strategic selectivity. The actual exercise of this strategic selectivity, in turn, has shaped how these discourses operate and relate both to one another and to development more generally. The agency's relationship with and use of geopolitics and geoeconomics in forming and enacting its development and aid strategies indicates the link between effective *spatial* administration and effective *institutional* administration across the multiple components and social forces that make up and animate the state.

The argument that follows addresses historical and political economic shifts between specific geostrategic approaches to development as practiced by and articulated through USAID and how such shifts relate to the institutional relationships that make the agency what it is. By this, I mean the institutionalized understandings of development broadly writ, and of the agency's own operation and mandate, that hold sway in and around USAID. The exact terms and articulation of this relationship are not pregiven by the agency's mere existence as an instrument for the global projection of American power. As an internationally oriented state institution with a goal of promoting economic and political development in line with U.S. foreign policy objectives, USAID is itself the product of numerous strategies adopted by other political and economic actors and forces (including other state agencies but also private capital, NGOs and civil society, and the objects of development intervention) and, as noted, a generator of strategies as well. Indeed, the way USAID "does" development significantly shapes the global development industry, even as the agency often has found itself in a rather weak and precarious political position relative to other actors, such as Congress, the State Department, and (more recently) the Department of Defense. These other actors themselves exhibit a triple identity as outlined above. The agency has on many occasions acted as a site for reworking the relations between such other actors with a stake in foreign policy, aid policy, and development strategies. In fact, USAID performs these roles—generator of strategies, product of strategies, and site of articulation—all at the same time. The focus here on how USAID has been subject and object of geostrategic discourses pulls apart these roles and provides a basis to analyze them both separately and in relation to one another.

Geostrategic Approaches to Development

In examining the institutional and historical specificities of usaid, I also address the broader question of how geostrategic discourses have shaped development theory and practice. This is likewise not a one-way street, in which geopolitical and geoeconomic discourses, framings, and practices determine once and for all the character, path, and outcome of development interventions and processes. Rather, as Lawson (2007, 80, emphasis in original) argues, mainstream development is better understood as "the coming together of geopolitical strategies, academic theories and actions in particular places in ways that *cannot be predicted in advance.*" The contingent nature of development in action, with the work across places, institutions, and scales that such action implies, occurs always within a set of material and intellectual conditions that shape how such action proceeds. Geopolitical and geoeconomic discourses are part and parcel of these conditions, and they have helped to shape development interventions by usaid, and development theory more generally, by framing how the actors involved understand sociospatial relations, and how they inform, incorporate, curtail, and legitimize certain forms of development intervention and assistance. In similar fashion, mainstream development discourse has shaped the geopolitical and geoeconomic realities in which development intervention is undertaken and so shape these geostrategic discourses through the particular configurations and actions of class-relevant social forces aligned with different geostrategic visions and projects (Glassman 2011).

For example, during the years immediately following World War II and into the early phase of the Cold War, Western theorists and practitioners of mainstream official development framed the process of development, their participation within it, and actual and preferred sociospatial orders largely in terms of the specter of communism and the need to foment modernization via capitalist economic growth and formal political democratization. The actual engagement that followed from this understanding of development was largely, though not completely, defined within the logic and assumptions of a specific Cold War geopolitics (see chapter 2), particularly as usaid and its predecessor and partnering agencies sought strategic sites for intervention in Europe, Latin America, and newly independent states in Africa, Asia, and the Middle East. How such development interventions actually occurred, and whether they were successful or not, was not easily predicted, and years of development aid and engagement in some locales proved frustratingly ineffective under the rubric of geopolitics that shaped them. This in turn forced reconsideration of and changes within geopolitics as a discursive framework directing development intervention through and by USAID, even as geoeconomic approaches, framings, and logics developed alongside of and intermeshed with geopolitical ones (see chapters 3 and 4). The contingency of institutional and political economic processes, of the exact contours and interactions of different discursive formations, and most of all of development success, all conspire to prevent easy analyses of development, its subjects, and its proponents.

Gillian Hart's (2002) discussion of articulation, as conceptualized by Antonio Gramsci and Stuart Hall, provides some theoretical grounding for how this analysis of USAID informs a broader analysis of development theory and action. In her reading of recent work on development from within critical development studies and development geography, Hart (2001, 2002, 2004) highlights the importance of material and conceptual inseparability in how the subjects of development make sense of, critique, and struggle against development processes. Importantly, this is also a struggle *within* the contexts and confines of these processes, as the emphasis on articulation points to the ways in which categories of understanding and meaning-making processes are always inextricably linked to forms and practices of domination that cannot be escaped or overturned simply by thinking differently or creating new abstractions or categorizations of social complexity. Hart (2002, 819) describes the stakes of this seemingly confounding academic exercise in defining and highlighting articulation in more robust political terms, arguing that a focus on articulation "in its extended sense . . . is useful not only in clarifying diverse and interrelated trajectories of sociospatial change but also in suggesting how struggles in different sociospatial arenas and across spatial scales might link with one another." Peering into the inner workings and external relations of USAID is one means of examining how such articulation occurs in relation to development—in other words, how development practice and theory have made one another, as structured by and through the institutional terrain of the U.S. state, and via broad discursive formations and strategic logics of geopolitics and geoeconomics.

Of course, the strategies, ideas, and projects that have driven and defined USAID's development work do not exhaust the realm of potential readings or practices of development, nor is the total history of postwar development perfectly captured by reference to USAID alone. Development is a contested terrain, with no consensus on its meaning, and certainly not on how best to achieve or maintain it. Stating such an obvious fact has become rote in critical development studies, but we are still faced with a dual task of making sense of development's tangled history and of providing some political, economic, and social ground for articulation as discussed above. If we return once more to Hart's work, the historical and geographic evolution of USAID offers a useful case study for examining two distinct but inextricably intertwined meanings of development: "'big D' Development defined as a post–second world war project of intervention in the 'third world' that emerged in the context of decolonization and the Cold War, and 'little d' development or the development of capitalism as a geographically uneven, profoundly contradictory set of historical processes" (Hart 2001, 650). The agency worked to articulate these two forms of development: large-scale intervention in line with particular political, state, and hegemonic projects emanating from U.S.-defined foreign policy and economic objectives and priorities; and development as an immanent process of capitalist growth and modernization, unfolding in a straight historical and geographical line from traditional preindustrial society to modern industrial, urban, westernized society. Yet the path of development never did run true, and this differentiation between *development* and *Development* requires, as Hart makes clear, historicizing the intellectual, institutional, and political economic interventions made and approaches employed.

In the remainder of this volume, I combine such historical analysis of USAID with attention to the space-making assumptions and processes that form the geostrategic backbone of the agency's work of articulation and development intervention. Interested from its origins in proving its worth as an agency capable of creating a better world defined by capitalist economic growth, material improvement in daily life, and a new modern ethic of rational individual self-interest in underdeveloped countries, it has also long sought to prove to detractors and advocates in the United States that it could do all this while advancing American foreign policy interests. The agency must balance several different and sometimes incommensurate strategic objectives, all under the rubric of development, against the larger strategic initiatives and priorities of the U.S. state and the interests of other development actors. Struggles with other agencies, elements of capital, and NGOs over the appropriate structure and deployment of USAID's resources have marked much of the agency's history and have significantly shaped how many working within and with it have understood USAID's mandate and how the agency is to fulfill it. This history also rests on a rather stable internal consensus on the basic elements and foundational principles of development, and how the practices and strategies of Development, as carried out by USAID, are to foment this process. While the trajectory of Development, and the relationship of such top-down intervention to development as process, has been destabilized by several factors discussed throughout the following chapters, USAID has long formed a primary mechanism of this articulation. The juxtaposition of conflict and consensus in and around the agency, and how agency staff emphasize the latter over the former in understanding and carrying out their work, was made clear to me in a July 2006 interview I conducted with a former USAID staff member, who had recently moved to another U.S. government agency. When I asked several questions about ongoing debates in USAID and the development policy community about the meaning and objectives of development, my interviewee stated that "consensus is the bane of academics, but it's the milk of policy makers."

Consensus was not always readily apparent in talking to other USAID staff, however, and the political and institutional pressures the agency has faced since the Cold War's end indicate that not everyone in the U.S. state sees development and USAID in the same light. The agency has dealt with numerous rounds of "streamlining," cuts, and reorganization over the years, and especially since the Cold War's end. A broad shift from geopolitical to geoeconomic calculation as the primary organizing and framing force for and within USAID occurred from the 1970s onward, picking up steam in the 1980s and becoming dominant through the 1990s. In the wake of the terrorist attacks of September 11, 2001, geopolitical aspects of development have been reasserted and rearticulated with geoeconomic aspects as development, along with defense and diplomacy, became a central plank of U.S. national security strategies under the George W. Bush administration. This so-called 3Ds approach to globalization, national security, and development progress has since become a new orthodoxy for the U.S. development policy community under President Barack Obama and Secretary of State Hillary Clinton. Like other global development institutions, however, USAID has had to work more closely with a range of NGOs, private charitable foundations, and even social movement actors, not all of which are easily positioned or accounted for in a geopolitics/geoeconomics framework. Likewise, not all of these varied actors are particularly happy about or welcome to participate in a development agenda that appears to many subsumed under the foreign policy and national security priorities of the U.S. government.

In practical research terms, the work undertaken to map out and make sense of USAID's place and role in the overlapping and sometimes contradictory articulations of development has drawn heavily on primary and secondary sources in the form of published documents and reports from U.S. government and development partner sources, with a handful of direct interviews and USAID interviews to back and direct analysis of these sources. As I noted above, the agency is both crystal-clear and defiantly opaque in how it presents itself and its work, and my struggle to obtain interviews with key insiders highlighted the tensions over form and process that comprise the flip side of the internal consensus on appropriate development. While it was surprisingly easy to obtain detailed reports, strategy documents, and other printed materials covering several decades and numerous projects and programs (indeed, USAID makes much of this material readily available for free over the Internet), actually talking to USAID staff about their work and the processes by which such reports and strategies are produced was a different story altogether. There is no reward for talking to a researcher who aims clearly to critique one's institutional employer and life's work, and little incentive to let an outsider in on how discussion and debate proceed within the agency as well as between it and its institutional partners within the U.S. state (especially those who are competitors for funding and clout). Perhaps such difficulties were due to my limited contact with USAID insiders, and an attendant lack of trust that would otherwise come from sustained personal contact and work with agency staff. Agency officials have little problem talking to other USAID staff, however, and my limited direct interview material is backed by several interviews with and by agency retirees conducted as part of the Foreign Affairs Oral History Program, managed by the Association for Diplomatic Studies and Training (ADST) in Arlington, Virginia.[2]

Snippets of conversations that took place over the phone in the USAID Public Information Center, or were overheard in the Reagan Building food court, where USAID staff eat hurried fast-food lunches alongside hordes of tourists, or with a contact who finally returned my call after almost a dozen attempts to reach him, pointed to deep reservations about the agency's future in a development system increasingly dominated by security-minded officials and numerous layers of subcontracting. These sources also emphasized USAID's strengths, especially the agency's vast field-level expertise in developing countries and capacity for anticipating critiques. Yet the familiar refrain of "one-half of 1%" that met me with each return trip to the agency's offices, and all that this figure and its announcement on USAID's public face implies, reinforces that the agency is part of an ongoing and contingent project of development, framed and enacted within broader geostrategic discourses of social and spatial order, and which practitioners themselves do not necessarily control or fully understand.

Layout of This Study

The remainder of this volume addresses USAID's place in the complex processes of articulation, development, and state institutional restructuring across historical and thematic axes, emphasizing the geostrategic character of the agency's work, its internal cohesion and structure, and its external relations with other development and foreign policy actors and institutions. This begins in the next chapter with a more detailed historical overview of USAID in order to demonstrate how, at its inception in the early 1960s and through the mid-1970s, a complex relationship between geopolitical and geoeconomic visions of world order and appropriate state action was written into the agency's mandate and structure. The geoeconomic was routinely subverted to the primacy of geopolitical frames and goals, though both discourses are evident in the agency's development throughout the Cold War period. Without wishing to repeat the conclusions of multiple other studies of USAID and American development strategies during this time, I concentrate on how development aid managed by USAID served instrumental political and economic purposes while also advancing an ideological commitment to what an early agency publication termed a "rational humanism" that, it was expected, would foster "individual choice, initiative and development" under American tutelage (USAID 1962, 22). Almost from its outset, however, conflicting pressures beset the agency, as economic, political, and humanitarian objectives and forces clashed within its institutional structure.

Chapter 3 moves the analysis to the aftermath of the Vietnam War, the late stages of the Cold War, and the double crisis of development geopolitics and of geopolitical development. By the 1970s and into the 1980s, the geopolitical framing of development within the U.S. state was beginning to face serious challenges from a more distinctly geoeconomic conceptualization of state action and appropriate development. It was during this era that neoliberalization took firm root within development theory and practice, with profound implications for USAID. Struggling with its mandate and buffeted from several sides by forces and actors hostile to its mission and even its very existence, USAID worked at the center of a significant transition in development thought and practice, accompanied by shifts in both the structure of the international state system and the geostrategic basis for American hegemony. The uneasy convergence of and competition between geopolitical and geoeconomic strategies of development and aid precipitated an institutional crisis for the agency, as USAID's mandate, purpose, and scope of action came under intense scrutiny from internationalizing fractions of capital, other arms of the U.S. state, and new challenges and movements on the ground in developing states. The agency became one important site through which a geoeconomic reconceptualization of aid and development, tied closely to processes of neoliberalization, was worked out against and amid the collapse of the Cold War's geopolitical logic.

Chapter 4 examines more directly the neoliberalization of development thought and strategy at USAID as it progressed through the 1990s and into the new millennium, which corresponds to a strengthening and maturation of a geoeconomic perspective within and through the agency. This geoeconomic discourse was tied strongly but narrowly to a specific reading of what constitutes appropriate development and world order, which itself built from neoliberal arguments about the primacy and desirability of free markets and certain political and economic reforms in developing states. In turn, this shift and its articulation within USAID had deep impacts on the agency's structure and strategic objectives. Here I emphasize how a particularly neoliberal form of geoeconomics came to dominate the development agenda at USAID following the Cold War's end, as evidenced by three concurrent trends: a crisis of geopolitical positioning and intervention as a raison d'être for American foreign aid, the restructuring and streamlining of USAID in line with neoliberal "smaller government" rhetoric, and the growing emphasis on "trade capacity building" and engagement in global market institutions as a primary programming focus for development action. These trends establish the reflexive constitution of neoliberal models of development and foreign aid (which emphasize global market integration and the state's facilitating role with respect to global economic positioning and the formal institutionalization of capitalist accumulation strategies at the global and local scales) with the restructuring and reorientation of development and aid institutions such as USAID (including the increasing role of NGOs and private aid channels, the streamlining and downsizing of agency capacities and personnel, and the political position of USAID relative to other state institutions and the private sector).

Just because geoeconomic discourse became more pronounced than geopolitical framings at USAID (and within development thought and practice more generally) after the Cold War, it should not be assumed that geopolitics completely disappeared from the agency during this period. Chapter 4 thus also provides a discussion of the place of development in post-9/11 official U.S. national security strategies, which emphasize the 3Ds approach to national security noted above and focus on the mutual coordination and reinforcement of defense, diplomacy, and development in U.S. foreign policy. While the elevation of development to the level of national security priority was articulated most directly following 9/11, this security-oriented understanding of development represents continuity with a longstanding geopolitical tradition in USAID rather than a radical break with past practice. Understanding the latest iteration of geopolitical discourse in and through USAID, however, means placing the agency in the context of a broader debate within mainstream development circles over the role of "soft power" (cultural, diplomatic, and developmental capacities exercised to structure the relations between the Global North and Global South) and "smart power" in national security. At USAID, this has meant articulating the relationship between geopolitical and geoeconomic discourses anew and recasting aid deservedness along axes that combine both political and economic conditionalities for developing states. This has induced a thorough soul-searching for USAID as an agency, continuing and intensifying institutional restructuring processes, but with concern for how the agency constructs, manages, and implements geoeconomic and geopolitical strategies in a complementary fashion. Key empirical focal points for examining the agency's role in producing this geostrategic nexus are the evolution of an approach focused on "transformational development" and "fragile states" and the construction and enactment of a new geographic categorization of developing states in the USAID's 2006 Foreign Assistance Framework.

I conclude in chapter 5 by examining the current moment of geostrategic positioning and engagement at USAID, which is full of both hope and anxiety for the agency. Not wishing to be speculative in approach, I focus, in the final chapter, on two recent programmatic and institutional changes and what they mean for the agency's position as site, strategy, and agent. First, I examine the Feed the Future (FTF) program, a development initiative launched in 2010 that highlights the present status and articulation of several interrelated trends addressed throughout the book. The FTF program is a government-wide response to the 2007–2008 global food crisis that sent food prices skyrocketing and pushed millions of poor and vulnerable people in the Global South into conditions of chronic food insecurity and hunger. It aims to comprehensively address a set of persistent development challenges (rural poverty and agricultural underdevelopment, hunger and food insecurity, environmental degradation, and the inability of small farmers and poor countries to compete in liberalized global markets) made worse by recent global economic and financial shocks and attendant political turmoil. The agency comprises a principal institutional component of this program, but FTF's formulation and implementation also reveal lingering tensions between geopolitical and geoeconomic approaches to development, the relative instability and precariousness of USAID's position within the American state and the global aid architecture, and the inability of neoliberal globalization to provide a stable, equitable, or just path to development. The second focal point in chapter 5 is the agency's role relative to internationalizing capital and other organs of the U.S. state, especially the Departments of State and Defense, in response to widespread and interconnected forms of systemic crisis, stalled development progress, and an emerging regime of neoliberal austerity. Despite an active embrace and reorientation of the agency in line with the geostrategic demands of neoliberal globalization, American informal imperialism, and post-9/11 national security strategies, USAID's future remains in doubt, with both its funding and institutional autonomy under threat.

CHAPTER TWO

"In the World for Keeps"

From the Marshall Plan to the Vietnam War

Geoeconomics, Geopolitics, and the Development Project

The history of post–World War II development theory and practice is a well-trod path, and scholars have approached it from multiple theoretical perspectives. Theorizing and implementing development amid and atop the crumbling edifice of colonial empires was a multifaceted process, drawing on and fomenting multiple intellectual traditions, precipitating a period of institutional ferment, and challenging long-held assumptions about interstate relations. At the same time, the postwar emphasis on development for the newly independent Third World reasserted some of the principal, taken-for-granted notions of state form and function in an international system that was rapidly expanding in scope and simultaneously settling into a binary system of Cold War great power politics. American foreign assistance and the U.S. Agency for International Development were born in the context of World War II's aftermath and the Cold War's early years, charged with geopolitical and geoeconomic aims and mandates: to promote the foreign policy goals and interests of the United States while assisting Third World states in their development. Although USAID's work was shaped by and shaping of both bodies of geostrategic discourse from its establishment in 1961 to the beginning of severe economic and political crises in the 1970s, Cold War objectives and geographies pushed geopolitical logic and action to the fore and made geoeconomic thought and practice secondary (but still vital) within the agency's structure, relations, and strategies.

Understanding how and why these missions and the discourses underwriting them were conjoined under the single roof of USAID, and how the agency managed tensions, contradictions, and overlaps between the geopolitical and the geoeconomic in fulfilling its mandate, requires a foray not only into critical geopolitics and the principal elements of development discourse and knowledge institutionalized at USAID but also into the political economy of development in an era of heightened territorial and ideological tensions. Relying on a purely discursive approach, without attention to the political economy of Cold War development intervention, produces an analysis overly focused on the textual formulation of geostrategic logic at USAID that does not adequately address how the agency's institutional materiality was built around and through the textual and discursive. Yet narrow political economy and institutional accounts ignore discursive processes and formations at their peril, focusing on structure while failing to interrogate the silences and gaps in strategic logic and decision making or the ideational work driving the institutionalization and professionalization of development and foreign policy expertise at USAID. Only through close attention to the evolution and circulation of geostrategic discourses *in concert with* the formation and exercise of political and economic decision-making powers can the spatial assumptions and projects underlying and animating USAID be understood in their full geostrategic importance. In other words, the content and use of development and foreign policy certainties produced by and through USAID stem from both the discursive formulation of knowledge and strategy within the agency and the material operation of USAID itself as a place (figuratively and literally) populated by experts situated within the political, economic, and cultural power of the U.S. state.

In an exegesis on the continued relevance of "critical geopolitics" as a distinct approach and subfield within political geography, Dalby (2008, 415) suggests that "there remains a necessity to engage with the spatial framing of politics and the geographical tropes used in security, defence and foreign policy thinking, a specific intellectual terrain that still justifies the moniker 'critical geopolitics.'" Dalby's plea for continued and rejuvenated attention to the themes and methods of critical geopolitics, first articulated in the work of Ó Tuathail two decades prior, stems from his examination of imperial imaginaries promulgated through the Bush doctrine of preemptive war and the associated war on terror that followed the terrorist attacks of 9/11. Specifically, Dalby (2008, 416) argues that the normative stance and discursive and cultural foci of critical geopolitics provide essential tools for "directly tackling the reasoning practices of statecraft" and the representations that legitimize and advance imperialism and other forms of domination. This builds from a new mapping of imperial geographies, with the territorial struggles between great powers that marked colonial and Cold War versions and visions of imperialism replaced by "[new] wars against militarily weak peripheral political organisations in distant lands," all underwritten by "clear moral cartographies, and a single overarching geopolitical division" outlined most directly in Barnett's "Functioning Core" and "Non-Integrating Gap" (Dalby 2008, 424).

Dalby's discussion highlights the continued need for critical examination of the cultural assumptions and chauvinism circulating among those who practice statecraft, and the popularized representations of geopolitical action and relations, though it also hints at the danger of forgetting these important questions so that messy and complex geographies of "grand strategy" are not reduced to presumed or simplistic caricatures of empire. This echoes Gearóid Ó Tuathail's (2000) argument, made almost ten years earlier, before 9/11 and the Bush doctrine, and well before talk of American empire had reignited in earnest across social science research and the punditry in American mass media. Despite the increasingly evident "postmodern geopolitical condition" of world politics, in which new forms of global interdependence and connectedness had thrown rigidly territorial and state-centric spatial imaginaries and categories of traditional geopolitics into crisis, Ó Tuathail (2000, 177) argued that "contemporary geopolitical discourses are still relentlessly *modernist* in method," eschewing complexity and de- or reterritorialized social relations in favor of hard and fast reliance on lapsed but deeply ingrained forms of territoriality and political authority. Calling for a *postmodernist* form of geopolitics, Ó Tuathail appealed for renewed critical attention to the culture of statecraft and the construction of geopolitical imaginaries and representations. The concern with advancing an explicitly normative critique of powerful geopolitical narratives, of their origins and silences, and of their use by both practitioners of geopolitics and the wider public formed the core of critical geopolitics as a field and methodology from its inception, primarily within Ó Tuathail's earlier work (1986, 1993, 1996). In his analysis of spatial constructions of the Middle East and Operation Desert Storm, for example, Ó Tuathail (1993, 4) stated unequivocally that "geographers have a moral and political obligation to confront and challenge the strategies by which the war was given to be seen by politicians, 'experts' and the mass media within the 'Western' world." The call for geographers' responsibility to challenge the spatiality of powerful discourses, and in particular those that justify or animate violence, subjugation, and domination, has since become generalized within critical political geography, though appeals to remember and foreground certain methods, themes, and central tropes indicate the extent to which critical geopolitics remains self-reflexive in outlook.

Certain key questions continue to stand out within critical geopolitics and are important to the analysis of USAID that follows. First are questions related to basic spatial metaphors through which geopolitical actors script and abstract the complex realities of geopolitical and other social relations, often in service to a particular political project or set of social forces. Examining how spatial metaphors structure the way we imagine geopolitical space and the actors in it, as well as the origins, circulation, and evolution of such metaphors, is an essential task for analyzing the operation of a state agency with a broad set of often-conflicting objectives such as USAID, as it must incorporate and respond to multiple kinds of geospatial metaphors. The second important set of questions centers on how the practices and discourses of geopolitical actors ignore and/or reproduce forms of inequality based on gender, race, ethnicity, and other forms of identity. I mean "identity" here in a broad sense, including conceptions of institutional culture. So, for instance, one might ask how the understanding of agency mission and mandate within USAID shaped relations between staff at that agency and other arms of the U.S. state; between USAID development experts and the supposed or intended beneficiaries of American development assistance in developing countries; and between competing ideals and theories of development espoused by various groups of experts with different institutional homes, social movement organizations, and the public at large (USAID's motto has long been, after all, "From the American People"). Finally, critical geopolitics focuses a great deal on geographical and cultural representation, especially within mass media and in relation to statecraft and military strategy, as a central of part of cultural logic and discourse. While I spend little time on the representation of USAID and development policy generally in the mass media, the concern with spatial representation remains important for this examination. As noted in chapter 1, USAID has long been concerned with its public image. It has been represented at different times (and sometimes simultaneously) as the expression and vanguard of Americans' noblest humanitarian impulses, a wasteful sinkhole for channeling taxpayer money to peripheral backwaters and corrupt dictators, and an essential component within a grand strategy of American leadership amid global interdependence and connectivity. Such opposed takes on the agency and the geographical character of its work suggest that questions of representation should not be left aside.

Questions and approaches drawn from critical geopolitics also emphasize the production of geospatial knowledge and, with it, development expertise in the historical context of the formation and deployment of geostrategic discourses. This allows us to interrogate, for example, the space-making aspects and effects of postwar development strategies undertaken by the U.S. state and bundled together in the institution of USAID in the 1960s. As discussed in more detail below, this was a period of Cold War rivalry, which not only attempted to divide the world into competing ideological camps, each with attendant spatial and geographical referents in the United States and the Soviet Union, but also sought to produce and enact a host of integrative practices and forms of political, cultural, economic, and environmental analyses through different U.S. state institutions, all under the rubric of fighting and winning the Cold War. These processes were not only geopolitical but also geoeconomic, as integration meant not just aligning state interests and political ideologies but also incorporating places, people, and capital into growing global circuits of capitalist expansion and commerce under the tutelage and hegemonic leadership of the United States. Matt Farish (2010, 3–4) highlights the interaction between these two tendencies within American Cold War strategies and the production of geospatial knowledge during the 1950s:

> If containment, in theory and in practice, provides an obvious example of Cold War geopolitics, then integration relied more directly on cultural and scientific (or social scientific) ideals and was occasionally presented in the dreamy language of global humanism. But integration was also an assimilative project rooted in a particularly iconic version of America whereby foreign areas and populations . . . could be domesticated and modernized, marked as successes on a checklist leading to a harmony that was more calculative than cosmopolitan.

Within Cold War–era U.S. development policies and strategies, the tension between the geopolitical move to territorially contain the identified threat of global communism, and to integrate allied and nonaligned states into a U.S.-led and U.S.-dominated system of economic and security interdependence, manifested in part through the institution of USAID itself. A geoeconomic imperative to facilitate global capital accumulation also found purchase in the agency's mandate, and the intertwined logics of economic integration and mutual security, both to be achieved through U.S. development strategies and interventions, offered ample opportunity for discursive and strategic differentiation. Such discursive shifts induced and were spurred by institutional reorganization within USAID, but in its earliest incarnation the agency was staffed with experts who actively intervened in developing countries to promote and implement development strategies based in both the universalizing prescriptions of modernization theory and the specific concerns associated with American geopolitical interests and foreign policy. USAID was also central to the production of knowledge about the Third World and appropriate forms and paths of intervention within it. In the context of the Cold War and the Keynesian class compromise that underlay relative domestic prosperity and labor peace in the United States from World War II to the late 1970s, the geopolitical imperative within USAID trumped and encompassed, for the time being at least, the geoeconomic impulse and its supporters. That is to say, while both geostrategic discourses were evident and integral in USAID's establishment and early operation in the late 1950s and early 1960s, the geopolitical held primacy over the geoeconomic in shaping the agency's mission, the way development expertise was produced and deployed, and the institutional contours and day-to-day operation of the agency itself.

This last point stands as an important bridge between the discursive and textual focus of critical geopolitics and the dynamic political economy of development intervention. While the analytical division between geopolitics and geoeconomics is useful for identifying and detailing different logics shaping how development practitioners and policymakers understood the world and acted upon it, *in practice* the two discourses overlap, intertwine, and intersect in ways that make such distinction between them difficult. These two geostrategic discourses were themselves linked to different social, political, and economic forces and actors (themselves, like USAID, sometimes deploying both discourses in often incompatible ways), with differential access to the levers of state power and legitimacy. Ardent cold warriors within USAID and other government agencies, private think tanks and foundations, and the business community made arguments and decisions based on both geopolitical and geoeconomic discourses and strategies. Under particular circumstances and moments of strategic calculation, one or the other might loom larger in decision making. Both provided ideological and intellectual tools and concepts for describing and planning U.S. intervention (or nonintervention, in some cases) in the name of development, which was in turn linked to modernization, capitalism, and national security.

Within postwar American development policy and USAID's mandate, the geopolitical and the geoeconomic were thus bound together institutionally and ideologically, though only imperfectly in the practical sense. This, in turn, is the result of the messy complexities of political affiliation and the relations between state institutional and class-relevant forces and groups that helped direct and implement strategies and policies associated with or coming from USAID. This does not imply that policymakers and development practitioners sorted through the various discursive strands available to them to find post hoc justifications for policies determined by class position or political ideology. Rather, specific political, state, and hegemonic projects of development emerged from the active and reflexive production, reproduction, and use of geostrategic discourses by agents who worked from differential positions of power within a broader global political economy of development produced and reproduced through multiple overlapping processes of intervention, articulation, and contestation. In addition to being an influential political, economic, and social agent in its own right, with the ability to make and enact development strategy, USAID was and remains a site and a strategy for other actors to participate in or shape the geostrategic logic and path of U.S. development policy and action.

As briefly discussed in the previous chapter, I build my argument regarding the political economy of development and the institutionalization of state powers related to development planning and intervention around the theoretical and methodological framework of the strategic-relational approach, outlined most fully in the work of Bob Jessop (1990, 2000, 2001a, 2001b, 2002a, 2002b, 2008). This approach rejects simplistic state/market and state/society dichotomies to concentrate on the state as a reflexive and recursive system structuring strategically selective political behavior, highlighting the role state institutions play as sites and strategies in broader processes and projects. These are *sites* in that state institutions are concrete spaces for the articulation of specific political strategies by social actors with access to the state apparatus, and they are *strategies* in that these institutions are marshaled for the enactment, legitimation, and maintenance of specific projects associated with class-relevant social forces.

Jessop (2002a, 42) suggests, then, that one way to study the state is by using the strategic-relational approach as a method to investigate not only the "formal institutional aspects of the state regarded as a social relation"—for example, the internal articulation of components of the state apparatus with one another (i.e., how different state agencies function and interact)—but also the "substantive and strategic aspects of the state regarded as social relation." In other words, the state is best understood by examining how different parts of the state apparatus are both sites for the institutionalization of particular social relations and strategies for their constant reinstitutionalization, which occurs amid and through context-specific political struggle, and always with failure and shifts in social and economic contexts as real possibilities. In this way, the strategic-relational approach examines relationships between institutions without assuming that all institutions matter in exactly the same way. This builds on Gramscian notions of the "integral state" and concerns with how discourse and class-*relevant* (rather than simply class-based or class-determined) social relations are legitimized, regularized, and regulated within and through the state. The concept of the integral state understands the state as encompassing civil society rather than just the discrete, formal institutions of the territorial nation-state or of political society. In this view, the state is not only "the organ or instrument of the oppression of one class by another" but also "the apparatuses of government and the judiciary and the various voluntary and private associations and parapolitical institutions that make up civil society" (Gramsci in Forgacs 2000, 429). Gramsci's conceptualization imbues the integral state with ethical or educative functions; that is, the capacity to contain, embody, and reproduce the social and political hegemony of a particular class or class alliance over society as a whole.

Addressing the qualitative changes in state form and function that accompany processes of broader social and political economic change requires, then, a means of conceptualizing the state as more than simply a power container existing at a given scale, able only to cede power to forces working above and below it as the march toward globalization began following World War II, and especially after the crisis of the Keynesian state and of Fordism generally in the 1970s. In contrast to this perspective, Glassman (1999, 673), following from Agnew (1994) and Agnew and Corbridge (1995), contends that the state itself has internationalized, a process by which "the state apparatus becomes increasingly oriented towards facilitating capital accumulation for the most internationalized investors, regardless of their nationality." Similarly, but with specific interest in the informal imperialism of American hegemony in the post–World War II international state system, Panitch and Gindin (2004, 42) define state internationalization as "a state's acceptance of responsibility for managing its domestic capitalist order in [a] way that contributes to managing the international capitalist order." The internationalizing state does not merely react to capital, nor is it limited to the strict territorial definition of sovereignty assumed in most theoretical treatments, what Agnew (1994) refers to as the "territorial trap." Instead, both state and capital are understood to consist of multiple and sometimes competing factions that align with one another around specific, class-relevant political, state, and hegemonic projects, so that the state aids capital's tendency to internationalize in search of greater rates of accumulation, a process that also unevenly reproduces state power and the international state system. Analysis of state internationalization should therefore take into account not only the many ways in which this undercuts some elements of state power through unevenly instituted and regulated systems of capitalist accumulation but also how some states or, more specifically, state institutions use internationalization to expand their capacities and reproduce themselves as part of a broader political economic system marked by the increasingly crisis-prone dominance of capital. In sum, the internationalization of the state must be understood as a contingent process of state transformation shaped in part by the discursive strategies and practices of relevant actors and agents, many of whom are part of the state itself, as well as the political and economic structures that constrain these, all of which operate in a dynamic, interdependent fashion.

This highlights a key innovation offered by a strategic-relational understanding of state-capital relations and the specific details of resultant institutional configurations and projects across different geographical contexts. Since there is no necessary or pregiven correlation between state action and capitalist interests, the state's regulation of capitalism should be understood by reference to the ways in which accumulation, including consideration for the alignment and relative power of different segments of capital (e.g., finance capital, agricultural or food corporations, small and medium-sized enterprises, large-scale manufacturing firms), has been incorporated into the logic and mechanics of the state as a whole and made a politically legitimate basis for social regulation more generally. This, then, represents the methodological rationale for centering analysis on specific political, state, and hegemonic projects that shape both the boundaries and details of specific policies and the governmental logic of the state in relation to "a broader—but always selective—political, intellectual and moral vision of the public interest, the good society, the commonweal, or some analogous principle of societalization" (Jessop 2002a, 42).

Here it is necessary to define what is meant by political, state, and hegemonic projects. Jessop's (2002a, 42) discussion of *state projects* refers to the ways in which the prevailing *political projects* of dominant social forces and actors "[seek] to impose an always relative unity on the various activities of different branches, departments and scales of the state system," while *hegemonic projects* "seek to reconcile the particular and the universal." While these levels of state cohesion and alignment do not map neatly onto scalar referents, they do connote a similar relational, nested character—hegemonic projects build from and encompass state projects (at least in the detailed historical analysis below), which in turn build from political projects that express the actions, interests, and framings of particular class-relevant social groups. This implies the imposition of a contingent and relative unity of purpose across different state institutions, altering and directing their strategic selectivity. This is a recursive relation, however, and actions taken by different arms of the state may work at cross-purposes in the context of shifts in political and state projects, precipitating changes in the balance of political and class forces or a reworking of institutional capacities within the state, transforming the character and enactment of state and hegemonic projects as a result. The relationships between different state projects (e.g., those in the United States and in various postcolonial states immediately after World War II) must also be considered, since internationalization implies correlation and articulation across, and within, national boundaries.

Returning once more to Hart's (2001, 2002, 2004) identification of a general process of development composed in part of multiple Development framings and interventions, and following from the work of Philip McMichael (2008, 2009) on the hegemonic force of U.S. development paradigms and strategies, I argue that post–World War II development as instituted by and through USAID constituted a hegemonic project. As a hegemonic project, it conditioned the environment of political, economic, and strategic decision making, while various context-specific mechanisms and policies of development intervention operating in different states and state institutions comprised and manifested different political and state projects of development. It is here that the differences and relations between geostrategic discourses of geopolitics and geoeconomics become crucial for fleshing out how and why U.S. development strategies and policies, as well as USAID itself, took the form they did during the early Cold War and into the crisis period of the 1970s. During this formative period for development theory and U.S. development strategies, USAID emerged as a principal site for articulating political and state projects of development tied to liberal internationalist visions of world order. The agency also acted as a key strategy for implementing this order and working out relations between and within those social forces aligned with each discursive formation. Finally, USAID acted as a generator of strategies itself, tied to but distinct from state organs managing other aspects of U.S. foreign policy, and with specific institutional interests and capacities all its own.

From the Marshall Plan to the Foreign Assistance Act of 1961

The agency, and American development assistance more generally, originated in the process of solidifying and expanding political, state, and hegemonic projects of development, driven by intersecting geoeconomic and geopolitical logics and strategies shaped by the early Cold War. This development project, argues McMichael (2008, 46), "was a political and intellectual response to the condition of the world at the historic moment of decolonization," imposing an economically reductionist vision of development that was growth-oriented, linear, and universalizing. Across the former colonies, newly independent states would develop socially, economically, politically, and culturally by following the template of national industrialization, leading to urbanization, mechanization and increased productivity in agriculture, and a diversified economic base supporting and supported by a state whose legitimacy depended on this project's success. McMichael (2008) notes that although the emphasis on national industrialization crossed the Cold War ideological divide, as Soviet development planners and assistance followed roughly the same linear framing of modernization, the particular project that held sway under U.S. hegemony centered on capitalist growth and development's importance as a bulwark against communism. There was specific political content to different state and hegemonic projects of development during the Cold War, with the state's role, and the state-capital relationship in promoting and maintaining development progress, crucial to differentiating them from one another. The road to development within the U.S.-dominated hegemonic project was relatively narrow, and the scaled power relations of capitalist growth constituting, reproducing, and enforcing this project strongly shaped and constrained the strategic selectivity of state institutions. The limited range of acceptable development strategies in postcolonial states, as Glassman and Samatar (1997, 181) argue, resulted from both the institutional capabilities of state managers and bureaucracies and the international alliances maintained by powerful class-relevant groups in those states, with non-class-based social hierarchies (e.g., ethnic divisions or kinship networks) and the class consciousness of specific leadership groups also important.

While the history of nation building, the construction of political and state projects around development and modernization, and the formation and role of national political and class elites within developing countries are important for understanding the active and often contested hegemony of the U.S.-led development project during the Cold War, I want instead to focus attention on the formation of a foreign development infrastructure *within the U.S. state* following World War II. It was from the crucible of wartorn Europe that USAID, and dominant discourses and strategies of foreign aid and development more generally, emerged. The eventual amalgamation into USAID of different agencies and accounts focused on development assistance and national security demonstrates that, despite claims to the teleological unfolding of advanced urban, industrial, and democratic development within the United States itself, the export of this model was a distinctly political undertaking. It required and was instituted through the organization of expertise and management in a state institution, such as the Agency for International Development, and the orientation of multiple state and civil society institutions toward the same goal (development through American aid and intervention) in a relatively unified manner. Yet the agency and the broader project of development were not cut from whole cloth, but rather evolved over a decade and a half following the end of World War II through the accretion and reshuffling of duties, powers, institutions, and objectives, all responding to a changing geostrategic environment and a growing concern with national security in the early Cold War. The articulation of the geostrategic discourses that so strongly shaped USAID in this formative period centered on questions of territorial influence and state formation, military and economic means of achieving national security, and the technical components of modernization that were lacking in other parts of the world.

The agency's antecedents were temporary programs with specific, discrete purposes: the post–World War II Marshall Plan, designed to rebuild wartorn countries in western Europe; various aid accounts and programs authorized under the umbrella of "mutual security" legislation; and several short-term economic and military assistance programs of limited duration and scope. Within this wide array, U.S. development policy bundled military and economic aid with technical assistance for development, targeting specific world regions or countries seen as strategically important in the context of American-Soviet struggles for power and influence across the globe. Even those programs that were primarily economic in nature, directing loans of American dollars and other forms of short-term economic assistance and development investment, were built on a firm foundation of geopolitical calculation with a focus on achieving mutual security under the hegemonic leadership of the United States. The establishment of USAID through the Foreign Assistance Act of 1961 extended and strengthened the emphasis on development aid as a geopolitical tool for building mutual security between the United States and its allies and dependents in Europe and the newly independent states emerging from crumbling colonial empires. The debate over foreign assistance in the 1950s, largely but not wholly internal to elite policy circles, became prominent in the 1960 presidential campaign between Richard Nixon and John F. Kennedy. This debate was couched in primarily geopolitical terms related to securing world order through U.S. leadership and blocking Soviet expansionism, even as most actual development assistance built from geoeconomic presumptions about the centrality of capitalist social relations and economic growth for proper development.

The agency itself, in an institutional history prepared in 1991, argues that the agency's creation on a permanent basis "most closely resembled a bureaucratic re-shuffling and a re-commitment to development purposes" in U.S. aid strategies and policies and that it unified multiple different programs and accounts under one institutional roof with a stronger emphasis on long-term planning (Duffy 1991, 1).[1] Prior to USAID's formation, American development assistance efforts concentrated on achieving short-term objectives through strategic aid to a limited number of states, with development planning designed to meet immediate foreign policy and military needs in a given place and time. For example, aid to Greece and Turkey in 1947 was primarily military, but it demonstrated to observers in Washington that American assistance could provide, in the words of Arizona Representative Morris Udall, "perhaps the decisive part" in helping prevent the spread of communism through Soviet policy and aid and domestic movements in foreign countries (Udall 1961). The Marshall Plan and the Economic Cooperation Agency (ECA) were authorized shortly after, with the Marshall Plan's successes achieved through only four fiscal years' worth of funding from 1948 through 1951 (though this totaled over $13 billion, a rather large sum for the immediate postwar period). Plan funding was concentrated in Western Europe and focused on rebuilding shattered industrial economies and political and military capabilities while building loyalty to U.S. leadership against the Soviet Union in world and regional affairs. European states' large trade deficits and social turmoil were eased by a "triangular trade" in which U.S. dollars were used to pay for raw goods from European colonies. European countries used dollars deposited in London banks to finance imports of American manufactured goods, while American investment in colonies stimulated markets for industrial exports from Europe (McMichael 2008, 56–58).

European economies rebuilt on American largesse were seen as bulwarks against the communist threat looming to the east, which made the Marshall Plan the political and ideological touchstone for U.S. development policy for decades after. Marshall Plan aid was both geoeconomic and geopolitical in outlook and structure, organized around economic aid and technical assistance designed to reformulate industrial relations in Europe, but with a broad strategic objective of territorially containing the Soviet Union and the expansion of its sphere of control. Taylor (1999, 9) describes how Marshall Plan assistance slowly but surely shifted from emphasizing increases in gross production in European economies to focusing on increases in productivity and industrial modernization in manufacturing processes and labor management, creating "a new politics" privileging economic growth, mass consumption, voter contentment, and "class compromise over class conflict." One USAID officer who spent his early career working on Marshall Plan implementation in France described this technical assistance: "What they would do is to organize a tripartite team, one third of it being from management, one third from labor, and one third from government, about 12 in all. These people would work together for several weeks, then go to the United States, industry by industry, and study how things were done in the United States in that particular industry, come back to their home country and write a report that was widely distributed throughout the industry" (Behoteguy 1999, 4–5).

It is no surprise that such shifts in the organization of social, political, and economic life in Western European states undercut the influence of communist and socialist parties and movements. They also paved the way for capitalist forms of state internationalization through new mechanisms to make and coordinate common economic policies and the deeper integration of Western European economies and business classes with their American counterparts (Panitch and Gindin 2004). Observers in U.S. foreign policy circles understood such shifts as one of the Marshall Plan's primary purposes in Europe. The wider objective, however, was geopolitical and centered on the largely defensive strategy of containment, in which the United States would prevent the extension of communism by encircling the Soviet Union and its satellites with friendly states built on principles of liberal democracy and capitalist economic growth. The Marshall Plan thus shaped and enacted geopolitical and geoeconomic discourses that laid foundational components for American development policy and strategy through the first three decades of the Cold War and that also helped shape the establishment and conduct of USAID as an institution. These discourses envisioned national and global versions of sociospatial order predicated on American political, military, and economic hegemony and forms of class compromise that negated radical challenges to Fordist and Keynesian models of economic growth, labor management, and political legitimation.

Despite fundamental differences between postwar Europe and newly independent countries across the developing world (and between these countries themselves), the Marshall Plan's successes loomed large in debates over U.S. foreign assistance following the plan's end in 1951, and this set the template for subsequent development strategy and institutions, including USAID. The development project that had its roots in the Marshall Plan became hegemonic in conjunction with the reorganization of U.S. foreign assistance programs in the 1950s and early 1960s, which pushed geostrategic considerations of development into the national political arena and strongly shaped the views of American policymakers and the American public about the meaning and exercise of American hegemony. Within this, the U.S. state project of development centered on long-term economic growth and intervention underwritten by the intellectual power of modernization theory, all incorporated into the geopolitical framework of the Cold War. The early Cold War framing of development strategy was driven by a view of interlocking states working under the leadership of the United States to resist, root out, and contain communist influence. In essence (though not always in practice), this was the Marshall Plan writ large and exported to the newly independent countries of the former colonial empires, which were seen as vulnerable to communist infiltration and dangerously outside the orbit of American influence and investment. This in turn had a significant geoeconomic component as market-based economic growth was the centerpiece of modernization and unlocked the secrets to development progress.

As Soviet industrial and military capabilities expanded through the 1950s, debates over American development assistance and programs to extend overseas aid to more countries became increasingly focused on the geopolitical content and goals of such assistance. When the Marshall Plan expired in 1951, it was replaced by the Mutual Security Program, which focused American assistance abroad on military aid, and a succession of relatively weak agencies were charged with managing aid programs and accounts (Udall 1961; Duffy 1991; USAID 2002b). The ECA was replaced in 1951 by the Mutual Security Agency, which was replaced in 1953 by the Foreign Operations Administration (this also absorbed the functions of the Technical Cooperation Administration); this in turn was replaced in 1955 by the International Cooperation Agency (ICA). The

ICA was an institution with a "vast and far reaching" set of functions, but also a weak structure and severe limitations (USAID 2002b, 2). Unlike its predecessors, ICA was not an independent and autonomous agency but worked under the Department of State, with no authority over military aid and only partial control over agricultural surpluses and food aid. Most lending activities were handled by separate accounts and agencies, while an increasingly influential multilateral organization of aid (marked by a strong U.S. presence, of course) began to overshadow American bilateral assistance (Duffy 1991, 2).

These shifts hampered U.S. development assistance in significant ways and tied it ever more strongly to often uncoordinated economic, political, and social objectives and programs, while an increasing amount of aid went to military purposes. As Representative Udall commented in his 1961 report on the Foreign Assistance Act, military assistance accounted for approximately 80 percent of U.S. foreign aid between the Marshall Plan's end and USAID's establishment. While the 1954 Mutual Security Act consolidated U.S. foreign assistance programs on a single legislative footing for the first time, it nonetheless set the stage for several years of debate within Congress over the utility of foreign aid expressed almost entirely in geopolitical terms, especially benefits to U.S. national security, with some attention to administrative rationales and the inefficiencies of spreading aid programs across multiple accounts and agencies. One foreign service professional with many years of experience across a wide range of U.S. development programs commented on the influence of security considerations in the decade prior to USAID's formation: "[T]he State Department and the Defense Department viewed economic assistance as an arm of military and political security. . . . They felt that, even if the Congress was interested in them purely from the standpoint of economic and technical assistance, those two departments felt that there needed to be . . . a security and a political aspect in order to go ahead with such programs" (Lowenthal 1996, 16). By the end of the decade, foreign aid was central to political debates over U.S. foreign policy. Several congressionally commissioned reports highlighted failures and gaps in American aid programs, while William Lederer and Eugene Burdick's popular and thinly fictionalized 1958 novel *The Ugly American* brought American diplomatic and strategic missteps in Southeast Asia, and the perils of incompetent and poorly planned development and military assistance, to wider public attention. In response, some congressional reports suggested the creation of a single government agency to replace ICA and oversee American foreign assistance programs on a more permanent basis, but they disagreed on the political and institutional relationship between social and economic development aid and military aid (Weidner 1961).[2]

The reorganization of American aid programs became a key political issue in the 1960 presidential campaign, and with Kennedy's victory in that election, significant changes to foreign aid became a top administration priority. This resulted in intense debate over foreign aid reform in 1961 and the eventual passage of the Foreign Assistance Act (FAA) in September of that year, followed in November by USAID's formation. The debate over the FAA and foreign aid's purposes and structure highlighted the increasingly residual character of opposition to aid within the American political establishment and the strength of geopolitical arguments in favor of a large coordinated aid program. A July 1961 article in *ICA Digest* (the official publication of the soon-to-be-defunct International Cooperation Administration) detailed congressional discussions over the FAA, highlighting critiques of the proposed program from both members of Congress and representatives of the American business class. The *Digest* reported that within this debate, "traditional arguments of thrift, economy and ingratitude have been revitalized" to oppose aid reform, while proposals to fund foreign aid with longer-term five-year appropriations from the Treasury predictably elicited "a substantial amount of criticism through the charge of 'backdoor spending'" (Duffy 1991, 17). Testimony provided by individuals representing the Citizens Foreign Aid Committee (which advocated against any foreign aid program) and the U.S. Chamber of Commerce attacked specific funding requests, and aid in general, as an expensive "give-away" that the United States could not afford (Duffy 1991, 17).[3] Opposition within Congress was concentrated in the House, where cuts to foreign aid programs had been both consistent and much higher than the average cuts made across government programs during the 1950s. What one contemporaneous observer labeled "bed-rock opposition" to aid legislation was concentrated largely but not entirely among representatives from the South and Midwest, where fears centered on aid's potential support to infant economic sectors in developing countries that would compete with regionally or locally important export industries in the United States. By the same token, public opinion from the end of World War II onward indicated "that the only genuinely unpopular item in [American] foreign policy is foreign aid, that support for it has been declining fairly steadily, and that opposition views on foreign aid are held a good deal more strongly than are supporting views," a situation that remains familiar today (Truman 1962, 69).

Supporters of the FAA argued that foreign aid was not an expense the United States could forgo and that a more comprehensive approach to managing aid, built around country-based strategies and long-term planning, would make aid more effective and strategically and financially sound. President Kennedy's initial message to the House of Representatives in March 1961 laid the technical and strategic groundwork for the new structure of American aid and sought to counter opponents' criticisms in both economic and political terms. The president criticized existing aid efforts as "[b]ureaucratically fragmented, awkward and slow," with administrative responsibilities "diffused over a haphazard and irrational structure" and based in multiple pieces of legislation that were "unsuited for our present needs and purposes" (Duffy 1991, 21). More stable financial and legislative footing would make the foreign aid program more effective and efficient; indeed, Kennedy argued that the then-current form of "uneven and undependable short-term financing has weakened the incentive for the long-term planning and self-help by the recipient nations which are essential to serious economic development" (Duffy 1991, 21). Rather than simply devising a new agency to resolve these difficulties, Kennedy called for "a new working concept" as well, one that was centered on "national development programs" to focus aid on social and economic development separate from military assistance and that could work from the stability of long-term financing to demonstrate to recipients and other potential donors (i.e., rejuvenated Western European countries) the United States' commitment to development progress (Duffy 1991, 24).

Similar arguments appeared in House and Senate committee discussions of the proposed Foreign Assistance Act through the spring and summer of 1961. A comprehensive section-by-section report on the proposed bill by the Senate Committee on Foreign Relations in July made clear that long-term planning backed by more flexible borrowing authority for the executive branch, which would partially dampen the efforts of aid opponents in Congress to effectively undo aid by rejecting appropriations on an annual basis, was central to any aid program's success, stating that "the long-term borrowing authority sought by the President is the most important part of this legislation" (U.S. Senate 1961, 10). The committee emphasized the link between more stable financing for development aid and the necessity of long-term strategic planning, quoting an administration official who stated, "We know in our hearts that we are in the world for keeps, yet we are still tackling 20-year problems with 5-year plans, staffed with 2-year personnel working with 1-year appropriations. It's simply not good enough" (quoted in U.S. Senate 1961, 7).

Even with such strong claims about the necessity of long-term government funding for development aid, the role of private capital in American development efforts overseas remained a point of contention for many years after. Despite assurances and mandates that the presence and use of private capital be maximized in U.S. foreign aid programs, a feature of all legislation dealing with foreign aid from 1948 onward, some observers argued that "administrators repeatedly have responded with little more than lip service and the most limited stimulation of private U.S. investment resources" (Clubb and Vance 1963, 475).[4] While this was based as much on private investors' reluctance to work in high-risk investment environments of which they were largely ignorant as on the recalcitrance of aid officials and foreign governments to deal with private American investors, it nonetheless helped solidify opinion among American business leaders that aid was muscling them out of position in new markets or helping to create unfairly supported competitors where none had existed before. The principles of "self-help" and program "graduation" (i.e., developing to the point where aid was no longer needed) were thus central to the geoeconomic framing and operation of American aid programs after 1961, and of USAID in particular. Kennedy himself noted that within the initial fiscal year's aid package of $2.4 billion, approximately $2 billion would flow back to American businesses because of procurement rules (Duffy 1991, 25). In the first few years following USAID's establishment, the agency provided numerous reports and informational resources emphasizing the importance of economic "take-off" and the mutual economic benefits of aid. Much of this argument was patterned on the experiences of Japan and Western Europe following World War II, and the success of aid administered under the auspices of the Marshall Plan, despite warnings from the Senate Committee on Foreign Relations (1961, 5) that such comparisons were best avoided, as the factors allowing Western Europe to rebuild under the Marshall Plan were "absent" from newly independent states struggling for development progress.

In the debate over the FAA, however, the crucial arguments that bolstered support and secured passage of the act were geopolitical in nature, and they highlighted the urgency of foreign aid reform in the late 1950s and early 1960s. A series of diplomatic and military incidents in 1960 and 1961 (the Soviet capture of an American U-2 spy plane, the failed Bay of Pigs invasion, the failure to move U.S.-Soviet relations forward at the June 1961 Vienna Summit, and the erection of the Berlin Wall in August 1961) made renewed and vigorous foreign policy action to improve U.S. geopolitical footing of utmost concern for American policymakers. More directly, foreign aid advocates identified an emerging "aid gap" between the United States and the Soviet Union that demanded immediate closure, akin to the "missile gap" that motivated expansion and upgrading of the U.S. nuclear weapon arsenal and the "space gap" demonstrated by the 1957 launch of the Sputnik satellite. The Senate Committee on Foreign Relations stated that one vital reason aid reform like that proposed in the FAA was needed was the clearly demonstrable effect of Soviet aid, which amounted to $1.2 billion in the previous year, and was concentrated in India, Indonesia, and the United Arab Republic union of Egypt and Syria (U.S. Senate 1961, 11). The committee stated that this geopolitical necessity would be achieved by aid reform that incorporated standard lending and finance practices, but with special consideration for the exigencies of developing countries receiving loans:

> The [FAA] is built on the premise that aid programs should be related to a country's growth process based on a broad development plan. We can scarcely expect the poorer countries to commit themselves to comprehensive development plans in the absence of reasonable assurances that foreign exchange requirements will be met and that programs undertaken will be supported through completion. The element of continuity is essential to all growth, including economic. It is the element common to all of the aid programs of the Soviet Union. (U.S. Senate 1961, 11)

The move to give greater and more flexible long-term lending authority to a single comprehensive aid institution housed within the executive branch was directly related to closing the perceived aid gap, as the committee stated that the immediate authorization of up to $1.9 billion in development loans "should, at least, balance whatever advantage the Soviet Union may be gaining as a result of the flexibility and continuity of its own aid program" (U.S. Senate 1961, 12). This was echoed by comments from the House Committee on Foreign Affairs, which stated that "this bill as reported provides the most effective means that it is possible to devise for attaining U.S. objectives in the cold war" (quoted in Udall 1961). While in the Senate, Kennedy himself had tried to defray concerns over the costs of foreign aid reform and expansion by making an explicit link between domestic economic growth (which had slowed considerably in the late 1950s) and foreign policy achievements abroad, stating in June 1960 that American economic vigor "greatly influences the countries to the south of us, and the countries of Africa and Asia, which are attempting to determine whether a free society is an effective way of mobilizing their resources, and developing their economy" (Duffy 1991, 35). American economic growth and political freedom depended on development, growth, and freedom abroad, which in turn depended on an American economy strong enough, Kennedy argued, to allow the United States to "afford to do the things which need to be done to build our strength abroad and meet our needs at home" (Duffy 1991, 35). Appeals to the necessity of foreign aid reform appeared in Kennedy's first State of the Union address in January 1961, in communiqués to Congress shortly thereafter, in private meetings with business and congressional leaders, and in congressional testimony by administration officials during the debate over the FAA. Kennedy even initiated the creation of a national campaign and advisory group populated by prominent business, educational, and diplomatic leaders, called the "Citizens Committee for International Development," to help build popular and legislative support for the FAA's passage (Duffy 1991), while the task force that drafted legislative proposals leading to the FAA counted among its members numerous career diplomats, academic experts, development administrators, and philanthropic foundation leaders (Weidner 1961).

Overall, supporters of the Foreign Assistance Act crafted an argument for significant reform of and increases to foreign aid that contained intertwined geoeconomic and geopolitical components, the former built on the absolute certainty that capitalist growth was both the prerequisite and outcome of liberal democracy, the latter on fears that Soviet aggression threatened capitalism, democracy, and freedom around the globe. Containment of this threat, they argued, must be supported by a robust program of development assistance to the undeveloped states of the Third World. Statements iterating the urgent and fundamental geopolitical necessity of aid in the seemingly precarious moment of the summer of 1961 rested on taken-for-granted arguments that developing countries must fall into one camp or another in the global Cold War struggle. Fears of communist infiltration and subterfuge, which had produced McCarthyism in the 1950s at home, were now turned outward, and the collapsing European empires and "banana republics" of Asia, Africa, and Latin America appeared as both a political vacuum prone to Soviet manipulation and control and a lucrative potential market anchored in a system of subordinate allied nation-states. Remaining nonaligned was, in the view of most American political and military elites, a temporary, economically aloof, and potentially dangerous status.

Secretary of State Dean Rusk thus argued before the House of Representatives in May 1961 that "[t]he battleground of freedom . . . is the whole southern half of the globe," and that "if the democratic world cannot satisfy this passion for modernization [among peoples in newly independent developing countries], then the Communists can leap aboard this great revolution, seize it, direct it to their own ends and make it the instrument of their own limitless imperialist ambitions" (quoted in Udall 1961). Even contingency and emergency disaster funding were seen in the light of Soviet influence: "Whatever their ideological disagreements the Communist powers are united on the policy of encouraging strife and rebellion in the less developed societies that they do not control," a situation that led many to believe "we are entering a period of multiple crises" (U.S. Senate 1961, 23).[5] President Kennedy himself returned from the Vienna Summit more convinced than ever that a reorganized and comprehensive permanent foreign aid program was an absolute necessity for U.S. foreign policy, especially as it confronted a more aggressive Soviet presence across the Third

World. He argued that "[a] small group of disciplined Communists could exploit discontent and misery in a country where the average income may be $60 or $70 a year and seize control, therefore, of an entire country without Communist troops ever crossing any international frontier" (quoted in Udall 1961).

In this light, aid was an indispensable tool for fighting and winning the Cold War. Kennedy's Chairman of the Joint Chiefs of Staff, General Lyman Lemnitzer, vouched for the program on military grounds as well, stating that the reform package proposed under the FAA "reflects a realistic, hardheaded, common sense approach to our very difficult security problems—problems which also confront the other free nations of the world" (quoted in Udall 1961). For supporters, foreign assistance had proven successful to date, and with the perceived "aid gap" between the United States and Soviets, undercutting aid or letting it continue in ramshackle fashion would be a foreign policy disaster that would only compound over time. Lemnitzer (quoted in Udall 1961) made this point by noting that "the assistance we have provided, and continue to provide our allies . . . has been a major factor in thwarting Communist aggression," while the powerful Senate Committee on Foreign Relations (1961, 5) argued that "[w]ithout American aid, many countries that today are independent might have been transformed into Communist puppet states," while numerous independent and nonaligned states remained and must also be assisted in their development. Indeed, the United States had a special responsibility to provide such aid as a component of its global leadership, and shirking this was seen as both dangerous and illogical. The Senate Committee thus strongly supported the principles of aid reform in the FAA when it stated: "Foreign aid is both an unavoidable responsibility and a central instrument of our foreign policy. It is dictated by the hard logic of the cold war and by a moral responsibility resulting from poverty, hunger, disease, ignorance, feudalism, strife, revolution, chronic instability, and life without hope" (U.S. Senate 1961, 4). Such geopolitical reasoning became impossible for opponents to overcome, and versions of the FAA passed in the House 287–140 and in the Senate 66–24 in August 1961; the bill went to conference before final approval the following month (Udall 1961). The act authorized the creation of the Agency for International Development, which began operations in November 1961 following Kennedy's executive order laying out its structure.

The geopolitical fears that motivated a good portion of the support for aid reform in 1961 resemble contemporary discussions of asymmetries encountered in fighting a global war on terrorism, in which security concerns and strategies are designed to meet the challenges posed by relatively small groups connected to networks of international financing and strategic support and with an intimate presence in the societies of which they are part. Development aid was fundamentally based not only on the transfer of capital and intellectual resources from the United States to the developing countries but also on the idea of creating the geopolitical and geoeconomic conditions of American hegemony in the fundamental social, economic, and political structures of national and global order. In other words, the task of American foreign aid, and of USAID as an institution, was to create the "geopolitical social" and "geoeconomic social" in recipient countries, as a means of spreading the principles and strategies of capitalist economic growth and combating the aggressive expansion of communism directed from Moscow and Beijing. The geopolitical and geoeconomic discourses embodied and instituted in the new agency were both distinct in their framing of aid's purpose, and the strategic logic of achieving and maintaining American hegemony in the world, and inextricably intertwined through the intellectual and practical work of development intervention on the ground. Importantly, the FAA separated administration of military and development assistance, with the former managed under the authority of the Department of Defense rather than USAID. Military assistance remained a sizable component of the aid program at $1.8 billion for the first two years authorized under the FAA, with funding remaining available until expended rather than expiring at a preset time (Duffy 1991; Udall 1961). Institutionally, then, there was some divergence between the geopolitical component of aid, which was viewed partly in military terms in its allocation and application, and the geoeconomic component, which anticipated the construction of orderly, modernized, capitalist societies through the catalyst of social and economic development assistance administered by USAID. As this all remained couched in the terms of grand geopolitical strategy, with an emphasis on nation building and directing aid to allies providing strategic territorial counters within the logic of containment, the geoeconomic impetus within aid remained secondary to the geopolitical in this period.

The dynamic interplay of geopolitical and geoeconomic discourses and strategies produced difficulties for USAID. Reports and other informational resources produced by the agency in its first few years of operation indicate lingering concerns about aid's impact on the interests of and opportunities for private capital. Within this were the seeds of tensions between a geoeconomic perspective favoring geographical connectivity, achieved through market mechanisms and viewing appropriate state action relative to these as distinctly limited in scope and scale, and a geopolitical perspective emphasizing nation building and the strategic necessity of containment and modernization policies facilitated by aid allocated primarily according to political and military rather than economic criteria. Early in its operation, USAID (1964, 5; see also USAID 1966) described its mission as one of "assist[ing] other countries that seek to maintain their independence and become self-supporting," linking the twin ideological foundations of capitalist economic growth and political resistance to international communism. The understanding and vision of development institutionalized in USAID, and within the broader state and hegemonic projects of development, was based largely in modernization theory, though other dissenting and diverging views of the process took root in developing countries.

Modernization theory, which began from a sociological focus on the characteristics and interaction between social, economic, and political systems in the process of development, was the major intellectual force supporting USAID strategies and programs. Development was understood as an evolutionary process occurring through systemic change, leading to the overall development of a whole society through a series of historical stages moving from traditional to modern, and measured by the yardstick of liberal, democratic, industrial societies led by the United States. The basic tenets of modernization theory should be familiar to observers and students of development policy and studies, but it bears repeating that in this theorization of development, developed (complex and modern) and undeveloped (simple and premodern) societies existed on the same historical continuum. While functionally similar, these were different in terms of the dominant norms, expressions, and structures of social behavior and decision making found in each type of society. Development could proceed only if both structures and social attitudes changed, and social attitudes only shifted by changing the structures that made those attitudes. In sum, development was envisioned as a totalizing process, encompassing all aspects of a given national society (Lawson 2007; Peet and Hartwick 2009).

This approach reached its clearest and most influential formulation in Walt Rostow's "stages of economic growth" formula, detailed in his book *The Stages of Economic Growth: A Non-Communist Manifesto*, first published in 1960. Rostow had a long and distinguished career in both academia and government, including service in the Office of Strategic Services (OSS) during World War II, as well as in the State Department and the Economic Commission for Europe following the war. In the 1960s, he worked in various high-level government positions for Presidents Kennedy and Johnson (including the task force that helped draft the FAA), but returned to teaching after Johnson left office in 1969. Apart from the particulars of Rostow's stages of growth model, the subtitle of his main work (*A Non-Communist Manifesto*) is important, as he focused not only on how developing countries could and should modernize but also on how to prevent these states from becoming aligned with the Soviet Union in the Cold War. Rostow's work also addressed prospects for peace and war between societies at different stages of modernization (such as the United States and Vietnam, for example). He was eager to show that Marx was wrong in both his supposed economic determinism and his political miscalculation of social bonds in advanced capitalist societies, though he did highlight the totalizing vision shared by communist development programs and his own stages of growth model.

As an evolutionary, sociological, and economic approach, the stages of growth framework focuses on all the aspects of modernization discussed above and their expression in different connected spheres of social life. Rostow's main contribution was to apply these ideas globally as a way of explaining and pushing for a particular form of modernization that stressed a sequence of stages through which societies must move to achieve modernization and development. This theory was both spatial and historical, in that by looking at certain aspects of social life (especially the economic system), one could determine where a given society (coterminous with the territorial state) existed on the social and historical continuum. The goal was to move from the stage where preconditions for take-off were prevalent, but not fully organized as the engines of social, political, and economic change; through to take-off, in which the forces of economic growth became dominant across a society; and on to stages of "maturity" and "high mass consumption." For modernization theorists, most countries needing or receiving aid were mired in the preconditions for take-off stage; aid was meant to provide the technical, capital, and political support to spark take-off and the drive to modernization. In the take-off stage, Rostow argued, economic growth became a virtue in its own right and would propel other social systems toward proper development, as "[g]rowth becomes [the society's] normal condition. Compound interest becomes built, as it were, into its habits and institutional structure" (Rostow 1990, 7).

Rostow (1990, 143) himself had argued in *The Stages of Economic Growth* that the movement toward development could be supported by foreign assistance, though this "must be organized on an enlarged and, especially, on a more stable basis," so as to provide not only the economic but, even more importantly, the political support needed for anticommunist elites in developing states to successfully push the transition toward take-off. The agency's most recent official history (2002b, 3) argues that Rostow's modernization theory "provided the premise for much of the development planning" the new agency undertook, and the geoeconomic and geopolitical components of his stages model stand out clearly as mutually supporting and reinforcing in the context of American Cold War strategies in the 1960s. Yet USAID was at pains from its establishment to make clear that its foreign aid and development programs did not undermine U.S. hegemony as a whole by working against the particular character of American economic power in the postwar world economy. First and foremost, the agency had to demonstrate that foreign aid did not drain American coffers, and that such expenditures would yield sizable economic and political returns even if development meant the growth of protected and even state-run domestic industries capable of competing with or limiting U.S. imports. As discussed above, this was not a new critique among the American foreign policy and business elite. To counter "misconceptions" about aid, USAID (1964, 8) made two points prominent:

1. American dollars are seldom given directly to foreign countries. Most economic aid involves the financing of U.S. goods and services for specific development activities.
2. Economic aid to the industrialized countries (Western Europe and Japan) was ended years ago. AID programs now are concentrated in the underdeveloped countries of Asia, Africa, and Latin America.

The agency worked to demonstrate that it did not deliver handouts of taxpayer money to countries where such funds were no longer necessary to spur investment, growth, and political reform. Instead, foreign governments paid American producers and sellers for military, industrial, and agricultural assistance with loans made in American dollars and managed by USAID. In fact, the FAA reorganization included a "guaranty program" that would "provide protection assuring United States business against certain risks of doing business overseas," encouraging private capital's insertion into the development financing process and continuing today via OPIC, the quasi-governmental Overseas Private Investment Corporation (USAID 2002b, 4).

Furthermore, the agency stated that economic and political development abroad was not an end in itself but an economic boon for the United States. This was particularly true for trade relations, as USAID (1966, 32) argued that "[d]eveloped countries are the best customers for American exports," citing Western Europe and Japan, beneficiaries of American aid in the immediate postwar years, as examples. In terms of food aid, which quickly became and remains one of the major components of U.S. development assistance and one of the agency's most important functions, USAID contended that development assistance provided in the form of food commodities would help not only poor peasants and growing urban areas in the developing world but also American farmers and food exporters. Food donations came from commodity stocks designated as surplus by the U.S. Department of Agriculture (USDA), while industrialization and urbanization in the developing world demanded the United States fill the subsequent gap in developing states' ability to feed themselves until agricultural modernization could provide national food self-sufficiency. Most important was USAID's (1963, 6) firm statement that "the aid provided . . . cannot substitute for trade," a point reiterated even more strongly today, as discussed in chapter 4. Aid programs were not to interfere with or displace normal channels of private trade, and USAID presented food and other forms of capital assistance as a path toward market development for future U.S. exports. Like most other forms of aid, food aid was not usually a direct government-to-government donation but a concessional sale made with long-term (up to thirty years), low-interest dollar loans from the U.S. government. Thus foreign exchange reserves were built up, accounts balanced, and political allies rewarded, all as USAID (1963, 18) assured American producers and exporters that this constituted an effective way to "maintain or expand present markets and to develop new outlets." Food assistance in the form of surplus food commodities distributed to geopolitically strategic developing states became a major component of U.S. state and hegemonic development projects, and the basis for U.S. "green power," a point discussed in more detail in chapter 3 (Garst and Barry 1990; Kodras 1993; McMichael 2000; McMichael 2008; Murphy and McAfee 2005).

In sum, the contest over foreign aid from the end of World War II and up to USAID's establishment demonstrated the strong overlap between geopolitical and geoeconomic discourses in the early Cold War, and the differential institutionalization of these discourses and the practices they informed within the U.S. state. Geopolitical logic garnered the support necessary for supporters of aid reform in 1961, leading to the creation of USAID and the consolidation of multiple functions and objectives related to development assistance under one institutional roof. The geoeconomic, however, always existed as a necessary but not sufficient rationale and structuring set of ideals for development aid; indeed, the debate preceding the Foreign Assistance Act in 1961 shows that the two bodies of discourse were never entirely separate and that they were dynamically articulated with each other and with specific strategic conditions facing U.S. policymakers at the time. Again, geopolitics and geoeconomics as geostrategic discourses do not map neatly onto a territorialized/deterritorialized rubric, but instead they build from, emphasize, and inform different frameworks for geospatial knowledge construction, state action, and development strategies. A look at the initial structure of USAID, and efforts to reform and reorganize the agency in the 1960s and early 1970s, shows the further elaboration of these discourses through and by the agency as well as the beginning of geoeconomic challenges to the dominance of geopolitical rationales in the U.S.-led development project.

From the "Decade of Development" to Institutional Crisis

When it began operations in November 1961, USAID ushered in what Kennedy dubbed the "decade of development" as a semiautonomous executive agency under the coordination of the State Department but answering to the president. In terms of bureaucratic structure, the agency (in its own words) entered into existence "like a blushing bride—wearing something borrowed and something new" (Duffy 1991, 60). The agency incorporated offices, functions, and staff of preexisting aid institutions, notably the technical assistance and social and economic components of the ICA and the financing capacities of the Development Loan Fund (DLF), while also creating four world regional bureaus—Africa and Europe, Far East, Latin America, and Near East and South Asia—each headed by an assistant administrator (Duffy 1991; Weidner 1961). These bureaus not only identified world regions of logistical and strategic action for envisioning and executing development action, usually planned and implemented at the scale of an individual country, they also helped to resolve differences between the fledgling USAID and the Department of State, creating a clear chain of command for development policy planning and enactment from field officers through embassies and to USAID head offices in Washington, imitating in part the structure and personnel titles of the State Department (Weidner 1961, 114–126).

This was something of a compromise between those who favored a geographic rather than a functional approach to development aid planning, which included most of the primaries on Kennedy's 1961 aid reform task force, and those who had long worked in aid programs organized along functional lines. Some aspects of the new agency's work remained tied to cross-regional or global offices organized around specific functions or support tasks, including financial accounting, personnel management, internal legal services, and commodity programs, including the Food for Peace food aid program (Duffy 1991; USAID 2007; Weidner 1961). While the functionally oriented offices remained important, the regional bureaus were a significant innovation in development aid planning and policy, and they strongly institutionalized within USAID the methodological nationalism of modernization theory and a form of organizational authority and hierarchy patterned on the more established and prestigious State Department. In this, USAID sought to ensure not only a place for itself within the policy environment of the Cold War American state but also to align the mission of development aid and the broader strategies of U.S. foreign policy, a necessary task for an agency whose mandate remained suspect to many lawmakers and the American public.

To get the new agency on its feet, Kennedy appointed Fowler Hamilton, a longtime government lawyer, as the first USAID administrator. Hamilton laid out USAID's emphases on country-level development planning and "self-help" facilitated by U.S. funding shortly after his Senate confirmation in October 1961: "In the administration of this program we will regard it as our first duty to help those of the less-developed friendly countries that make efforts to help themselves, and we will regard as the best evidence of their desire to help themselves their willingness to undertake changes, *if necessary even in their internal organization*, that will enable us to take what is after all seed money, small in amount but we hope effective in consequence" (Duffy 1991, 59, emphasis added). With USAID's mandate and structure laid out, the new agency became a central site within the U.S. state for managing aid to developing countries, crucial to the interscalar coordination and reproduction of state and hegemonic projects of liberal internationalism. The broad economic development and foreign policy objectives of USAID's mission, and the ideological link between the two, produced a wide range of points for intervention in developing societies and states by U.S. development planners. In turn, this created the need for professional expertise in outlining, managing, and assessing such intervention. Weidner (1961, 135–160) details wrangling over personnel and staffing as early as the spring of 1961, when the task force drafting legislative proposals for aid reform sought to create an administrative system that would favor principles of country planning and self-help rather than the functionalist and piecemeal approach under which existing aid program staff worked prior to USAID's establishment. Reformers on this task force saw absorbing staff wholesale (from ICA in particular) as problematic, and they pushed to integrate and ingratiate the new agency with the State Department via a unified personnel system. This resulted in some overlap with that department, and a reduction in existing staff after 1961 to make way for newcomers attached to views of development and aid more in line with those of reformers.

The training and expansion of a large pool of experts specifically focused on development, especially development as understood through the lens of modernization theory, was a key part of USAID's evolution in the decade following its founding and moved it away from its roots in personnel who came from the crucible of the Marshall Plan and the agency's predecessors. Within just a few months of taking his post, for example, Fowler had reviewed the files of 700 ICA and DLF staff shifted to the new agency with marginal performance assessments, and he let 350 of them go (Toner 1962). The hiring of new field officers and administrators with training in development was crucial to the agency's success in exercising its mandate and working with other government, inter-governmental, and private institutions. One USAID officer who spent his early career in several Central American posts in the 1960s and 1970s stated:

> We stood out as the first USAID generation of trained development professionals. We were among the first to come out of the U.S. university system with formal course work and graduate degrees in international development. Our predeces-sors, and in some cases our mentors in the field, who participated in earlier U.S. government overseas assistance going back as far as the Marshall Plan in Europe and the Point Four plan in Latin America, were all career specialists in engineer-ing, agricultural marketing, research and extension, infectious diseases, or educa-tion administration. None were development practitioners by trade and training. (Church 2001, 12)

The focus on development as an interdisciplinary object of intellectual inquiry and professional training cannot be understood apart from the geopolitical discourse that centered on national states in the developing world as taken-for-granted objects of theoretical and practical work, distinct from their counter-parts in the developed world but still subject to the same universalizing pro-cesses and part of the same politically charged and divided state system. Nor can it be divorced from the geoeconomic emphasis on social change ignited by capitalist growth and "self-help" triggered by the technical support and "seed money" U.S. assistance provided. The geoeconomic and the geopolitical were bound tightly together in USAID's initial operation, and continual reorganization efforts indicated the extent to which the agency worked to fully align them.

Yet emphases rooted in U.S. foreign policy meant USAID's development work in the field was often planned or assessed through a geopolitical lens first and foremost, with an eye toward making foreign aid a short-term strategic tool for achieving foreign policy objectives as well as a long-term tool for a given country's economic and sociopolitical development. The former could under-mine the latter or lead to programs and projects without clear objectives or follow-through. A longtime agency officer who worked in the Afghanistan mis-sion during the late 1960s argued that USAID's presence and operations in front-line Cold War countries was dominated utterly by geopolitical considerations: "[S]urely the sole reason for our massive presence was one associated with try-ing to preserve the independence of Afghanistan and a line against Soviet en-croachment into the region beyond the Amu Darya. . . . We were, of course, engaged in the Cold War and our presence was to try to preserve our position, the Western position in Afghanistan" (Kean 1995, 45). The geopolitical rationale driving development aid under USAID auspices in such locations resulted in massively expensive projects designed primarily to counter a Soviet presence or to influence the local population and government in a favorable way. Whether such projects or the USAID mission resulted in long-term development achievements and geoeconomic transformations in the country's social, political, and economic fabric was quite often a secondary concern in this period.

Thus, while USAID officials and field officers worked to make development progress a key part of broader geostrategic thinking, and took on technical and financial work in planning, developing, and (less so) implementing long-term projects, the agency and its development mission remained strongly framed by geopolitical concerns. So, for example, the Alliance for Progress program, launched in 1961 and designed to direct a significant amount of aid to Latin America for social and economic development programs, had as a primary animating force the urgent necessity to combat communism and "Castroism" across the region. An early request to Congress for funding noted that "a political struggle is in progress between the opposing ideologies of communism and the Free World" that could only be won by providing development assistance that would achieve pro-poor reforms without fomenting class warfare and violent revolution (Duffy 1991, 72). The fear of unrest provoked by underdevelopment and manipulated by the forces of international communism drove the push for aid and put USAID at the forefront of enacting geopolitical strategies. The agency's Latin America regional bureau was merged with its parallel regional bureau in the State Department (Kleine 1996), a unique situation that gave USAID staff, and their focus on national and regional development, a direct seat at the foreign policy table. Ronald Venezia (1996, 17), a USAID official who worked in the Latin America bureau at the time, noted that USAID "had a strong back to back relationship with the State Department" that placed the agency's Latin America offices "in the midst with foreign policy" and gave them a strong ability to "get things done"; sharing office space and functional duties with the State Department meant that, in Latin America at least, "We [USAID] were a machine. We could do things."

By the early 1970s, the Alliance for Progress was winding down in an effort to "graduate" countries from development aid, demonstrating "success" to Congress and placating long-standing worries that aid programs were open-ended with little chance of actually generating capacity for self-help among recipients. Field officers and embassy staff resisted ending Alliance programs in Latin America for fear that without substantial aid to offer the region's governments, they would lose influence and the U.S. image would be tarnished (Herrick 1996;

Kleine 1996). Yet USAID efforts in Latin America were meant to graduate countries based not only on development progress, measured by reduced need for capital and financial inflows, but also by the creation of an intellectual strata that would make American experts unnecessary in the long run. A USAID officer who spent several years in the region during the Alliance for Progress period argued that while the State Department was very concerned with the political aspects of U.S. development strategies in Latin America, USAID was much more focused on providing "[s]upport for the individual economists and others of the countries who were dedicated to development, many of whom had been educated in the United States" (Herrick 1996, 24).

The effort to institutionalize a cadre of U.S.-trained professional development experts was a key component not only of the nation-building aspect of USAID's presence in Latin America but also of intellectual and political battles over the theorization and framing of development, especially as the dependency school of thought rose to prominence and challenged many aspects of modernization theory (Peet and Hartwick 2009; Slater 2004). Aid also continued to serve instrumental geopolitical purposes in the region, however, as demonstrated by the decision to cease funding for new projects in Chile upon the election of leftist president Salvador Allende, and the subsequent restoration of aid funding at even higher levels following the U.S.-supported military coup that overthrew Allende. In the words of Herman Kleine, head of the USAID Latin America bureau and the Alliance for Progress, Secretary of State Henry Kissinger's goal in restoring aid to Chile was to "strengthen the Chilean economy under its new leadership" and "throw out the Communist influence that Allende had been attempting to bring about" (Kleine 1996, 63). In this, the geoeconomic was both a means to achieve the geopolitical and a desired outcome of geopolitical strategy.

In such moments, these two geostrategic discourses, and the aid and development practices they informed, coalesced and diverged, abetting a discursive, strategic, and practical evolution that made the subjugation of geoeconomic impulses and forces to geopolitical objectives increasingly difficult to manage. The agency found itself caught in the middle of these pressures as developmental, foreign policy, and national economic strategies and objectives began to shift in the 1970s, and tensions between geopolitical and geoeconomic framings and strategies often found expression in reforms of USAID structure and operations. This can be seen most clearly in the agency's involvement in the Vietnam War, the failures of which led to serious reconsideration of both aid's purpose and the institutional mandate and standing of USAID within the broad scope of American national security, foreign policy, and development strategies. Most importantly, the Vietnam War strongly tainted congressional and public views of direct intervention in foreign countries as part of a Cold War grand strategy, undermining support for aid generally and USAID specifically. Through staff in the field and its East Asia bureau, USAID had played a pivotal role in American intervention in South Vietnam from the agency's inception, with the main thrust of agency operations "focused primarily on counterinsurgency, at least in the broader sense of addressing conditions that facilitated the successes of the Viet Cong" (USAID 2007, 5). This included assistance to rural pacification efforts (no surprise given the agency's technical and programmatic expertise in rural and agricultural development), as well as support specifically to areas affected by military operations. But USAID was not just a handmaiden to military operations in South Vietnam. The agency worked diligently toward economic stabilization and "national cohesion" in its American ally against the communist North and the Viet Cong (USAID 2007, 5).

From 1967 to 1972 the agency's mission in Vietnam shifted with changes in military strategy, as the U.S. military took on pacification duties and moved toward the "Vietnamization" of the war, focusing on training and equipping the South Vietnamese army. The agency, in turn, focused more heavily on economic stabilization, humanitarian assistance to civilians affected by the war, and "developing Vietnamese institutions and economic and social services" (USAID 2007, 5). The agency's staffing levels, in Vietnam and globally, hit all-time highs in 1968, and dropped thereafter; at its largest, the agency had over 18,000 personnel working globally, including almost 5,100 in Vietnam itself, with almost two-thirds of those being foreign nationals (USAID 2007, 6). After the American military withdrawal in 1973, USAID's efforts and presence in the country dwindled, concentrating on humanitarian assistance and supporting the fiction that South Vietnam was a viable state that could support a national economy. The last stages of the Vietnam War were difficult times for the agency, and it struggled with goals and programs in Indochina that put the entire foreign aid program in the crosshairs of its detractors in Congress, and made development policy completely subject to the geopolitical rationales and logic of policy "hawks" intent on supporting South Vietnam and continuing the war. Miles Wedeman, who served in the agency's Cambodia office and as the director of the Office of Vietnam Affairs in the East Asia Bureau, suggested that the war strongly influenced staffing decisions, and that by the war's end, significant differences in perspective were to be found in the field in Indochina and in Washington headquarters. While the "people in [the Department of] State responsible for Cambodia were not great enthusiasts for the war in Vietnam" (Wedeman 1995, 25) and sought policy and development officers without experience in Vietnam for posts in Phnom Penh, decisions in Washington remained in the hands of those advocating for the war's continuation:

> I didn't like working on Vietnam. I said at the time, "All but the superhawks have fled." Everybody, not in AID necessarily, but people who were influential in State, and particularly on the National Security Council staff, and the Ambassador in Saigon, still thought it was a war to be won. And, won in a sort of conventional sense, that somehow the North Vietnamese were going to be beaten. It was clear this was not going to happen. But here we were, still busy, planning for future fiscal years. . . . Certainly the people who worked at AID on Vietnam were uneasy about it, but our Ambassador in Vietnam was very, very insistent on a big AID program, that sort of thing. (Wedeman 1995, 38)

With the clear deterioration of the U.S. position in Vietnam, and USAID's central if increasingly reluctant position in the execution of American strategy in the region, criticism of aid ramped up and initiated strong challenges to the agency's mandate, funding, and structure. Some in Congress began to criticize USAID for "having too many people in Washington," a situation remedied by transferring personnel to other agencies, while a more general program of reducing American military and foreign service personnel abroad resulted in attempts to increase the relative importance of field officers and the regional bureaus, as well as large reductions to USAID staff, especially in Washington (Mustard 2003, 42; USAID 2007).[6] While USAID maintained strong influence over the work of development specialists in other agencies both directly and indirectly, the loss of personnel should not be regarded as simple bureaucratic weight-shifting. Such moves signaled a serious challenge to USAID's mission and political standing and to the hegemony of the liberal internationalist development project as a whole. In light of persistent economic stagnation and failures in Vietnam, the entire purpose and structure of U.S. development policy was challenged during this period. Criticism became so strong that "in 1971, the Senate rejected a foreign assistance bill authorizing funds for fiscal years 1972 and 1973," the first outright congressional rejection of foreign aid authorization since before the Marshall Plan (USAID 2002b, 4). Congress also placed strict constraints on aid to Laos, Vietnam, and Cambodia, preventing its use for military and security purposes in those states, and the agency began to contract out more of its work amid tightening budgets and waning support on Capitol Hill and in the White House (USAID 2007).

If a fundamentally geopolitical rationale had garnered the ideological and political support necessary to get USAID on a firm footing after World War II and into the Cold War's early years, both geopolitics *and* geoeconomics informed the agency's activities and made U.S. development policy and strategy a form of nation-building designed to expand commercial opportunities in an interdependent world of liberal democratic states while containing the spread of international communism. By the mid-1970s, Congress, the White House, and even USAID itself were undertaking numerous moves to significantly alter the agency's geostrategic foundations and approach to development by emphasizing the geoeconomic more strongly, especially as neoliberalism increasingly began to shape the political environment. Geopolitical framings and objectives remained important, however, as the Cold War entered a new phase and USAID's instrumental purposes within U.S. foreign policy were reiterated.

CHAPTER THREE

Geoeconomics Ascendant

Development, Interdependence, and Neoliberalization

THE U.S. AGENCY FOR INTERNATIONAL DEVELOPMENT'S (USAID) annual budget request and accompanying justification for fiscal year 1982 stressed mechanisms and themes that sought to reorient the agency and the overall U.S. assistance program toward greater participation with and reliance on market mechanisms and the private sector. As new agency head M. Peter McPherson stated in his introduction to USAID's proposed budget, the administration of Ronald Reagan was "committed to increased opportunities for the private—both commercial and non-profit—sector to participate in AID programs" while maintaining foreign aid's role as a vital element in protecting and advancing American interests abroad (USAID 1981, 2). The following year, McPherson used his introductory budget statement to more robustly state the new tack USAID would take on the private sector's role in U.S. development and aid strategies. Following an October 1981 speech in which President Reagan posed a complementary and facilitating relationship between government and private enterprise, McPherson outlined several principles to guide USAID as well as American development policy more generally. First among these was that U.S. development policy should "stimulat[e] international trade by opening up markets, both within and among countries," while also working to improve the "political atmosphere" and the "climate for private investment and the transfer of technology accompanying such investment" (USAID 1982, 2).

Such statements indicate a sea change in thinking and strategy at USAID in the early 1980s, ostensibly toward a more fully geoeconomic (and thoroughly neoliberal) approach to foreign aid and international development. This approach put private capital, liberalized trade relations, and international market forces at the center of development processes, with USAID and government more broadly acting primarily as facilitators of economic connectivity and growth. Yet it would be incorrect to assume that, in this period, geoeconomics firmly and fully supplanted geopolitics as the underlying discourse shaping the agency's activities, structure, and strategies. The Reagan-era shift toward a market-oriented approach to development and aid was the product of several years of intermittent crisis within the geopolitically driven development strategies that had shaped USAID from its inception through the Vietnam War, and it was but a midpoint in the process of institutional reform and geostrategic change that took the agency from the Cold War mindset of its initial two decades of operation to the post–Cold War era of neoliberalization. Both the Reagan and George H. W. Bush administrations reasserted the agency's instrumental geopolitical uses, especially in directing aid to anticommunist allies and movements in Africa and Latin America. On the other hand, the agency had strived in the latter half of the 1970s to distance itself from the geopolitical maneuvering of the Vietnam era and adjust to a "basic needs" approach to development, with a firm footing in a distinctively geoeconomic understanding of the poor's capacity to participate in development as rational economic agents.

Accordingly, USAID found itself amid the wreckage of Vietnam at the center of a double crisis of development geopolitics and geopolitical development. By this, I mean the geopolitical discourse that framed development largely in terms of the ideological struggle between the democratic, liberal, capitalist United States and the centrally planned, authoritarian communism of the Soviet Union began to fray as a dominant mode of development thought and a blueprint for development strategy and policy. At the same time, the actually existing model of development and aid enframed and enacted largely (but not entirely) through this discourse—and expressed primarily through the prescriptions of modernization theory, the foreign policy strategies of the United States and its client and allied states, and the institutional structures of USAID—were increasingly seen as failures at worst and misguided and ineffectual at best. A strong sense that the challenges posed by international development and growing global economic interdependence were rapidly outpacing the ability of existing institutions, especially USAID, to answer them, lay at the root of this double crisis, though it is important not to discount the shifting political and economic bases of American hegemony as well.

Beginning in the early 1970s geopolitics faced serious challenges as the dominant geostrategic framing and rationale for USAID, U.S. development policy, and development intervention generally. By the middle of the 1980s, this challenge had crystallized around a more fully geoeconomic conceptualization of state action and appropriate development steeped in emergent processes of neoliberalization. It was during this period, amid recurrent global debt, energy, and food crises, the failures of nation building in Vietnam, movement toward liberalization in the international trade system, and the last stages and subsequent end of the Cold War, that neoliberalization took firm hold within development theory and practice. Within this transition, USAID worked to reconcile geopolitical and geoeconomic discourses and strategies of development, while political actors in the executive and legislative branches made repeated attempts to reorganize and reorient the agency. Many of the changes occurring at and through USAID hinged on the structure and character of the state in the developing world, relative to the balance of class and internationalizing market forces, as well as lingering geopolitical concerns associated with the Cold War. The increasing insistence that USAID promote institutional and political restructuring to facilitate liberalization and other market-oriented policy reforms in developing states became so dominant by the late 1980s, however, that it formed the basis for a fundamental rethinking of how the agency made and enacted development strategies and, perhaps more importantly, how it produced, legitimated, and managed geographical knowledge about development processes and programs.

New Directions and the "Art of Development"

In 1973 Congress significantly amended the Foreign Assistance Act (FAA) of 1961, the result of lawmakers' dissatisfaction with the track record of USAID and American development assistance during the Vietnam War. The changes in policy and strategy outlined in the 1973 legislation enacted much more than basic institutional or programmatic tinkering, putting in place a set of objectives and approaches that, over time, significantly altered the geostrategic framing and operation of American development assistance and the inner workings and external relations of USAID. The initial House resolution (H.R. 9360) to amend the FAA had proposed changing the lead U.S. development and aid institution's name from the "Agency for International Development" to the "Mutual Development and Cooperation Agency," to better "reflect the emerging view that this country has a direct self-interest in the development of the low income countries" because of their potential influence on "the functioning of the world's cooperative systems in such fields as trade, monetary affairs, and investment" (U.S. House of Representatives 1973, 2).

This legislation was sent to committee in summer 1973, and was replaced in the end by a bill (S. 1443) whose provisions were less far-reaching yet nonetheless retained an emphasis on "mutual cooperation" with developing countries in devising and implementing development and aid strategies. The overall shift laid out in the 1973 legislation, which came to be known as the "New Directions" policy, stressed a new target for American development aid in the "poor majority" of developing states, a new approach to implementing and channeling aid across economic and social sectors toward "basic needs," and a re-organized portfolio of technical and commodity forms of assistance rather than the large capital investments that had previously marked much of the USAID-administered funding envelope (U.S. House of Representatives 1976; USAID 2002b). For USAID, this meant new priorities for overseas missions, programs, and projects as well as "organizational restructuring that merged generalist and technical staffs," establishment of a new liaison structure with the State Department, and the relative strengthening of field staff and regional bureaus within the agency (USAID 2007, 7).

While the New Directions policy was formally outlined in 1973 and implemented in the years following, the increased strategic and programmatic importance it placed on the development role of private and voluntary organizations (PVOs; referred to in different contexts as charitable, philanthropic, and civil society organizations) and private capital had been articulated as a way forward for American aid as early as a May 1969 message from President Richard Nixon to Congress (titled "New Directions in Foreign Aid"). In this message, Nixon staked out his administration's support for a robust foreign aid program, but with important new elements that would "redirect" and rejuvenate American development policy and assistance. Chief among these was the need to "enlist the energies of private enterprise, here and abroad, in the cause of economic development . . . by stimulating additional investment through businesslike channels, rather than offering ringing exhortations" (Nixon 1969, 3).[1] While the president's message stressed that private enterprise, facilitated and encouraged by appropriate government action, was historically the most effective engine for development progress, it also noted that increased participation by private capital and stronger flows of private investment were necessary to maintain the aid program "[in] this time of stringent budgetary restraint" (Nixon 1969, 11). To this end, the policies Nixon outlined in 1969 also called upon other industrialized states (particularly those in Western Europe, which had previously benefited from American aid but which by the 1970s were becoming serious economic competitors) to shoulder more of the political responsibility and financial burden of development aid. He also argued that USAID itself should shift to emphasize provision of technical forms of assistance and institution building, especially in agriculture, family planning, and education and health. All of these elements eventually made it into the 1973 legislation, though it was also the Nixon administration's expansion of war across Vietnam, Laos, and Cambodia that helped grease the wheels of reform for USAID and its approach to development.

The changes outlined by Nixon, taken up by Congress, and eventually enacted within USAID indicated the extent to which a geoeconomic framing of development was gaining traction, as well as how the geoeconomic social was to be envisioned and constructed in developing countries. The geoeconomic discourse and its strategic and institutional expressions remained somewhat fettered by the institutional structures and cultures of a weakened but still dominant geopolitical orientation. Thus, while the New Directions policy induced strong changes in the focus of U.S. foreign development assistance and USAID, the concepts that underlay aid targeting—basic needs and the poor majority— were not fully clarified or worked out in terms of USAID's strategic and programmatic functioning. Though increasingly oriented toward the involvement of private actors in project implementation, American bilateral aid remained a government-to-government program, and thus it was subject to the demands of American foreign policy strategies and interests rather than a strictly economic rationality or the promise of specific returns to U.S.-based financiers and investors. In beginning to alter the geostrategic framing and enactment of development toward a more fully geoeconomic basis, however, the New Directions policy also launched a series of functional and administrative changes within USAID that led eventually to a profound shift not only in the content of the aid portfolio (from infrastructure and capital financing to more technical, institutional, and commodity assistance) but also in how the agency produced, structured, and deployed knowledge about development, including geospatial knowledge. This change was linked to the increasing importance placed on USAID's coordinating role within an expanding set of development actors, including not just PVOs and private capital but also other official development assistance (ODA) agencies, multilateral organizations, international financial institutions, development consulting firms, and even the intended beneficiaries of aid, the poor themselves.

This last point is vital for understanding how the implementation of the New Directions policy led to further restructuring at USAID, as the difficulty of defining, let alone directly reaching and involving, the poor majority in the development process proved difficult for the agency. It likewise demonstrates the lag between shifts in development theory and development practice, the institutional inertia that often results when such shifts are articulated into specific policy and strategic changes, and the contingency of political outcomes across the discursive and political economic terrain of geostrategic decision making. The two major emphases of the New Directions policy were its insistence on better aid targeting to reach the poor majority within developing countries and its reorientation of aid to provide "basic needs" to improve the quality of life for this majority. The former was a product of the latter, with the basic needs approach quickly achieving widespread acceptance among both mainstream and radical development theorists and practitioners in the 1970s. Under the leadership of Robert McNamara (formerly architect of the U.S. war effort in Vietnam), for example, the World Bank adopted a basic needs approach that worked toward "enabling decent living conditions (food, clothing, housing, services)" for those living in poverty in order "to raise the productivity of the poor, enabling them to be brought into the economic system" (Peet and Hartwick 2009, 88). This was to be achieved through a sort of "global Keynesianism," using rapid growth in both relative and absolute productivity to bring people quickly out of poverty and "to use the resources made available . . . to expand public services" (Peet and Hartwick 2009, 88). This version of basic needs relied on developing states to provide or facilitate such services. By the early 1980s the World Bank had scrapped key elements of this approach and moved strongly in a neoliberal direction, painting the state itself as an impediment to development-promoting market growth, a view also adopted by the Reagan administration with significant implications for USAID, as discussed below.

The basic needs approach also appeared in stronger, more radical forms, growing out of criticisms, especially from dependency theorists and popular social movements representing or incorporating the poor, about the lack of poor peoples' inclusion in the development process and mainstream institutions' general neglect of and resistance to redistributive policies within dominant development models. Lawson (2007), summarizing the work of Wisner (1989) on differences among versions of the basic needs approach in Africa, argues the weaker version of basic needs that held sway in mainstream development institutions like USAID and the World Bank deflected concerns over structural inequalities in land, capital, and access to decision-making authority within development processes. Rather than confront the challenge of genuine, popular political participation and decision making by the poor, the weak basic needs approach instead encouraged them "to participate in development projects, such as building infrastructure, taking out credit, and so on" (Lawson 2007, 101). This has, according to this reading, evolved into contemporary development approaches that emphasize building human resources and social capital at the expense of democratic inclusion of the subjects of development. The focus on social, political, and economic inequalities *within* developing countries, concentrated on channeling development aid more directly toward the poor, likewise generally neglected the wider context of global inequalities between the global North and South. This gap fueled a concerted effort within the international state system, especially by the developing countries in the UN's Group of 77 (G-77), calling for fundamental reform of the international economic system to open up developed country markets to developing country goods, and to improve terms of trade, financial access, and technology transfer for Third World states (McMichael 2008, 121).

The agency's 1975 report to the House Committee on International Relations on its implementation of New Directions highlighted the problem of definition in planning development for the poor majority and the agency's understanding of the basic needs approach, especially in the context of existing institutional networks that favored intergovernmental relations and official bodies rather than direct connection to the poor themselves. The agency noted that in implementing New Directions, it sought to make development a more participatory process for poor beneficiaries, thereby bolstering the effectiveness and reach of development aid while "avoiding any suggestion of a handout," but numerous factors conspired to make such wide-ranging strategic and programmatic change difficult and slow (USAID 1975, 3). Such changes involved hard economic and political choices within the strategic planning of developing countries, and USAID was careful to highlight not only that significant resources and time were needed to effect such a monumental strategic shift but also that outcomes and appropriate mechanisms were not always entirely clear. Pointing out that "[we] have not had universal success in our own country in eliminating poverty," USAID (1975, 5) attempted to head off further congressional criticism and challenges by asserting the necessity of time, unequivocal political resolve, and legislative deference to agency expertise in defining and assessing development success.

How to define and reach the poor majority, and how to assess and measure development progress in an ongoing fashion, were the basis of such expertise. These were precisely the problems faced in implementing a new geostrategic basis and modus operandi for development assistance and USAID. In laying out what was meant by participation, the agency also had to confront the wide thematic priorities for development prescribed in the New Directions policy—food and nutrition, population control and family planning, and education and health. These were, Congress and USAID outlined, those aspects of developing countries' social, economic, and political systems through which the poor were most likely to be reached and from which they would most directly benefit (USAID 1975; U.S. House of Representatives 1976). Thus, those projects proposed by developing countries most likely to be funded via USAID-managed aid accounts, and supported through technical assistance provided by USAID, were those that addressed these functional themes and proceeded on the basis of participation by the poor (especially women) in the project's execution. Participation formed a significant measure of selectivity for aid allocation, and the agency interpreted its new focus as one in which aid resources were to be concentrated in "countries whose development policies we can support and that can utilize our assistance effectively," especially in priority functional areas, implemented through a participatory approach incorporating other donors and the poor majority in developing countries, and gauged through "selected pilot programs testing new approaches with potential for affecting many people, thus encouraging the experimentation needed to advance the art of development" (USAID 1975, 7).

Aside from its selectivity application, participation remained a slippery concept around which to organize internal and external change at USAID, partly because the poor majority themselves were a difficult population to define in the first place, and partly because numerous factors countered poor people's effective and direct engagement with development projects and programs. The agency identified three such constraining factors in its 1975 report to Congress: the role of local and national institutions and developing country policies and structures; widely variable understandings of and approaches to land tenure and reform; and entrenched social and economic impediments to improving labor productivity (USAID 1975, 15–17). A further challenge to implementing participatory basic needs approaches, and one that development theory and practice was increasingly forced to confront beginning in the 1960s and 1970s, was the status of women. The agency built consideration of women's role in development into project proposal assessment and program evaluation and emphasized the necessity of women's integration into the formal economy not only as a means of opening economic opportunity more fully to them but also as a component of family planning policies. In sum, participation by the poor majority in development projects funded or administered by USAID became, under the New Directions policy, a fundamental means of assessing development progress, measured and rewarded with further aid. As the agency stated in its implementation report, "Increasingly, our decisions on project funding will depend on the degree to which participation at the local level is a reality" (USAID 1975, 15).

Yet the question remained of how exactly to identify the poor majority so as to better facilitate their participation in development and thereby assess the outcomes and impacts of development projects and aid programs. One aspect of the definition USAID adopted relied on setting benchmarks to accurately measure poverty. Annual per capita income below $150, average daily per capita intake of less than 2,160 to 2,670 calories, and an array of health and population indicators (infant mortality over 33 per 1,000 children, birthrate over 25 per 1,000 population, and less than 40 percent of the population having access to basic health services) were all minimum indicators of poverty (USAID 1975, 6). While such benchmarks served a very basic categorizing purpose, the agency struggled with a unit of analysis problem in putting them into practice. Such rough measures were "intended to apply to varying proportions of country populations, not to countries as a whole," though some are primarily individual measures and others social, calculated on national or regional bases (USAID 1975, 6). Further, the reliability of such data was always suspect, as the poor majority were primarily rural and often existed on the political, economic, and social margins. While the emphasis on rural development gave the agency's technical expertise on agricultural issues new grounding, the political sensitivity of instructing partner governments in developing countries to pay better attention to domestic inequalities and the poor majority when devising long-term development strategies and short-term development projects was not lost on USAID (see Morss 1980). This clarified for Congress the agency's interpretation of what was meant by "direct" assistance to this large proportion of the developing world's population (800 million people, or three-quarters of the developing world), arguing that the agency sought under New Directions to "support activities which directly benefit the poor majority or *support, through assistance in planning and institution building, LDC agencies that deal directly with the problems of the poor majority*" (USAID 1975, 7, emphasis added).

This recalls the statement made by USAID's first administrator, Fowler Hamilton, discussed in the previous chapter, that U.S. development assistance must be predicated on developing countries' "willingness to undertake changes, if necessary even in their internal organization" in order to make "self-help" a reality (Duffy 1991, 59). It also points to the tension between USAID's political and institutional position as an official organ of the U.S. state and its rearticulated development mission under the New Directions policy and the basic needs approach. Despite strategic shifts made under New Directions, the agency was obligated to carry out American development assistance *and* foreign policy, with bilateral aid designed as a government-to-government program; within the participatory basic needs approach, the agency was to promote and assist development progress by ensuring that the poor majority benefited from aid provided more directly to them, and that they participated in the development process. In between were the structures, interests, and idiosyncrasies of developing state apparatuses; an array of international, civil society, and intergovernmental bodies and institutions; and the particular internal relations of the American state and the agency's place within it. On this front, and citing the limits faced due to tightening budgets, USAID fell back on its most important institutional asset to argue for its place at the budget trough and in strategic decision making:

development knowledge and expertise. The increased emphasis on and funding for technical rather than capital assistance in the aid budget built from this particular agency strength. This had two ramifications for the agency's internal organization, which in turn had important consequences for the geostrategic discourses that framed and enacted USAID's work.

First, the agency began to move toward a long-term development planning system emphasizing program and project evaluation in order to help augment annual budget requests with measures of development progress and aid effectiveness and create new modes and applications of expertise based around project review and analysis. This meant changes to USAID's development planning and staff training procedures as well as a more general transformation of how development knowledge was produced, managed, and deployed at and by the agency. In the mid-1970s, long-term analysis and review of aid projects was novel within development institutions but demonstrated how challenges to the hegemony of the U.S.-led development project (and to development aid funding) induced significant changes in the production and reproduction of development knowledge in those agencies. On these innovations in planning and analysis, USAID argued that while "[m]ost LDC governments are not enthusiastic, and there are few knowledgeable experts in this area . . . improving our [program evaluation] capacity—and that of the LDCs—will be slow but extremely important to pursue" (USAID 1975, 27). Second, to improve its evaluation capacity, the agency had to develop new approaches to staff training and personnel management. Noting that it was "deeply conscious of the long history of criticism and charges of overstaffing" leveled against it, USAID sought nonetheless to maintain a considerable field presence in developing countries and to undertake a wide range of training and retraining programs while also contracting some work out to experts and skilled personnel from other U.S. and developing country government agencies and private organizations (USAID 1975, 33). As already noted, USAID staff increasingly concentrated in Washington during the 1970s as the agency reduced its permanent personnel complement under political and budgetary pressures. It relied more on short-term contract staff for project implementation while maintaining and even expanding control over evaluation and the definition of development expertise.

Implementing New Directions was not solely, however, a matter of proper definitions enabling better accounting of the poor majority and changes to the management of agency personnel and expertise. Also important was the fact that USAID and American development policy and assistance remained subject to foreign policy prerogatives and objectives. According to the assessment of a USAID official who had worked under New Directions in Bangladesh, an important member of the G-77 and a major recipient of American aid, the "U.S. Embassy's agenda was securing Bangladesh votes on United Nations issues of importance to U.S. interests" (Church 2001, 18). The foreign policy elite within the U.S. state apparatus viewed economic and humanitarian assistance managed by USAID primarily in the context of winning political support in a contentious state system. Indeed, the definition of the poor majority, the best means of facilitating their economic if not political engagement in development, and mechanisms by which to improve their life conditions and opportunities were questions of strategic significance for the United States generally. Yet this did not mean that ideals and strategies articulated by USAID, or within the optimistic humanitarian components of New Directions and other associated institutional and bureaucratic changes, were not also grounded in and bolstered by arguments based on national security considerations. Framings of development, USAID, and basic needs that foregrounded aid's national security benefits did so by melding geopolitical and geoeconomic tropes.

Most prominent was the argument, appearing in discussions around the 1973 FAA amendment, the 1975 report discussed above, and thereafter in USAID's annual budget justifications to Congress, that developing countries possessed large stores of raw materials vital to American military power and economic growth, making aid and foreign development more important to national security than ever. Developing states providing crucial raw materials could experience political, social, and economic upheaval due to unfulfilled popular demands for development progress and a higher quality of life. Such potential and actual moments of crisis posed significant threats to American national security and global hegemony in ways that development aid appropriately aimed at the poor's basic needs could soothe and undo. That it was also morally right to provide the poor majority with better life conditions and enable the development of their societies was a wonderful, if contingent, coincidence. In its comments on the original House version of the 1973 FAA amendment, the Committee on Foreign Affairs argued that "[as] a nation which consumes 40 percent of the world's annual output of raw materials and energy, the United States needs access to the resources of the developing nations which . . . control large untapped resources," as well as to embryonic but growing Third World markets (U.S. House of Representatives 1973, 7–8). Foreign aid restructured around a basic needs approach could also help "in preventing the tumult and unrest from social disintegration in poor countries," and it would foster cooperation with Third World states on controlling cross-border and global problems such as "narcotics control, terrorism, and environmental pollution" (U.S. House of Representatives 1973, 8). Thomas Ehrlich, head of the International Development

Cooperation Agency (IDCA), an umbrella agency established through executive order in 1979 and meant to coordinate USAID and other American development efforts and programs, identified the link between globalization's dangers and promises in a February 1980 hearing before the House Committee on Foreign Relations.[2] Arguing that "[t]hose who fight for peace are also required to struggle against poverty," Ehrlich (1980, 2–3) stated that the United States "must forge an American response to the twin problems of growing interdependence and world poverty." More than just problems to be solved and threats to quash, however, Ehrlich (1980, 3) emphasized that directing development efforts more fully toward the eradication of poverty would be a boon for American interests, as "our own economy and society will be strengthened by the growth and adaptation that our response will require."

Amid ongoing energy, financial, food, and diplomatic crises in the 1970s, USAID reiterated these points in assessing its implementation of New Directions, stressing heightened interdependence between the United States and the developing world in economic and political terms, and arguing strongly that the "era has passed in which our size, our strength, our technology and our resources posed no limits to our economic expansion and rising living standards" (USAID 1975, 35). Subsequent annual budget requests hammered this point home, articulating U.S. interests in Third World development simultaneously along political, economic, and humanitarian lines (see figure 2) and always with the looming possibility of developing countries' social collapse. This inevitably would be followed by reduced American access to strategic raw materials and regional or global disorder threatening the United States' ability to exercise hegemonic leadership and maintain its own domestic tranquility. Framing developing countries as spaces that simultaneously promised threatening social and political upheaval *and* lucrative market expansion and international cooperation was not necessarily new, though the geostrategic context and emphases were. Economic interdependence of the sort identified in the statements above posed new challenges to both the state system and state form itself. Not only did the United States require access to oil, metals, and other primary resources actually and potentially exported by developing states, U.S. manufacturers and financial interests increasingly looked toward Third World markets as outlets for goods and services, while domestic stagflationary pressures in the U.S. economy were closely pegged to global energy and commodities markets (USAID 1975). Aside from the beneficial impacts aid could have on global North–South political relations and its ability to build export markets and assure continued access to raw materials, USAID also pointed to the fact that the majority of American development assistance, "almost 75 cents of every

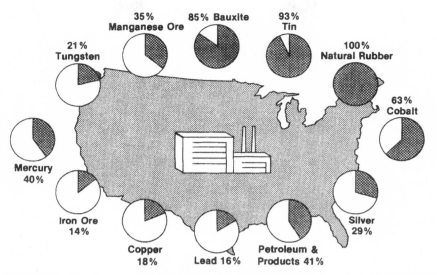

FIGURE 2. U.S. Dependence on Raw Materials from the Developing Countries, 1977 (Imports of Raw Materials from Developing Countries as a Percentage of Primary Consumption). Source: USAID 1978, 4.

foreign aid dollar," was actually spent in the United States itself, extended in a variety of forms that necessitated the purchase of U.S. goods and services, including commodities, technology, and expertise, by both developing country and U.S. governments (USAID 1979, 18). While the concern with geopolitical positioning and assistance to allied states prone to communist infiltration had not entirely disappeared from the discursive construction and justification for development assistance by the late 1970s, such arguments sounded increasingly like relics amid the growing concern with economic interdependence and the necessity for cooperation in combating poverty and other transnational ills.

Thus, while similar geopolitical concerns continued to animate political and budgetary support for USAID and development assistance generally, the deep global crises of the 1970s fostered intensive geostrategic change in USAID's form, function, and worldview. With New Directions, the agency sought to both cre-ate and adapt to a new geoeconomic social emerging at the global and national scales, using development aid to incorporate class-relevant actors in capital and the philanthropic sector more fully into state and hegemonic projects of development. This still relied in part on a geopolitical framing and rationaliza-tion of U.S. aid programs, though economic relations and cross-border flows increasingly mattered more than the ideological threat of Soviet expansionism and the territorial chess game of containment. Yet institutional changes within and around USAID pushing development strategies toward considerations of equitable growth and the poor's participation in the development process, as well as efforts to include more countries (especially in Sub-Saharan Africa) in USAID's reach, suggested that geoeconomic discourses, strategies, and relations remained in flux. In addition, a humanitarian streak entered aid policy more strongly under President Jimmy Carter as USAID implemented this approach, exemplified in the agency's expanded presence, justified on humanitarian grounds, in Sahelian countries experiencing drought and famine. A USAID official who worked in the Sahelian Development Program in the late 1970s argued that not only was this new, it was at odds with the foreign policy establishment's reading of U.S. strategic interests in the region:

> [T]he U.S. interest in the Sahel was expressed solely in terms of humanitarian and developmental goals. This shift was in some ways rather radical. . . . My State Department colleagues had written that, "Chad was strategically located in the heart of Africa." In terms of U.S. political and security interests, this was way off base. However, during the Carter Administration, the rationale for the programs in Chad and the Sahel were much more humanitarian and development-oriented in keeping with the New Directions legislation. (North 1995, 55)

While such humanitarian impulses could not be fully disentangled from concerns over access to raw materials and new market opportunities in developing states, centering human rights and basic needs (however weakly expressed) as principal objects of development policy and agency action opened the door to a quite different geoeconomic discourse and strategy than the deeply neoliberal one that eventually crystallized within the agency in the 1980s. Other factors, however, worked to shut this door and pave the way for the neoliberalization of development and USAID.

The Shifting Basis of American Postwar Hegemony

The political and economic basis of American hegemony was also shifting during this period, and with it USAID's strategic selectivity, which partly depended on the contingent outcomes of these shifts and the political and economic decisions guiding them. By the mid-1970s U.S. policymakers began to realize that former aid recipients in Europe and Japan were not only back on their economic feet but becoming formidable competitors in manufacturing, finance, and trade, even as the national and regional economies of Japan, Western Europe, and the United States became more tightly integrated. Budget woes coupled with intensified international economic competition and integration placed enormous pressure on the postwar global trade regime instituted under the General Agreement on Tariffs and Trade (GATT). This induced some strategists in the United States to push more aggressively for market liberalization and expanded use of U.S. economic leverage against competitors, leaning on American comparative advantages more directly.

One such advantage was in the grain-feed-livestock sector, and U.S. "green power" was one muscle to flex in increasingly bitter and protracted contests over relative economic power within the world trading system. Within the hegemonic development project of the postwar period, the United States solidified its position as a food exporter from the 1950s onward through a state strategy of green power, which emphasized the aggressive export of American agricultural products backed by food aid programs, protection and subsidization of agro-food production and exports, and efforts to open new markets. From the 1950s through the 1970s this strategy allowed the United States to double its share of the world grain trade, reaching 60 percent of total trade at one point, while the agricultural sectors of the United States and the European Community became closely integrated through a complex combination of trade restrictions and moves toward strategic liberalization (Friedmann 1993; McMichael 2008). The flip side of this was American producers' greater dependency on exports of basic food commodities for sustained profitability; by the late 1970s, agro-food capital in many European countries faced the same need to export. As Friedmann (1993, 37) argues, the U.S.-European agricultural trade relationship "was the hinge for the reconfiguration of the food relations of Asian, Latin American and African countries," many of which became dependent on food imports and food aid as components of their own national development strategies. Given the geopolitical context of the Cold War and the domestic political machinations surrounding agro-food policies and subsidies, the U.S. state often wielded its green power as a bludgeon, or as Mayer (1983, 121) puts it in his anecdotal study of American agricultural diplomacy, "U.S. politicians [were] always tempted to regard access to American food exports as a privilege that should be denied the truly naughty."

In this context, and alongside the specific technical and strategic changes ongoing in USAID discussed above, the relative failure of the 1973–1979 Tokyo Round of GATT talks demonstrates how the political economy of American hegemony changed in the crisis moment of the 1970s. The strategic value and political and economic costs of deeply subsidized agricultural production in Europe and the United States, which fueled the persistent congressional dilemma over whether and how to advance global efforts at market liberalization, came to the fore with the Tokyo Round. The United States shifted its stance on international agricultural trade in this round of trade negotiations. It sought to place pressure on European and Japanese rivals by strengthening American comparative advantages in specific agro-food sectors through a GATT-centered internationalization strategy and the threat of economic retaliation if liberalization did not go forward. This intensified struggles within the United States to find an acceptable path toward liberalization without further upsetting the international state system and the United States' hegemonic place within it, and it illustrated the class, political, and economic tensions created and exacerbated by processes of state and capital internationalization.

Some, including advisers close to President Nixon and officials in the Department of Agriculture, pushed U.S. negotiators to seek full liberalization of the grain-feed-livestock sector, commodity-by-commodity agreements for other agricultural products to ensure American access to foreign markets and to placate regional interests, and linked negotiations on monetary, industrial, and agricultural issues. Agriculture had been largely absent from previous GATT rounds and liberalization generally had proceeded in a piecemeal and haphazard fashion, but U.S. strategists argued that the benefits of this new approach to liberalization were "threefold: a substantial improvement in the balance of payments; an important reduction in government expenditure; and a significant increase in farm income" (FAS 1973, 10). Acknowledging the break with past GATT positions and approaches, U.S. trade officials wanted instead to use GATT mechanisms to ensure the complete market orientation of a whole range of interconnected commodities in which, most importantly, the United States held significant comparative advantages, while explicitly linking trade and monetary issues. This negotiating position should be enforced, it was argued, by dangling the threat of U.S. withdrawal from the GATT and the return to a more robust and thorough economic protectionism (FAS 1973). This would appease domestic capital and political forces important to further liberalization in later GATT rounds while also demonstrating to trading partners and rivals alike that the United States retained primacy in setting the global economic agenda.

The largely secretive nature of these recommendations, not shared with Congress until leaked to Senator Hubert Humphrey, who read them on the Senate floor so they could be entered in the *Congressional Record*, made their reception rocky and prevented this negotiating position from receiving full political consideration going into trade talks (U.S. Congress 1973). In the end, the Tokyo Round proved only moderately successful overall, and it failed to significantly open international agricultural trade, due in part to global grain shortages in 1972–1973 produced by emergency sales to the Soviet Union, which had experienced intense drought and was threatened with potential famine (Friedmann 2005). When negotiations were concluded, the U.S. position moved to one supporting GATT in general rather than seeking specific, far-reaching changes in the international agricultural trading system and the removal of high levels of domestic support for agriculture in other countries. Dissatisfaction with GATT remained strong within the U.S. policy elite, who continued to grasp for solutions to stagnant growth, high inflation, and fraying class compromises that threatened the social order and a return to profitability at home and the ability to project American economic, political, and military power abroad. The failure to achieve significant liberalization in favor of U.S. strengths via the established trade policy processes and mechanisms bolstered calls for a more thorough change in American global economic and trade strategies based on neoliberal principles.

This came in the Uruguay Round, launched in 1986, and only after the Reagan administration assigned top priority "to preserving the multinational system and the open American market, not to helping domestic industries deal with import-related competition more successfully" (Lovett, Eckes, and Brinkman 1999, 87). This move signaled that the executive wanted to ensure the continued viability of multilateral trade institutions, even if this meant giving less priority and less direct aid to U.S. industries that could not compete in an increasingly open and global marketplace. It also demonstrated the emergence of a more coherent state project of neoliberalization, which, in the context of the debt crises in the early 1980s (in both developing states and the U.S. farm economy), had agricultural trade liberalization as a central pillar. This likewise demonstrated the final limits of the previously hegemonic development project and induced changes in U.S. foreign policy and development thinking more generally, altering once more the context in which USAID worked and the approach and internal functioning of the agency. With Ronald Reagan's election and a turn toward the socially and fiscally conservative political right after 1980, USAID's strategic options narrowed rapidly to those based on neoliberal policy prescriptions and advancement of a wider process of neoliberalization. This was more than simply a matter of realists replacing liberals in the ideological persuasion of American foreign policy, as development and aid strategies are not fully contained within the realm of foreign policy. Nor are broadly realist and liberal approaches to and theories of international relations sufficient to accurately describe changes in American hegemonic relations with the developing world, the communist bloc, and its economic partners-cum-competitors in the European Union and Japan. Instead, as argued above, the changes to USAID and American development and aid policy that occurred beginning in the 1980s were the outcome of both protracted crisis in geopolitical approaches to and framings of development and the further articulation of a more strongly geo-economic strategy and discourse of development, based largely on neoliberal theory, ideals, and policies.

Neoliberalization under Reagan

The steady neoliberalization of mainstream development theory and practice has received extensive treatment in critical social-scientific accounts, but it remains nonetheless important to specify what is meant here by *neoliberalization* in relation to development, and how it in turn relates to the dynamic articulation and reconfiguration of geoeconomics and geopolitics at USAID during the 1980s and early 1990s. Within processes of international development, the application of neoliberal theories of economic and political governance, focused on the centrality and necessity of unfettered free market mechanisms in allocating wealth and risk, moved from a diffuse and scattered collection of varied policies and approaches to a more solid and coherent basis following the debt crises that rocked many developing states in the late 1970s and early 1980s. This emergent coherence was worked out across innumerable sites where economic and political decisions were made regarding development strategy and progress, but by the early 1990s it came to be known as the "Washington Consensus" because of the powerful influence of three Washington-based institutions with considerable pull in the definition and financing of appropriately neoliberal development: the World Bank, the International Monetary Fund (IMF), and the U.S. Treasury (Peet and Hartwick 2009).

Although initially applied narrowly to a specific set of economic and political reforms recommended to various Latin American states struggling with debt amid the collapse of Keynesian-Fordist policies and import substitution models of industrial development (Williamson 2008), the term *neoliberalization* eventually referred to a much broader set of neoliberal reforms applied across a range of developing countries and backed by the power of the United States, the IMF, and the World Bank. These institutions, and, as Harvey (2005) points out, like-minded and politically organized capitalist interests in the international financial sector, articulated, advanced, and enforced throughout the 1980s a set of neoliberal policy prescriptions that emphasized deregulation and liberalization, capital mobility and internationalization, and the erosion of state systems of social support and economic protectionism. More than just a simple rollback of Keynesianism, however, the construction and enactment of political and state projects of neoliberalization in this period meant the rollout of new neoliberal state forms. The neoliberal state was tied intensively and inextricably to the needs and desires of the most internationalized capital fractions, and it worked to facilitate the "flat" world of pure, unfettered economic exchange envisioned by neoliberal theories of economics. As site, strategy, and agent, neoliberal state institutions presented a new terrain for social and political economic struggles, including those related to development (Harvey 2005; Peck 2001; Peck and Tickell 2002). While this meant the full political rupture of delicate class compromises in the United States and many other developed states, in the developing world it implied an assault on the often-meager systems of public support that stood in for Keynesian-Fordist models of socioeconomic regulation, and the intensified exploitation of the global North–South gap that structured underdevelopment in the first place.

The next chapter provides a more complete discussion of the neoliberalization of development as a hegemonic project, but here it is necessary to remember that this process was and remains incomplete, contested, and marked by various ideological and political compromises. The agency's experience of neoliberalization, particularly as it took shape under the political leadership of Ronald Reagan, demonstrates this well, and indicates the extent to which political actors working to reshape and reconcile geopolitical and geoeconomic approaches to development and aid yoked the agency to a particular form of neoliberalism that, in turn, reshaped those geostrategic discourses. More specifically, under the Reagan administration, USAID emphasized a somewhat contradictory set of strategies. The pursuit of economic liberalization, along with an overall free market orientation in developing country policies and structures as the only acceptable path to development and rubric for aid programming, were combined with a strong return to the geopolitically instrumental use of agency funds and resources. The difficulty lay in reconciling and making complementary these sometimes conflicting strategies and views of development, aid, and the agency's place within an evolving system of American hegemony. The simmering contradictions between visions of development, aid allocation schema, and agency objectives and structures—one, roughly speaking, built on conceptions of good governance defined in relation to free market reforms in developing countries, the other on geopolitical utility in the last stages of an aggressively pursued Cold War—threatened the agency's long-term viability during this period. Structural and policy reforms at USAID in the Reagan years therefore worked to foster and consolidate a profound change in the agency's institutional culture, with a focus on building a new geoeconomics around neoliberal prescriptions and ideals that could also meet the national security requirements mandated by a hostile world and USAID's own legislated mission.

Importantly, the implementation of structural and policy changes around neo-liberal plans and goals demonstrated emphatically that if American development strategies aimed to fundamentally remake developing states as facilitators of globalizing free market forces, they also provided the cornerstone for similar ongoing changes in the American state and especially within USAID.

Beginning in 1982, for example, USAID found itself home to a new bureau dedicated to facilitating and expanding American foreign direct investment and local capitalist ventures as a mode of development. The necessity and utility of USAID's new Private Enterprise Bureau were explained in a video, produced and distributed internally within the agency, in which a small panel of high-level agency administrators answered preselected questions from USAID staff and discussed the means by which programs emphasizing private capital and entrepreneurship would be implemented. While the Private Enterprise Bureau initially targeted a select set of only ten countries for the launch of the agency's private enterprise policy, one assistant administrator noted that "a general agency-wide private sector policy that will address all of the countries that fall within AID's purview" was on tap in the near future (USAID 1983). Country selection for inclusion in the private enterprise development programs proceeded in conjunction with the agency's regional bureaus, specific country missions, developing country governments, and the State Department, signifying the broad appeal and increasing strategic and political purchase of "free markets" and "private enterprise" in U.S. bilateral relations with developing states and among American foreign policy elite. It is important to remember, however, that this instructional video was *produced for* and *directed at* USAID's own staff around the world. The high-ranking panelists featured in the short film argued that such internal instruction was necessary because past efforts to include private capital more fully in development planning and implementation had failed partly because agency field officers often misunderstood the private sector's vital role in development. It was noted that those who *did* understand this role and wished to move into the new bureau should have certain skills and experience, such as an MBA degree, experience in the agency's International Development Intern (IDI) Program, and "enthusiasm" (USAID 1983).

Reagan-era reforms thus began to validate, emphasize, and create new forms of development expertise within the agency, while building new institutional relations and mechanisms and reorienting existing ones in order to consolidate and strengthen the agency's nascent neoliberalization. For example, despite cuts to agency personnel, two of USAID's most important assets remained the extensive field experience of its staff in developing countries and the associated knowledge of social, political, and economic conditions that such experience entailed. The agency's personnel possessed technical and practical knowledge regarding rural areas, infrastructure, and agricultural production that lay beyond the scope or capacity of most other U.S. state institutions. The agency thus proved useful during the Uruguay Round of GATT negotiations, when a detail of USAID officers was assigned to assist the Office of the U.S. Trade Representative (USTR) in discussing agricultural trade, an area in which USTR negotiators squared off against European and Japanese counterparts reluctant to liberalize. A USAID official who served on this trade detail argued that the expertise of agency staff was called in because American negotiators "wanted to gain developing countries as our allies" in liberalization efforts, and they "needed help in communicating [their] concerns to the developing country GATT members, whose votes [they] sought in crafting a final GATT agreement" (Church 2001, 29). In such ways, USAID staff, geospatial knowledge, and institutional relations were reorganized and incorporated into broader political and state projects of neoliberalization within the contours of the U.S. state, and within the broader Washington Consensus emerging from the nexus of U.S. development, trade, and economic policy and institutions with the international financial institutions of the IMF and World Bank.

The specifics of neoliberal reforms to American development policy and strategy, and the geostrategic implications for U.S. relations with developing countries, were laid out more fully in 1985 in the agency's first long-range strategic plan, titled *Blueprint for Development*. This plan incorporated "four pillars" identified in the previous year's budget request and around which development policy and the agency itself were to be reoriented: emphasizing technology transfer to developing countries; a more robust contribution from and engagement with the private sector; an expanded and intensive new dialogue with developing states on policy issues; and renewed efforts at institution building in developing countries (USAID 1984). The comprehensive 1985 strategy went a step further than an annual budget request could, and linked these broad objectives not only to specific long-range development targets and benchmarks for the aid program but also to a more comprehensive vision of development progress and how USAID would work to achieve it. The strategy provided a framework for organizing internal resources across USAID's many foreign offices, managing relations with other political and economic actors and development institutions in the U.S. state and beyond, and assessing agency activities and success.

In clearly laying out a more thoroughly neoliberal vision of development, USAID's *Blueprint* presented a striking set of continuities and breaks with past agency modes and forms of planning and strategic decision making. It stated unequivocally that, while the agency and U.S. development policy maintained the central importance of basic needs as a program focus,

> what has changed is our way of approaching these fundamental development problems. We are seeking to achieve systemic changes in recipient countries that reach far beyond the direct beneficiaries of specific projects. We are concerned with the fundamental structures within which development occurs. Our concern is with policies, institutions, technologies, free market forces and the involvement of the private sector. How a country treats these issues is the essential factor in stimulating or blocking development. (USAID 1985, 4)

The emphasis on free market forces, private capital, and systemic structural and policy change was posed as a direct challenge to the capacities and propriety of state direction of economic activity and resources. The *Blueprint* presented this as a fundamental shift from views and practices that had previously held sway at the agency, arguing the new strategy had "broken with any assumption that government is in all areas the most effective agent of development change," stressing instead "the contribution that human energies and initiatives through the private sector can make to solving development problems" (USAID 1985, 4). As already discussed, critics and reformers of USAID and development assistance had long labored under the persuasion that the agency ignored, misunderstood, and even worked against the interests and abilities of private capital. Now this argument had been intensified and expanded to include the suggestion that not only had USAID not properly engaged and employed private capital and institutions but it had done so under the assumption that state institutions were the only appropriate economic mechanism for achieving development progress. While this was not accurate as a representation of USAID's historical perspective on the state's position vis-à-vis economic, social, and political development, it nonetheless sent a strong signal within the agency and to its partners in governments, international organizations, and the private sector that free market forces were to be prioritized across the whole terrain of development policy.

The emphasis on setting benchmarks and targets for measuring development progress likewise formed an important facet of USAID's early neoliberalization, tying both short- and long-term agency objectives and assessment functions, as well as program funding decisions, to quantifiable measures of economic growth, educational attainment, and health improvements. Overarching emphasis was placed on economic growth as a problem area for strategic action, and the agency set a target of "an annual rate of growth of real per capita income of not less than 2%" as a requirement for supporting other development efforts and programs (USAID 1985, 24). Economic growth, especially that which improved the incomes of and met basic needs for the poor, was in turn predicated on the increased productivity of labor in combination with policy reforms linked to market liberalization and the inclusion of private capital in development processes. As discussed in chapter 2 and above, placing stress on improvements to labor productivity was neither new nor controversial in understandings of development or strategies adopted at USAID. Indeed, increased labor productivity had long been seen as essential to adequate development progress within mainstream development theory and policy, as it unlocked time and resources for other necessary social and economic activities and implied technological advancements and labor specialization.

The explicit link made in the *Blueprint for Development* between increased productivity and policy reform, however, must be seen in light of the neoliberal revolution underway within and around the wider array of development theory and institutions, including USAID. The neoliberalization of USAID's geostrategic underpinnings, and the theoretical, ideological, and practical frameworks for development policy and strategy generally, were manifested in the specific kinds of reform envisioned for developing states and the broader context in which increased labor productivity could, would, and should mutually reinforce economic growth. Stating bluntly that the agency "believes there are many things that government cannot do, or cannot do well," and "reject[ing] the idea that government is the sole instrument for delivering the goods and services vital to the development effort," the *Blueprint* articulated a development program based on the comprehensive structural reform of developing country institutions toward the facilitation of internationalizing market forces and the support and strengthening of local private sectors within aid recipient states (USAID 1985, 19). Increasing labor's productivity was vital because, the strategy argued, most developing states possessed a relative surplus of labor. Yet this surplus was not adequately or efficiently employed because "substantial barriers exist to capital flows, internal and external, inhibiting investments that can create employment," or because bad policies "[had] the effect of encouraging capital intensive technologies and industries that fail to use the labor resources of the developing countries" (USAID 1985, 26). Therefore, government action should be directed toward facilitating greater and more efficient use of labor resources, improving agricultural production, and putting more people to work in the formal industrial sector, in turn sparking economic growth that would further improve social conditions and provide basic needs and higher incomes for the majority of the population. All that was needed to unleash the rising tide of free market forces was to bust the dam of government restrictions, regulations, and controls on capital and innovation.

The policy reform envisioned in the *Blueprint*, then, applied neoliberal ideals of unfettered free market mechanisms and voluntary action to all the major issue areas of programmatic concern highlighted for USAID's specific attention: hunger (e.g., stimulating agricultural production by removing price controls and taking advantage of global market opportunities rather than focusing single-mindedly on national food self-sufficiency); health and education (e.g., the innovative application of user fees in health systems and "private production and distribution of health care supplies" as "a preferred alternative to public channels"); education (e.g., the greater involvement of private-sector employers in providing training and skills to employable populations); and population and family planning (e.g., use of private market channels to distribute contraceptives) (USAID 1985, 43). Within each of these issue areas, the *Blueprint* explicitly linked development progress to economic growth achieved through the private sector and removal or rollback of state controls, protections, and publicly owned and operated competitors. Societies suffering from hunger, disease, illiteracy, population growth that outstripped economic growth, and an overbearing and oppressive state were unlikely to find themselves in a position where economic interdependency, foreign investment, and local innovation could produce comprehensive transformational development, as measured by the rubrics outlined in the strategy.

Accordingly, the *Blueprint* was quite specific about the policy changes developing states must make to efficiently use American aid and to deserve its continued flow into their countries. These included the reduction, removal, or alteration of policies that imposed import tariffs and capital and investment controls, set interest rates artificially low, and established other "non-economic business barriers" such as "unnecessary regulation" (USAID 1985, 26–27). In addition, the strategy highlighted the benefits of privatization of state-run and parastatal enterprises, tax reforms (especially for agricultural producers), and energy pricing policies that "reflect the need to curb demand and stimulate supply" (USAID 1985, 30). In practice, such changes were not simply rollback forms of neoliberalization but also *rolled out* new institutional configurations in line with a broader shift in the policymaking environment and discourse itself (Peck 2001; Peck and Tickell 2002). Such proclamations about the absolute necessity, efficiency, and rightness of free market forces echoed contemporaneous statements from the World Bank and IMF, while the strategic policy and structural changes desired and prescribed in the new USAID strategies reflected and reinforced via American aid the move toward conditionalities on loans found in Structural Adjustment Programs (Lawson 2007; Peet and Hartwick 2009). Yet USAID, as part of the U.S. state apparatus and with a personnel complement steeped in the traditions of the Foreign Service, did not copy or exactly mirror the approaches found in the international financial institutions but developed its own specific methods and models of neoliberalization as outlined in the *Blueprint*.

In Honduras, for example, USAID facilitated the creation of a management and vocational training program and skills certification organization, initially in conjunction with several leading businessmen but eventually incorporating representatives from labor and government as well. This organization (the Honduran Advisory Council for Human Resources Development, or CADERH) worked to revamp a government vocational training program with which many in that country's private sector were unhappy. The creation and financing of CADERH through USAID included a trip to the United States to observe vocational and business education management practices and institutions, and participants returned to Honduras with new appreciation for private-sector direction of skills training and the intention of becoming an advisory group within Honduras to better guide state action (Bernbaum 1999). Such new institutional arrangements, working in parallel with and sometimes in lieu of state and public institutions, have become a hallmark of neoliberalization (Essex 2007; Harvey 2005; Peck 2001). While the example of CADERH in Honduras demonstrates that processes of neoliberal restructuring within state and civil society institutions work across an uneven political and economic terrain that requires political and class compromises (for example, the inclusion of labor representatives in what was ostensibly a businessmen's organization for certifying work training programs), it nonetheless speaks to how USAID missions and officers took on their role as agents of neoliberalization via agency programs. As one official who had worked in Africa and the Philippines argued, the main strategic and programmatic question for USAID in the 1980s became "what the government has to do to put in place an environment that will allow the private sector to grow," part of a broader process of strategic change driven by both "political differences in the United States" and "the fact that the private sector . . . has become such an incredible source of finance in the developing world," itself a result of widespread neoliberal policy reforms (Love 1998, 98).

Following from internal agency reforms that emphasized neoliberal ideals in producing, managing, and applying development expertise, and shifts in the agency's institutional structure and relations toward increased emphasis on free market mechanisms and collaboration with private-sector actors, not to mention Ronald Reagan's landslide reelection in 1984, the *Blueprint for Development* seized on a key moment to consolidate the shift toward a geoeconomic vision of development that built from and sought to expand a broad process of neoliberalization. While the strategy made overtures toward the unique circumstances of individual developing countries and the flexibility required by agency programs to meet such circumstances, it nonetheless proposed a comprehensive and universalizing framework through which USAID would help build the neoliberal state in every developing country in which it operated. By the end of the Reagan years, agency higher-ups had made leveraging USAID development funding and expertise to promote neoliberal reforms in developing countries the new mantra for all agency activities, though they still ostensibly recognized the uneven geography of underdevelopment across different parts of the Global South. As USAID Administrator Alan Woods stated in his introduction to the agency's budget request for fiscal year 1989, which broke with past practice by providing a lengthy discussion of agency vision and strategy rather than a short summary of figures and objectives: "There are no textbook answers that tell us exactly how to stimulate economic growth in a developing country—even if we know that a market orientation is to be preferred" (USAID 1988, 14).

Such statements demonstrate how the robust articulation and enactment of a geoeconomic discourse based on neoliberal assumptions became the primary basis for USAID structures, strategies, and relations. These assumptions naturalized capitalist markets as the appropriate locus and arbiter of economic action and social organization, and understood state institutions as interfering with the normal and proper channels of free market exchange, both in developing countries and in those countries' engagement with the wider, interdependent global economy. Yet geoeconomic thinking is not essentially or necessarily neoliberal; the emergence of a more coherent, persuasive, and specifically neoliberal geoeconomic discourse in and through American development policy was predated, as discussed above, by forms of geoeconomics that made a strongly interventionist Keynesian-style welfare state a fundamental component of successful development and that introduced "poor majority" and "basic needs" considerations into agency strategies and development thinking. In the process of neoliberalization, decision makers and ideologues selectively recalled and built from these antecedents. Administrator Woods argued, for example, that, even amid geographical diversity, the experience of "places as diverse as post-war Europe, post-war Japan, [South] Korea, Taiwan, Hong Kong and Singapore" demonstrated that appropriate growth and development were based almost entirely on "the extent to which [these countries] relied on market forces and open trading systems to ensure the efficient production, distribution, and pricing of goods and services" (USAID 1988, 2–3).

This was in fact inaccurate, as massive inflows of strategically targeted American aid and highly protectionist forms of economic policy had shaped the development, growth, and reconstruction of many of Woods's examples as much as free markets and free trade. While the basic needs approach, global Keynesianism, and neoliberalism all concerned themselves intimately with improved labor productivity, the provision of social services, and the social wage as objects of geoeconomic discourse and practice, the consolidation of the neoliberal project within, around, and through USAID required shedding some (but not all) baggage from geoeconomic antecedents. Dismissing a wide swath of Keynesian policies and most forms of state economic planning while absorbing the focus on the poor's basic needs as a means to open new arenas for privatization, international investment, and capitalist accumulation, the process of neoliberalization pushed the agency even more fully toward technical rather than capital assistance and new ways of creating, circulating, and legitimizing geospatial knowledge about development and developing countries.

Yet institutional change often follows only slowly from ideological and political transformations, and USAID had difficulty keeping pace with the geoeconomic shift. Field staff often found the free market orientation of Reagan-era strategies unworkable, and the agency retained an important geopolitical role that gave the lie to the overarching rhetoric of facilitating free markets and promoting private-sector leadership in agency activities. With respect to the first of these, the geostrategic and ideological moves accompanying the change in political administrations after the 1980 election, while not completely unwelcome among the agency's field staff, proved nonetheless abrupt and, for some, extreme. Discussing the sharp departure from the New Directions policy under Reagan, one officer with experience in policy and program assessment stated that, "In retrospect, I doubt whether the agency really gave the New Directions approach much of a chance to be tested out" (Vreeland 1998, 10). Noting that USAID followed the strong turn toward liberalization and the emphasis on free market mechanisms that was reshaping development thinking in important global institutions like the World Bank during the 1980s, Vreeland (1998, 35) recalled that "[f]or a while . . . it seemed as though the role of the public sector in development might be discounted altogether . . . I had become heartily sick of the unqualified adulation of the 'private sector' by the end of that decade."

Likewise, Haven North (1995, 58), who worked in agency missions across Sub-Saharan Africa, argued that the "Reagan Administration came with a highly ideological orientation. . . . It was also extreme in its anti-communism views, which caused it to underestimate local and historical factors in some of the developing countries." In this context, political pressure on USAID and developing countries led to unrealistic expectations and unattainable targets for neoliberal reforms, such as privatization:

> I don't think there was enough time to really see that blossom. There was a lot of pressure on developing country governments to undertake reforms, to divest themselves of public enterprises, which is an extremely difficult process. . . . There was a great deal of pressure, and the administration of USAID went so far as to set targets for each country requiring so many privatization acts which was quite unrealistic given the extreme difficulty developing countries find in the privatization process. (North 1995, 58)

North concluded that, although the move toward a market orientation was "healthy" for the long-term economic development of Third World countries, Reagan-era policies were perhaps too extreme, and "constructive views of appropriate government roles were not evident or considered" (North 1995, 59). Similarly, Allison Herrick (1996, 75), another USAID officer with experience in both Latin America and Africa, recalled the sometimes brash dismissal of previous agency policies, practices, and ideas by Reagan appointees, implicitly rejecting the notion that developing country circumstances did in fact differ widely or that existing field-level expertise offered a viable basis for strategic planning:

> I recall one time [in 1984] . . . [Assistant Administrator Richard Durham] told me he was very proud that he personally had rescinded the AID policy on land reform. What happened was, he had looked at the policy and had read that productive resources in Africa are often collectively owned. So, considering that he "did not come to AID on behalf of the Reagan Administration to support collectives," he decided we needed a totally new policy. That was very upsetting to some of the staff who had hoped he would gain some understanding of the African situation.

Despite the wholesale adoption of neoliberal rhetoric and prescriptions in agency strategies, then, internal tensions at USAID remained strong, driven by ideological and political differences, struggles over the valuation of staff knowledge and experience, and disagreement over the extent, speed, and implementation of new approaches.

The agency also faced a strategic quandary as it attempted to fulfill its geopolitical mission in relation to lingering Cold War fears and policies, and it continued to pursue aid policies and programs that often had little to do with promoting viable economic growth or improving basic living conditions for the poor in developing countries. This meant some compromises were to be made in reworking and cementing the intellectual, institutional, and political relationship between geoeconomic and geopolitical discourses and strategies. Aggressive moves toward liberalization and the construction of neoliberal state institutions rested uneasily alongside aid provided as support to friendly and strategic states in the geopolitical contest between the United States and the Soviet Union. Aid resources were increasingly directed to new countries of Cold War geostrategic importance, especially in Central America and Sub-Saharan Africa, where many aid recipients maintained macroeconomic policies distinctly out of joint with the widespread application of and consensus around neoliberal reforms. Thus, while USAID missions under Reagan (and, after 1989, George H. W. Bush) worked to promote neoliberal changes to the policies and structures of numerous developing countries, they also helped channel money and other forms of aid to places and regimes where free market reforms were not imminent but a strategic ally was maintained (e.g., Zaire), where states supported important U.S. military objectives and strategies (e.g., the Philippines), and where civil war raged and the United States hoped to use aid to sway the outcome toward a preferred combatant (e.g., El Salvador).[3]

When such efforts to assert USAID's geopolitical instrumentality bogged down amid rules regarding how and where aid resources could be used, "Reagan foreign policy elites frequently turned to a special aid account called Economic Support Funds (ESF)" (Auer 1998, 85). These ESF accounts, included under USAID's broad budget umbrella, faced few restrictions and did not need congressional approval, providing a flexible means of directing aid money toward countries where geopolitical logic dictated the United States had national security interests. The Reagan administration further angered lawmakers (especially those who wished to cut aid amid the pursuit of "smaller government") by sending foreign aid budget requests to appropriation committees in Congress, buried within omnibus and continuing resolution spending bills, rather than putting them through the usual authorization process, which would have meant freestanding bills to fund aid programs. This limited Congress's ability to shape aid and development policy and removed opportunities for critics (typically from the president's own party) to amend or even kill aid funding (Auer 1998; Obey and Lancaster 1988). The agency identified ESF accounts, as well as food aid, as offering "considerable leverage and support for fundamental policy efforts to enhance development programs" (USAID 1985, 63). By the late 1980s the agency was up-front about ESF's utility in "leveraging policy reform," especially "in the context of major multi-donor structural adjustment programs" (USAID

1988, 118). The fiscal year 1989 budget noted that ESF accounts had been useful in supporting "allies and developing nations heavily burdened by high costs of their own defense" (especially Israel), rewarding countries providing the U.S. military with basing and access rights, and (because they were flexible in terms of approval and deployment) in temporarily suspending development funds to countries that failed to meet policy reform and other conditions for aid (USAID 1988, 119).

Such uses of USAID resources eventually spurred the creation of a congressional task force designed "to rescue an aid program that was, in many lawmakers' view, held prisoner by cold warriors in the Reagan White House" (Auer 1998, 85). Struck in 1988 and headed by Representatives Lee Hamilton (D-Ind.) and Benjamin Gilman (R-N.Y.), the task force reported back to the House Committee on Foreign Affairs in February 1989. Arguing that development, food, military, and other forms of aid were necessary and beneficial components of American foreign policy, the U.S. foreign assistance program nonetheless suffered from numerous problems and needed a complete overhaul to meet the demands of a changing strategic environment (U.S. House of Representatives 1989). Pointing to multiple ambiguous and inconsistent aspects of the extant authorizing legislation (the Foreign Assistance Act of 1961, with amendments), the Hamilton-Gilman task force recommended the passage of a new aid bill, the proposed International Economic Cooperation Act of 1989, to separate development and economic assistance from ESF and military aid and to replace USAID with a new Economic Cooperation Agency (ECA) tightly bound to the strategic pursuit of four policy objectives: economic growth; environmental sustainability; poverty alleviation; and political, social, and economic pluralism (U.S. House of Representatives 1989). By contrast, the task force had identified thirty-three separate objectives within the FAA, noting that one USAID document listed seventy-five different priorities for economic assistance; meanwhile, military aid had become "overly politicized" and did not efficiently or usefully meet broader strategic objectives (U.S. House of Representatives 1989, 27). The result was a bureaucratic, administrative, and strategic mess, in which the mix of "security, military, development, and humanitarian objectives makes evaluation and Congressional oversight difficult" (U.S. House of Representatives 1989, 27).

Importantly, the task force reinforced the strategic direction toward market liberalization and global economic interdependence put in place over the previous nine years, and it argued strongly for the separation of military aid from economic development and other nonmilitary forms of assistance to continue advancing this vision. The Hamilton-Gilman report noted that while the budgetary size of the total aid program had fluctuated considerably from the 1977 to 1989 fiscal years (and actually decreased in real dollar terms), much of this was due to oscillations in outlays for military aid and ESF, with an overall 36 percent increase in military assistance over this period (U.S. House of Representatives 1989, 8). In addition, aid expenditures were heavily concentrated in countries with "a strong security relationship with the United States," a category that included nine of the ten countries receiving the largest amounts of American aid between 1977 and 1989, and accounting for roughly 70 percent of all U.S. aid in this period (U.S. House of Representatives 1989, 12).[4] Accountability, oversight, and strategic clarity were, according to the task force, in short supply with respect to military aid, and the comingling of different types of objectives across the fractured institutional landscape of development and aid policy weakened the entire program as it entered a new era of profound global change.

The Hamilton-Gilman report offered a reconciliation of geostrategic differences by highlighting, like previous USAID reform efforts, growing global economic interdependence and the importance of U.S. engagement with developing states on a collaborative economic basis. But 1989 was not 1973, and the task force deviated sharply from past geopolitical emphases by foreseeing, if not the Cold War's end, then at least its residual character as an organizing principle for U.S. security, economic, and political strategies. Noting that the "lessening of tensions between the superpowers and the possibilities for settlement of some regional conflicts create new challenges and opportunities for peace and development," the task force observed a developing world in flux, in which rapid urbanization, massive debt, and entrenched poverty were matched by rapid technological progress, new inflows of foreign capital, and eagerness to take advantage of global market openness (U.S. House of Representatives 1989, 24). Economic policy, and especially the desire to liberalize markets and expand trade, now dominated the global agenda and formed the backbone of international order and engagement, not the fading ideological battle between the United States and the Soviet Union. Only a thorough and fundamental shake-up of aid programs, the report concluded, could position the United States to enter this new era on a footing that would maintain and enhance U.S. influence relative to its economic and political rivals and provide new arenas for collaboration and trade with developing states.[5]

An Agency Adrift

The far-reaching changes proposed by the Hamilton-Gilman task force were never enacted, however, and USAID floundered into the post–Cold War period amid mounting tensions over strategy, budgets, and oversight. Struggles sparked during the Reagan years over USAID's place and structure, as well as the overall orientation and execution of U.S. development and aid policy, resurrected many of the problems the agency had faced at the close of the Vietnam War. The agency continued to pursue numerous, conflicting objectives and priorities across its broad geographic and thematic scope of operations, struggled to reconcile different geostrategic bases for and in its programs, and worked within a wider state apparatus in which its role as site and strategy for competing social forces made it an easy target of critics hostile to aid and development for a variety of reasons, including isolationism, domestic protectionist impulses, ideological fervor, hawkishness on deficit matters, and even criticism of family planning measures.[6] The agency was thus also caught in contests between other U.S. state institutions, especially the executive and legislative branches, though congressional concerns over military aid and strategy and administrative oversight also presaged changing relations with the Departments of State and Defense. The Cold War's end and the strong articulation of fully neoliberal visions of development, globalization, and state form and function complicated ongoing efforts to use aid as a blunt instrument of foreign policy. By the end of George H. W. Bush's term in office, USAID found itself institutionally and geostrategically adrift, with few political supporters, and out of alignment with an increasingly hegemonic state project of neoliberalization, despite the agency's decade-long effort to orient itself toward free market mechanisms.

Given the geostrategic shift that had occurred around and in part through USAID, the agency's future was not, paradoxically, uncertain. As demonstrated by the findings and recommendations of the Hamilton-Gilman task force, the most comprehensive congressional overview and attempt at development policy reform since the 1970s, a strong consensus had emerged around global economic connectivity and market interdependence as bases for U.S. foreign and development policy. Geostrategically, the discursive framing of development and aid were moving from a foundation dominated and driven by Cold War geopolitical logic, concerns, and rationales to one based in geoeconomic logic, and specifically grounded in neoliberal theories of free markets and state facilitation of capitalist internationalization. Indeed, by the time Bill Clinton took office in 1993, free market champions in Congress and key sectors of capital were chomping at the bit to not just significantly cut development aid, and with it the Agency for International Development, but perhaps even do away with them altogether.

More broadly, mainstream "cartographies of development" were themselves becoming fully neoliberal as the ideological challenge to capitalist globalization and liberal democracy posed by one-party state socialism collapsed with the Soviet Union and "market triumphalism" became the central logic of official development institutions (Peet and Watts 1993). In this environment, two political and strategic options stood available to USAID: undertake painful reforms to reassert the agency's purpose, mandate, and utility on a more appropriately geoeconomic and neoliberal basis; or face constant political and budgetary attacks that would likely result in dissolution over the medium to long term. While such attacks occurred regardless, the reforms USAID undertook following the Cold War's end were part of a longer process of neoliberalism's post–Cold War geostrategic articulation, in which the terrain across which geoeconomic and geopolitics were built and deployed also shifted. More specifically, USAID sought in the 1990s to reestablish itself within a new era and geography of informal American imperialism, in which a more aggressive geoeconomic vision of global order, development, and American hegemony shed some aspects of past geopolitical frames and practices while maintaining those which supported forms of political, economic, and military interdependence and influence consistent with neoliberalism. In other words, geoeconomics did not simply refute and replace geopolitics at USAID after the Cold War. Instead, the agency sought to combine and deploy these in new and dynamic ways, seeking flexibility and stability in a rapidly changing context of new threats, challenges, and institutional configurations. The next chapter details the course of these changes from the early 1990s through the terrorist attacks of 9/11 and the "global war on terror."

CHAPTER FOUR

Two Decades of Neoliberalization

From the Cold War to the War on Terror

THE SHIFT TOWARD NEOLIBERALISM within USAID and the broader world of development theory and practice should not be read simply as a product of the U.S. state's ideologically driven strategists and handlers forcing an unwanted set of policies and structures upon developing states. This would ignore neoliberalism's complex and uneven morphology, and the entanglements, compromises, and concessions made in processes of neoliberalization across multiple scales and sites. Indeed, the chorus of consenting voices that made the neoliberal project hegemonic in the 1990s included public- and private-sector leaders, intellectuals, and institutions from the Global South. Other scholars have aptly discussed the internationalization of capitalist class relations as a major component of both economic globalization and state internationalization (see Cox and Sinclair 1996; Glassman 2005a; Jessop 2008; Panitch 1994; Panitch and Gindin 2004; Robinson 2004; Sklair 2001). As I discussed in the first chapter, my objective is not to trace and analyze such circumstances and processes as they have been worked out in specific developing-country contexts, though the many ways in which these have in turn shaped USAID and its strategic selectivity are an important part of the story. That the Cold War basis of American development policy, and USAID itself, were after 1991 thrown into turmoil, or that economic growth faltered and highly centralized modes of development planning and policy ultimately fell out of favor in many developing states, are not matters of debate. Yet the elaboration of political, state, and hegemonic projects of neoliberalization alongside and in conjunction with these shifts was neither preordained nor guaranteed to produce the flat world of unfettered economic exchange its proponents envisioned. The agency adapted to neoliberalization and the associated geostrategic shift in novel ways, reasserting its role as a vital component of American informal imperialism and retaining its status as junior partner and, sometimes, punching bag in American foreign and economic policy circles.

In McMichael's (2008) terms, the previously hegemonic development project had been supplanted by the early 1990s by a hegemonic project of globalization (or, more specifically, neoliberal globalization, given the many countervailing forces implied by the term *globalization* alone), in which new configurations and mechanisms of socioeconomic regulation solidified around processes of state and class internationalization. National states themselves authored or underwrote the globalizing forces that ostensibly eroded their territorial sovereignty, particularly where management and regulation of economic connectivity was concerned. McMichael's framework provides a useful heuristic account of how the continuities between these two hegemonic projects, such as the way international market orientation in economic growth policies, or the institution of global trade rules through the General Agreement on Tariffs and Trade (GATT) and the World Trade Organization (WTO), reproduce the international state system and capitalist class relations despite deep changes in the accepted role and structure of the national state. It is important to build on this presentation, however, by referring to the concrete, differential ways in which such projects have been instituted and struggled over, to avoid presenting neoliberal globalization (and its status as a hegemonic project) as a uniform or uncontested process. Doing so recognizes what Castree (2006, 4) calls the "contingently occurring processes and outcomes that may well have operated differently if the 'neo-liberal component' had not been present," and highlights the "articulation between certain neoliberal policies and a raft of other social and natural phenomena." Importantly for USAID, the maintenance of a strong link between development and aid policy and foreign policy meant that the geostrategic waters in which it swam remained muddied by concerns with national security. The agency's embrace of neoliberal policy prescriptions and visions of development had to contend with forms of geopolitical discourse and action based on the desire to maintain U.S. superpower status, tempered by cutthroat economic competition.

While neoliberalism, geoeconomics, geopolitics, globalization, and hegemonic projects are in one sense abstractions, referring to processes, relations, institutions, and discourses constantly in flux and never as fixed as such terms' usage might suggest, real material processes and changes were nonetheless hard at work. Development practitioners, lawmakers, and a raft of experts in positions of official power reached an uneasy but relatively coherent consensus by the early 1990s that there was one best road to development. For developing countries, this road led through policies of liberalization, privatization, and other measures designed to remove intrusive state institutions from market dynamics as much as possible, while also altering state form and function so that national states worked to manage and coordinate the increasingly thick and multiscalar nexus of institutions constituting the primary modes, forums, and executors of governance within the nebulous thing called *globalization*. While the once-rancorous debate over globalization's novelty has by now grown stale, it remains important to emphasize that the transition between state and hegemonic projects of Keynesian-style development and neoliberal globalization were marked by strong continuities as well as ruptures. In this context, the oscillation between and articulation of geopolitics and geoeconomics at and through USAID are vital components of the material production and organization of neoliberal globalization as a hegemonic project. The primary questions here are how exactly geoeconomics became the primary geostrategic framework for agency structure and action beginning in the 1990s, and how USAID has worked to reintegrate and rearticulate geoeconomics with geopolitical framings emphasizing global integration, state failure, and, after 9/11, the global war on terror.

The particular combination of geopolitical and geoeconomic strategies employed by and through USAID since the Cold War's end have largely sublimated the geopolitical within a geoeconomic frame based in the market triumphalism and economic connectivity of neoliberal globalization. The geopolitical component of this discursive framing and its concomitant strategies are, however, like their predecessors concerned with the objectives and conduct of American informal imperialism. By this I mean the ways in which the U.S. state acted as manager, coordinator, and mediator of relations across the international state system and between states, including its economic rivals, as well as *within* states. This is distinct from formal imperialism, since, as Panitch and Gindin (2004, 21) argue, informal imperialism "requires the economic and cultural penetration of other states to be sustained by political and military coordination with other independent governments" rather than through direct rule from a foreign capital. I have already discussed USAID's role in the historical trajectory of American informal imperialism following World War II and through the Cold War, and the processes and objectives through which the agency sought to remake developing states and bring them under the umbrella of American hegemony. Panitch and Gindin (2004, 40) contend that through such strategies, the United States advanced "the reconstitution of states as integral elements of an informal American empire" to organize and regulate the larger international capitalist order, with the nation-state forming the primary agent of domestic social cohesion, global economic integration and accumulation, and the reproduction of capitalist social relations.

This, as discussed extensively in chapters 2 and 3, was the mission of USAID and American development policy from the Marshall Plan through the end of the 1980s, with the specter of Communist aggression and other disruptive nationalist, anticolonial, and nonaligned movements forming the backdrop for geopolitical preeminence in agency structures and strategies. When this danger evaporated after the Soviet Union's dissolution, American informal imperialism entered a new phase in which the interpenetration and interdependence of capitalist states and economies increased while the United States maintained and even enhanced its coercive and military apparatus in line with the mushrooming of new geopolitical foci, from shadowy terrorist networks and climate change to nuclear weapons proliferation and the rise of new regional military powers and economic rivals. This reaffirmation of geopolitical concerns and logic is not divorced from the neoliberal underpinnings of post–Cold War geoeconomics. Indeed, they have become intimately and inextricably connected, with the terrorist attacks of 9/11 and the subsequent execution of the global war on terror giving new urgency to the articulation of geoeconomics and geopolitics, and sparking continued restructuring within and through USAID over the last decade. The agency has sought to craft a geostrategic framework that can provide it some political clout within the U.S. state, displace or resolve lingering geostrategic tensions, and map out a new cartography of development to accommodate the neoliberal vision of the nation-state as facilitator of capitalist internationalization while maintaining the state's role as guarantor of security in an unruly world of multiple risks and threats.

The remainder of this chapter follows these processes both chronologically and thematically according to a rough geoeconomics/geopolitics division. Looking at the former first, I examine how, after the Cold War's end, the agency focused on processes of internal institutional streamlining and the adoption of trade capacity building (TCB) as a principal component of development programs. Trade capacity building in itself is not new, with an emphasis on institutional reform and capacity building in developing states dating back to the agency's founding, and a particular stress on making such institutions responsive to and integrated with global market forces a central concern of strategic shifts beginning during the Reagan years. In combination with the collapse of geopolitical framings based on combating a global communist threat, the role of free trade and developing states' ability to engage in multilateral economic institutions and encourage capitalist internationalization became more than just the centerpiece of geoeconomic discourses and strategies. It also became linked to discussions about what national security meant, and how best to achieve and maintain it, in a state system defined by multiple poles of political and economic strength and a pervasive neoliberal rhetoric stressing global interdependence, trade openness, the increasing irrelevance of borders, and the victory of free market mechanisms over all other forms of social organization and regulation.

While TCB plays an important role in ongoing efforts to reorient state institutions within a more general process of neoliberalization by marshaling development discourses, practices, and agencies, including but not limited to USAID, in support of trade liberalization and capitalist internationalization, it also must be understood in relation to U.S. geopolitical and security objectives that emerged in the 1990s. The agency's adoption of trade capacity building constituted a central part of a much broader reconfiguration of development and security that sought to narrow both to functions of global market logic enforced by and internalized within the state. As discussed at the end of chapter 3, and following from Peck (2001), Peck and Tickell (2002), and Harvey (2003, 2005), the hegemonic project of neoliberal globalization did not imply the simple weakening and dismantling of states, but instead depended on institutional rollout and the reorientation of state institutions away from wage-based social equity and economic redistribution and toward the facilitation of private market forces and the intensive internationalization of capitalist relations. In doing so, neoliberalization alters the character and logic of the strategic planning and policy-making environment, as well as how political, economic, and social forces operate and interact within this environment. Peck, Theodore, and Brenner (2009, 105) emphasize the constant articulation of neoliberalism as "a politically (re)constructed, nonlinear, and indeed mongrel phenomenon." They argue that neoliberalization produces and thrives across a dynamic institutional and regulatory landscape, shaping the rules and forms of geospatial, social, political, and economic relationality: "Regime competition and regulatory adaptation are not externally determined under these conditions, but underlying forces of 'dull compulsion' effectively channel regulatory restructuring strategies along broadly neoliberal pathways—variously reinforced by hierarchical pressures from strong states and multilateral institutions; lubricated by networks of experts, practitioners, and advocates; and reproduced through the adaptive behaviors of social agents and institutions" (Peck, Theodore, and Brenner 2009, 107). Capacity building to engage in liberalized trade relations is part and parcel of constructing the neoliberal state, charged in turn with expanding and maintaining a neoliberalized geoeconomic order in which the U.S. state and finance capital retained hegemonic roles, but also in which neoliberal globalization developed through intersection, co-optation, hybridization with, and destruction of other systems and projects.

In this vein, Roberts, Secor, and Sparke (2003) demonstrate how neoliberalization has also reproduced traditional realist geopolitical practices and imaginaries under the gloss of multilateral integration, while Harvey (2003) and Glassman (2005a) point to the tensions between competing logics of American hegemonic power embedded within the state and different fractions of internationalizing capital. Such insights help direct attention back to the geopolitical and the ongoing struggles over USAID's national security function. The agency had to perform a strategic two-step after 2001, seeking once more to strengthen the geopolitical components of its strategies, logic, and functions as the 9/11 terrorist attacks sharpened tensions over the direction and conduct of American informal imperialism. Whereas the flow of agency resources toward narrow geopolitical and military ends had served as fodder for critics in the past, following 9/11, USAID's relatively weak expression of national security and geopolitical aims provided a basis for new critiques that saw the agency as out of alignment with changing imperial needs and practices, and it induced a scramble to once again adjust the agency's mission, structure, culture, and instrumental capabilities. An examination of USAID's Foreign Assistance Framework, first released in 2006 and providing both a comprehensive categorization of developing states in relation to aid deservedness and a strategic blueprint for managing and aligning agency resources as part of the post-9/11 articulation of neoliberal globalization, demonstrates how the agency has attempted to meet this challenge.

Remaking USAID for the Post–Cold War World

Without specifically referring to the agency, the U.S. government's 2002 National Security Strategy (NSS), the first outlined after the terrorist attacks of 9/11 and the first released by the George W. Bush administration, asserted two goals relevant to USAID that demonstrated how the neoliberal project had solidified over the decade following the Cold War's end. The first goal stated that U.S. national security depends on a "strong world economy," best built and maintained through "[e]conomic growth supported by free trade and free markets" (The White House 2002, 17). While such broad sentiments about the intimate link between free markets, economic interdependence, and national security are old hat, the 2002 NSS offered a much more specific indication of the policy framework in which such benefits would be achieved. The success of the free market/ free trade/national security equation required appropriately liberalized trade policies that "can help developing countries strengthen property rights, competition, the rule of law, investment, the spread of knowledge, open societies, the efficient allocation of resources, and regional integration" (The White House 2002, 19). Echoing arguments from the late 1970s, the NSS pointed out that if developing countries were potential partners in economic integration and the realization of American security objectives, they were likewise threatening spaces of potential state failure, abject poverty, and terrorism. The second major NSS goal relevant to USAID thus highlighted the security risks produced by underdevelopment, and called for both "an expanding circle of development . . . and opportunity" as "a moral imperative and one of the top priorities of U.S. international policy" and increased aid resources for those "countries that have met the challenge of national reform" in liberalizing trade and investment and advancing formal democratization (The White House 2002, 21).

Underscoring this ostensibly new understanding of and approach to development and aid policy was the supposition that "[d]ecades of massive development assistance have failed to spur economic growth . . . and often served to prop up failed policies," a clear rebuke of past iterations of development strategy and an implicit critique of USAID as the primary agent of development and aid policy (The White House 2002, 21). Such criticisms were repeated in the 2006 NSS (The White House 2006), despite a 2004 agency white paper, titled *U.S. Foreign Aid: Meeting the Challenges of the 21st Century*, which outlined a program of internal change designed to redefine the objectives of foreign aid programs, reassert the connections between development and security, and reinvigorate USAID's relevance within foreign and economic policy. Strongly adopting and internalizing the connections between development, security, and interdependence highlighted in the National Security Strategy, USAID (2004c, 7) noted that "development progress has been prominently recognized as a vital cornerstone of national security" in the post-9/11 world, with "weak states" providing the most critical points for "widening the circle of development" and combating global terrorism.

The 2002 and 2006 NSS documents present a reading of American development and aid strategy and policy in which past critiques and agency reforms, as well as the instrumental use of both aid and USAID to meet formerly pressing geopolitical objectives, are curiously absent. Indeed, such intense skepticism about aid's effectiveness in promoting sustainable economic growth, democratization, and trade openness could just as easily have come from critics highlighting USAID's failures at almost any point in the agency's post-Vietnam history. Likewise absent was consideration of USAID's efforts to implement programs and strategies in tune with the centering of market forces and trade liberalization over the previous three decades. It is worth looking at these changes more closely, since they coalesced around a set of internal management and strategic reforms that, while deepening and consolidating the agency's neoliberalization, did not apparently do much to improve the view of USAID among American policymakers and foreign policy elites. So what did the agency do following the Cold War, and why was it, after the 9/11 terrorist attacks, still not enough, especially since these attacks did not fundamentally alter (and in fact strengthened) strategic emphases on economic openness and trade liberalization as prerequisites of development progress?

As detailed, USAID faced withering criticism in the 1980s from those in government and business circles who favored greater trade liberalization and an end to the state-centric developmentalism that had supposedly dominated agency thinking since its establishment. Although the foreign aid legislation proposed by the Hamilton-Gilman task force in 1989, which would have replaced USAID and narrowed aid's objectives, failed to pass Congress, several subsequent government audits and reports piled up, all emphasizing the agency's ineffectiveness, diffuseness, and lack of direction. Yet a second comprehensive legislative attempt to replace USAID with a restructured and more flexible executive agency also failed to pass Congress in 1991 (GAO 1993; USAID 2002b). The 1991 rewrite of the FAA proposed by the Bush administration allowed considerable agency discretion in managing aid accounts and disbursing aid, but it left many in Congress leery of growing executive branch power at the expense of legislative oversight and approval. A draft bill written by the Senate Committee on Foreign Relations actually went even further than the Bush administration's original proposal in terms of agency flexibility, but it also included elements reflecting committee members' pet interests (such as "abortion-related provisions and provisions expanding merchant marine subsidies") that provoked a veto threat from the White House (USAID 2002b, 6). This instigated a legislative game of chicken, as the president hoped a vetoed bill could be voted on again with the controversial sections removed. The bill was defeated in the House, however, as economic recession and foreign aid's persistent unpopularity spelled its demise (USAID 2002b).

An internal government review of U.S. foreign aid and development programs following this second failed reform bill argued that the agency was "buffeted by (1) the competing agendas of other federal agencies, (2) the role Congress has taken in programming decisions, (3) the lobbying efforts of outside special interest groups, and (4) fundamental differences among and within these groups on how foreign aid money should be spent and what it should accomplish" (GAO 1993, 4). Under these conditions, and with profound changes in the global geopolitical balance, USAID had seen its programmatic emphases expand to cover a panoply of emerging issues for which it was ill-prepared, increasing fragmentation within the agency and hampering both development efforts and agency management (GAO 1993, 2003a). With a muddled institutional structure, a growing set of objectives, and a changing balance of political forces within the U.S. state and globally, USAID found itself in a situation that made internally managed reform difficult, if not impossible. Legislative reform likewise continued to elude Congress and the White House. A presidential commission recommended fully incorporating the agency into the State Department in 1992, though ongoing battles over agency mission and mandate made such a move "premature" according to the government's General Accounting Office (GAO 1993, 21; Ferris 1992).[1] Following this, the Clinton administration took its turn at reform, but the proposed Peace, Prosperity, and Democracy Act of 1994, intended to replace the FAA and radically alter and make more flexible authorization processes for all U.S. development aid programs, failed to even make it out of congressional committee (USAID 2002b).

External criticism of aid and the agency also sharpened, as global economic growth, trade liberalization, and capitalist internationalization became the paramount objectives of state and hegemonic projects of neoliberal globalization. Although this did not translate into support for making aid programs and USAID into outright funding agents for *direct* promotion of American exports, as in many European and Japanese aid and export credit programs (see Lancaster 2000, 27–28), critics nevertheless sought to reinforce as much as possible the agency's market orientation and utility. Export-oriented segments of agro-food capital were especially pointed in their critiques, despite the fact that U.S. agricultural producers had long found a ready outlet for surplus disposal in the agency's food aid programs. Such sentiments were summarized by Richard Krajeck, vice president of the U.S. Feed Grains Council, who stated before Congress that "there have been countless instances where AID agricultural programs have been counter to U.S. agricultural interests . . . [and to] objectives of increasing agricultural exports and eliminating trade barriers" (U.S. House of Representatives 1994, 40). Krajeck expressed frustration with USAID's inability to align development and trade, and he offered a blunt assessment: "The AID program is funded at $6.2 billion per year and has been primarily a foreign aid program that has been shaped by U.S. political and strategic interests during the cold war. *Those days are over* and the mission of AID and its role in developing agriculture must be reviewed" (U.S. House of Representatives 1994, 106, emphasis added). Unable to navigate the pressures of political gridlock between Congress and the White House on comprehensive legislative reform; the demands of internationalizing capital, which saw USAID's development work as a fetter to accumulation; and a general but intensive move toward neoliberalization across the U.S. state as a whole, the agency was caught in a powerful vise. The agency offered in 1993 to become a "reinvention laboratory," implementing new forms of personnel, data, and resource management through internal bureaucratic, procedural, and technological changes in line with new public management philosophies and centered on "customer focus," staff accountability and team-work, and "managing for results" (GAO 1998, 134).

The outcome was a series of internal reforms that, in keeping with the "smaller government" rhetoric of the time, cut USAID's budget and workforce and streamlined bureaucratic structures. The fiscal year 1996 budget of $5.7 billion was, for example, 13 percent less than that of the previous year, while congressional and executive earmarks expressly directing how USAID funds could be used increased from 59.8 percent of the agency budget in fiscal year 1995 to almost 70 percent in 1997, a move *away from* flexibility and toward more external control over agency resources and their use (GAO 1998, 133–134). The agency also cut its global staff significantly between 1993 and 1997 (from over 11,000 to 7,600 total staff, with a growing number of these being contract staff and foreign nationals hired abroad), closed two dozen overseas missions, and implemented new regulations for coordinating overseas and headquarters staff (GAO 1998, 133). This streamlining was part of a broader reform of the agency's internal management systems, and it entailed key changes in how USAID overseas missions operated, including "taking a team approach to management, accepting increased accountability through the authority and flexibility given [missions] by USAID, and increasing the participation of development partners in the design and implementation of projects" (GAO 1998, 136).

In 1996 the agency also implemented a wholesale "reengineering" of internal financial and aid program data management processes, dubbed the "New Management System," with disastrous results. The GAO concluded that the computerized system had not been effectively tested before its launch and that it did not in any case meet federal requirements. Its use was suspended after just a few months, though not before it cost the agency an estimated $100 million over the following two years (GAO 1998, 135). In addition to the failure of this technological fix, a number of other conspiring factors, including a 1996 Reduction in Force (RIF) mandate, produced a "human capital crisis" for USAID. Several senior and experienced staff left the agency, others were forced to "bump" according to civil service personnel rules, and, shockingly, leadership and several other training programs for new and midcareer staff were eliminated (USAID 2007, 9; 2004a, 16; see table 1).[2] These issues continued to reverberate within the agency for years after, with a 2004 personnel management strategic plan noting that "decisions made in the 1990s left us without the depth of expertise, new leadership, and numbers of staff needed to address today's challenges and mandates" and "placed USAID's institutional memory in jeopardy" (USAID 2004a, 16).

Restructuring in the 1990s also included the beginnings of more intensive interaction and alignment (but not consolidation) with the State Department,

TABLE 1 USAID Staffing Levels, 1965–2005

Year	U.S. direct hires	Total staff
1965	6,828	15,098
1970	6,959	15,050
1975	4,365	6,591
1980	4,058	8,256
1985	3,623	8,017
1990	3,488	11,401
1995	2,981	9,152
2000	2,124	7,474
2005	2,398	7,320

Adapted from USAID 2007, 1.

altering the bureaucratic chain of command so that the agency administrator reported to the secretary of state rather than directly to the president (GAO 1998). In addition, the State Department exercised considerable authority over USAID staffing levels at overseas agency missions, housed in American embassies, and over the agency's ability to manage offices and personnel at its foreign posts. This influence extended to the State Department's reluctance and refusal to close USAID missions in which the USAID presence was sometimes merely token and turn them into regional offices, even when the agency itself requested such closures in order to find efficiencies and consolidate smaller posts. As the GAO recounted, the State Department feared such closures "might be misinterpreted by the host country and subsequently damage bilateral relationships"; when requested closures and regional consolidations did occur, it was only after USAID conducted "protracted negotiations" with the State Department (GAO 1993, 29).

The agency's absorption into the State Department remains incomplete today, but the agency's struggles with its larger and more politically influential sister department in the 1990s revealed two tensions that cut across the changing geostrategic terrain in which these instruments and agents of American foreign policy worked. First, USAID's relative weakness belied the fact that the State Department also felt the pinch of geostrategic change following the Cold War, as it too was hit by downsizing, confusion over objectives and mandates, and competition for staff from the private sector. Having been encouraged to "do more with less" for two decades, the State Department faced a human capital crisis of its own, with "empty desks at more than seven hundred foreign service and six hundred civil service positions" by 2001 and a raft of outmoded, obsolete, and inadequate facilities, equipment, and management practices (Kopp and Gillespie 2011, 35). A 2001 "Diplomatic Readiness Initiative" (DRI) sought to add over one thousand new employees to the department to fill lingering gaps, provide more and better training to department personnel, and reduce workload to prevent stopgap solutions and relieve overburdened staff (USAID 2004a, 37).[3] While the State Department's larger size, greater clout, and Cabinet-level influence made reforms easier to navigate, the past decade has nonetheless seen stronger integration of USAID into the State Department in ways that demonstrate the latter's weaknesses as much as its strengths. This is discussed in more detail below and in the final chapter with respect to joint efforts at strategic planning and the incursion of still other federal institutions (most importantly the military) into development and aid programming, financing, and implementation.

Second, the Cold War's end, the USSR's dissolution, and the expansion of thematic concerns for U.S. foreign policy meant that by the middle of the 1990s, USAID was working in far more countries than it ever had before, albeit with proportionately fewer resources and a much smaller personnel complement. By fiscal year 2002 the agency was managing U.S. foreign assistance to 159 countries, with direct-hire American personnel stationed in 71 of those, almost double the number of countries (82) in which it worked at the Cold War's close in 1992 (GAO 2003b). The expansion of USAID program responsibilities during the 1990s alongside declining levels of direct-hire American staff was an important facet of the agency's neoliberalization and its evolution from an institution wherein American Foreign Service experts designed and implemented aid and development programs "to one with a declining number of direct-hire staff that oversee the contractors and grantees who carry out most of its day-to-day activities" (GAO 2003b, 2). Despite downsizing and other resource issues; low morale; a plethora of management problems; and sharp criticism from other organs of the U.S. state, private capital, and the American public, USAID nonetheless saw a rapid expansion of its presence, and on a new geostrategic basis, in a changing system of American informal imperialism in the 1990s and into the twenty-first century.

Tensions between institutional and strategic flexibility and rigidity strongly influenced the course of geostrategic decision making at the agency, as it sought for over a decade to clarify its mandate and improve its political standing and institutional effectiveness. Underlining all of this was the requirement that the agency ensure its programs stimulated economic growth through the facilitation of trade openness and global economic integration. The restructuring

USAID underwent beginning in the 1990s focused on aligning the agency's development mission with state and hegemonic projects of neoliberalization; altering agency personnel and management practices according to neoliberal rhetoric; and emphasizing cost-cutting, outsourcing, and smaller, more flexible, and streamlined government institutions. Developing and implementing coherent strategic plans and objectives for foreign assistance programs was no easy task amid the swirl of political criticism, management reforms, and institutional restructuring described above, but the one overarching goal that remained intact across this period stated that aid must ensure liberalized economic relations and formal democratization as the only sure path to development for developing and post-Soviet transition countries.

Even bills aiming to slash foreign assistance, such as the Foreign Aid Reduction Act of 1995, combined persistent critiques made by deficit and defense hawks with a thorough embrace of the fundamental components of neoliberal globalization, albeit in constrained fashion tied directly to U.S. economic interests. Emphases on economic growth and democratization were not, of course, fundamentally new, as USAID had long maintained the necessity of development progress based on liberal democracy, capitalist growth, and mutual cooperation. Senator Jesse Helms (R-N.C.), arch-conservative and vociferous foe of foreign aid, identified the goals of the 1995 bill, which he sponsored, as ensuring that: "(1) U.S. national security interests are protected; (2) export markets are increased for U.S. businesses; (3) transnational threats to American security [. . .] are reduced; (4) private sector economic growth and democracy take hold around the globe; (5) and the U.S. Government maintains tools to respond effectively to urgent international humanitarian crises" (U.S. Senate 1995, 2).

This bill never made it to a vote, yet the context of intensive neoliberalization, and general consensus among decision makers on the necessity and desirability of the changes this implied, gave to the broad objectives outlined both in the bill's policy statement and over decades of USAID activity new meaning and a new geostrategic mapping amid a neoliberal realignment of state/market/civil society relations. At the center was a geoeconomic vision of interdependent states managing and facilitating capitalist internationalization, a process that relied in turn on appropriately liberalized trade relations and state structures. The agency's own turn toward downsizing, contracting out, and streamlining left it little to lean on as a basis for articulating its relevance or utility in maintaining and expanding U.S. hegemony in this project. What did emerge, however, were emphases on the agency's technical and policy expertise and its extensive reach into the political and economic structures of developing states. This made institutional capacity building in developing countries, particularly that aimed at implementing and cementing trade liberalization, a central component of USAID activities as the agency aligned itself with the project of neoliberal globalization.

Trade Capacity Building at USAID

The adoption of trade capacity building as a central plank of post–Cold War strategies at USAID was neither immediate nor easy, as the agency had to negotiate the difficult internal reforms detailed already while seeking clarity and stability with respect to its own capacities from Congress, the White House, the State Department, and other development institutions. Indeed, *trade capacity building* emerged as a distinct term and concept only during the World Trade Organization's 2001 Doha Round of negotiations, though it had existed as a point of pragmatic and strategic emphasis long before that. The meaning and implementation of TCB in the 1990s and early years of the twenty-first century were meant to move aggressive efforts at global trade liberalization forward, after these had stumbled upon the objections of many developing country governments that they were not benefiting from liberalization, structural adjustment, and global market integration as promised, not to mention an explosion of social movements stressing the democratic deficit of international financial and trade institutions like the IMF, World Bank, and, after 1995, the WTO.

While TCB has been put into practice in ways that reinforce and extend neoliberalization, focusing development resources on building political and economic capacity to participate in liberalized trade and global markets, it remains vague and difficult to assess as a development strategy. Advocates of TCB as a path to development argue that liberalized trade drives economic growth and that state institutions and civil society must be brought into line with market mechanisms—civil society through active cultivation, and states through the expansion of their abilities to promote and guarantee a sound investment climate and international market linkages, as well as social cohesion and national security. This is all to be achieved through trade capacity building, the transfer, production, and reproduction of knowledge, practices, and skills within and between institutions charged with implementing, expanding, and overseeing trade liberalization and economic globalization. Phillips and Ilcan (2004, 397) describe capacity building as one of the primary political technologies for constructing and spatializing neoliberal governmentality, those "ways of governing populations that make individuals responsible for changes that are occurring in their communities," with responsibility exercised and enforced through markets and increasingly emphasizing "skill acquisition, knowledge-generation, and training programs."

This perspective highlights the ways in which discourses and practices of capacity building center on the creation and reproduction of social categories that mark off populations as either responsible members of open, market-based communities moving toward development or irresponsible and potentially dangerous outliers. Moving from the latter group to the former depends on acquiring the skills and knowledge that permit individual actors to practice responsible behavior and enforce or receive discipline via market mechanisms. In the case of TCB and its link to development and aid strategies, these categories remain tied to and dependent on the territorial nation-state as the primary unit of analysis, object of development, agent of policy implementation and enforcement, and (a rather porous) container of economic, political, and social relations. Diffusion of skills, knowledge, and training—investments in "social capital" and "human capital"—are the driving forces of this vehicle of neoliberal globalization and development (Rankin 2004; Walker et al. 2008). Yet there remains a need to go beyond simply recognizing the categorization of populations and places along axes of responsibility and, as emphasized by the strategic-relational approach, to consider more thoroughly how such processes are part of larger hegemonic projects tied intimately to the relations between and strategies of class-relevant social forces and state institutions. In other words, to what specific ends are such technologies and strategies put in articulating, defending, and maintaining neoliberal globalization as a project? A closer examination of how USAID has instituted TCB, and what this means for its strategic selectivity, as well as that of other state institutions in the United States and developing countries, helps answer this question.

In a comprehensive 2003 report on its TCB activities, USAID (2003c, 3) outlined a three-part framework for enacting successful development through trade capacity building in developing countries: participation in trade negotiations, implementation of trade agreements, and economic responsiveness to new trade opportunities. This report followed on the heels of an extensive government-wide survey carried out by USAID (2001b) to assess the entire range of official resources devoted to technical assistance and capacity building for trade liberalization in developing countries. This survey revealed that almost thirty government agencies, including USAID, provided some form of technical assistance for trade capacity building to developing and transition countries, with the dollar value of this assistance increasing rapidly and totaling $556 million in fiscal year 2001 and over $750 million in 2003 (USAID 2001b, 4; USAID 2003d, 2). This TCB assistance took many forms, including training and consultations on WTO accession and compliance; aid for construction of or improvements to trade-related physical infrastructure such as ports, airports, and telecommunications systems; and technical assistance for policy reform in areas such as competition, labor standards, and financial regulation. Much of this implied or demanded changes to recipient countries' economic regulatory systems, the drafting and passage of new legislation, and extensive training for public- and private-sector officials.

The actual content and implementation of representative TCB programs are discussed below, but it is important first to highlight how reframing foreign assistance in relation to trade liberalization consolidated the geoeconomic basis for USAID strategies and activities in line with state and hegemonic projects of neoliberal globalization. A key point in the agency's 2004 white paper was that greater interdependence, multilateralism, and trade openness posed opportunities and challenges for states, capital, and civil society. In this context, the "rewards for good policies and institutions—and the negative consequences of weak policies and institutions—are greater than ever," making "the need for better coordination and harmonization" a priority for development aid and programs (USAID 2004c, 7). This framing positioned the agency's work as a form of institution and network building that can ensure the success of development, trade liberalization, and globalization efforts by assisting developing countries in constructing and maintaining a proper policy environment. It also extended the agency's historical focus on restructuring developing state institutions as a means of promoting development progress according to U.S. foreign and economic policy needs and strategies, and fully fleshed out a sentiment articulated in the 1980s, when USAID sought to build a "policy dialogue" with developing countries. In the 1985 *Blueprint for Development* strategy, for example, USAID (1985, 60) stated that it would "use the policy dialogue process to bring perceived trade problems to the attention of recipient countries . . . [and] use programs and projects to encourage the removal or modification of policies and practices that inhibit trade and retard the development process." This required close coordination and dialogue not only with developing country governments but also with the IMF and World Bank, with whom USAID had several "shared policy concerns" in the areas of trade and macroeconomic policy, and other developed country governments, whose aid programs were portrayed as distorting development and free market mechanisms (USAID 1985, 60).

That the agency did not fully implement this deeply geoeconomic approach to development aid until the turn of the century was due to both internal disorder, as discussed above, and the political context, with electoral shifts, gridlock in the WTO, and the foreign policy response to the 9/11 terrorist attacks providing space for articulating geostrategic discourses in new and complementary ways. Yet moves to emphasize technical assistance aimed at institutional and policy reform in developing states were ongoing throughout the 1990s, which was well before the full delineation of such strategies between 2001 and 2004. During the 1990s, as the Cold War threat of communism receded ever further into the past, USAID highlighted more strongly the importance of expanding and liberalizing global trade as a fundamental component of the American national interest, though early on it placed as much stress on increasing incomes in the developing world as on macrolevel concerns with altering the policy environment through technical assistance and training. Budget requests from the early and mid-1990s stressed sustainable economic growth, achieved through greater integration into international markets and multilateral economic institutions, as a strategic priority for foreign assistance programs. A principal point in this was developing countries' lucrative and rapidly expanding market potential for American exports. The fiscal year 1993 budget, for example, stated that while the United States annually exported $130 billion worth of goods and services to developing countries, "poor people make poor markets" (USAID 1992, 9). Sustained income growth would be necessary to ensure that consumers in developing countries could afford American imports, which in turn supported American jobs in a competitive global economy, with the agency estimating that 2.8 million jobs in the United States depended on exports to developing countries (USAID 1992, 9).

The agency expressed the paired themes of maintaining American economic and political hegemony and opening new markets in the developing world even more strongly in the following year's budget. Here USAID (1993, 2) identified U.S. domestic economic growth as "a primary foreign policy goal," with American competitiveness in a cutthroat and interdependent world reliant on the "ability to compete and trade in the context of a global economy." It likewise made an explicit link between democracy, human rights, and free markets in a single strategic objective, with the promotion and protection of these in developing countries a cornerstone of American foreign policy and national security. This in turn was linked to market potential and policy reform in developing countries, as the agency highlighted the fact that "U.S. exports expanded much more rapidly to countries making progress in economic policy terms than to others," with "American exports to AID-assisted countries classified as 'policy reformers' increas[ing] by 126 percent, compared with 46 percent for non-reformers" between 1985 and 1991 (USAID 1993, 2). Policy reform went only in one direction in this geostrategic framing of aid and development: toward liberalization, privatization, and structural adjustment. Just two years later, the programmatic emphasis specifically on capacity building and policy reform became even more pronounced, with the agency arguing that "USAID's development programs are helping to create tomorrow's markets today. By helping poor countries with institution building, training and technical assistance in all facets of their economic, political, social and environmental development, we are making sound investments which will pay handsome dividends in the next century" (USAID 1995, 6).

By the time the agency presented its fiscal year 1998 budget to Congress, this perspective had solidified into the beginnings of a strongly geoeconomic rubric for determining not only the objectives of aid but also which countries deserved aid. Stating that USAID programs "will succeed only in those countries where all parties . . . share a commitment to the development process," the agency bluntly concluded that "we can no longer afford to provide assistance to countries that fail to incorporate basic principles of good governance and sound economic liberalization into their development strategies" (USAID 1997, 1). As noted above, the number of countries in which USAID directly and indirectly worked increased rapidly during this period, highlighting the growing consensus on and constitutionalization of trade liberalization and international economic integration within USAID and, more broadly, in the development industry and global aid architecture. A study by the Congressional Budget Office (CBO) identified this consensus on the benefits of liberalization and other measures that formed the backbone of neoliberal globalization: "Developing countries seem to realize in increasing numbers that the more they liberalize trade, privatize state industry, and adopt open, market-oriented economic policies that encourage integration in the world economy, the more likely they are to see sustained economic growth" (CBO 1997, 19).

Although USAID's embrace of its role as capacity builder for developing countries' liberalization efforts was by this time well underway, and resulting in a slow return to greater funding for the agency, it remained under intense political pressure to reform itself and justify its existence. The role of USAID programs and expertise in fostering economic policy reform in developing countries, for example, often received short shrift from Congress and the White House, with the agency forced to eliminate both its Office of Economic Analysis and its chief economist position in the early 1990s (Pillsbury 1993). This made interagency coordination and partnership vital to USAID's efforts to achieve appropriate neoliberal reforms both for itself and for developing countries via its foreign assistance programs, and especially in trade and other capacity-building programs. As the agency stated in its 2001 TCB report, USAID and U.S. development policy are "committed to working in partnership with developing and transition economies to remove obstacles to development, among which are barriers to trade" (USAID 2001b, 3). The 2003 report likewise singled out free trade agreements as a powerful growth engine for developing countries, so long as they are supported by "sound institutions" that can "ensure transparency and predictability in economic governance, reinforcing economic reforms that are critical for successful development" (USAID 2003c, 7).

Such reforms would be successful only in a wider web of mutually reinforcing rules and fundamental, locked-in changes to the policy environment itself, in which USAID would play a vital coordinating role with respect to the production, circulation, and legitimation of knowledge about appropriate policy change and development progress, all grounded in the geoeconomic discourse underwriting the project of neoliberal globalization. How closely the actual implementation of TCB hewed to these conceptualizations is slightly more problematic. The often vague, catchall character of TCB in practice suggests that it was (and is) less a fully coherent, radically new blueprint for official development assistance, provided and managed by USAID, than a repackaging and strategic elevation of existing programs and activities, meant to bring both developing countries and USAID in line with state and hegemonic projects predicated on economic liberalization. Examples of TCB in practice often center on facilitation of specific policy reforms, development of new institutional partnerships, or provision of targeted training programs. Noting, for example, that in "many developing countries, it is the business community that is most cognizant of the benefits of free trade and therefore takes the initiative to advocate for trade policy reform," USAID highlighted its assistance to a business association in Mozambique, conducting "a countrywide series of discussions of the opportunities and costs of liberalization" for that country (USAID 2001b, 47). This business association succeeded in convincing the government of Mozambique, emerging from over a decade of civil war, to liberalize its trade policies, join the Southern African Development Community free trade area, and follow up on its WTO commitments. This was followed by USAID-funded efforts to "mainstream" trade policy considerations (i.e., liberalization) into ongoing development planning and institutional reform in Mozambique (USAID 2001b, 47).

Similarly, USAID (2001b, 25) helped provide training on international accounting standards and market-based financial information systems to financial-sector managers and officials in several former Soviet republics. The agency worked with other aid donors to help countries in Eastern and Southern Europe harmonize their financial accounting standards and systems with those of the European Union. This not only helped modernize the financial sector in those states but also greased the wheels for foreign direct investment, privatization efforts, intensive financialization of national economies, and accession to larger multilateral and intergovernmental organizations. Much of USAID's trade capacity building assistance focused on such "behind the border" activities, and especially on a wide range of technical changes to trade-related policies, standards, and enforcement systems, often linked to preparations for trade negotiations, as well as compliance with bilateral and regional free trade agreements and WTO obligations (USAID 2003c). In Indonesia, a USAID project provided the Ministry of Finance with technical training and data resources to strengthen that agency's "institutional capacity for analysis, leading to key tax reforms and the use of fiscal sustainability indicators" (USAID 2003d, 10). Such changes not only, in USAID's analysis, assisted with financial stabilization, export orientation, and poverty reduction in the Indonesian economy but also positioned USAID as a central node in the complex global network of development knowledge and information.

The diversity of programs, projects, and strategic objectives bundled together under trade capacity building, however, suggests that much of the agency's TCB concentration consisted of recategorizing already-existing programs and activities under new headings, in order to align the agency more clearly with the extremely strong liberalization agenda pursued after President George W. Bush took office in 2001. While a good deal of continuity existed between Bush and his predecessors on the necessity of trade liberalization, this strategic push was strengthened after 2001 as it became more tightly linked with national security concerns and strategies. One USAID official remarked to me, for example, that initial attempts to institute TCB within the agency cast a very wide net, in which "virtually anything that we were doing in the economic growth sphere could be described as trade capacity building" (Anonymous, 2004). The broad definition of TCB, coupled with the increased emphasis on international market integration as the best means of alleviating poverty and spurring economic development, belied continuities between the focus on trade liberalization and previous overarching aid and development objectives. The same USAID official continued, describing the purpose of government-wide TCB surveys the agency conducted:

> My understanding . . . was that [developed countries] would ask the developing countries, what do you need in terms of trade capacity building, to get you ready to participate in the WTO and globalized trade regimes? And they would give these long laundry lists that would run into the hundreds of millions of dollars, and the developed countries would go, "whoa, we can't do all this.". . . So we started developing these inventories of all our trade capacity building investments, and one of the objectives of those inventories was so we could talk to the developing world and tell them, look, we're doing all this stuff in trade capacity building already. (Anonymous, 2004)

Despite this, there *were* two important changes that occurred with the agency's centering of TCB within development assistance strategies and programs. The first relates to the institutional relations through which USAID operates; the second centers on changing understandings and practices of security and state weakness, discussed more fully in the next section. As stated above, the geoeconomic emphasis on liberalization's centrality to appropriate development places the onus for successful development on "responsible" states that can adequately facilitate capitalist accumulation via free trade and economic openness. This has necessitated that USAID alter the character and intensity of the partnerships through which it defines particular development problems or gaps, and then plans and implements capacity-building and other development programs in response, especially through multiple layers of contracting and subcontracting within a global system of development expertise and consulting that includes both NGOs and for-profit institutions (Lancaster and Van Dusen 2005). How USAID serves as both site and strategy for class-relevant social forces institutionalized in and by the state has changed as well. The most important partners with which USAID has strengthened or pursued relations to advance TCB programs have been internationalizing fractions of capital and those state agencies most closely attuned to the ideological foundations of neoliberal globalization, such as the Office of the U.S. Trade Representative, which is itself tightly intertwined with various segments of internationalizing capital (Essex 2007). It is important then to understand TCB not simply as mere technocratic jargon or the shuffling of column headings on budget reports, but as another means of reproducing and reinstitutionalizing class-relevant forces and social struggles in and through the national state. Providing assistance to capital markets and financial service providers, supporting business associations in specific trade-policy lobbying efforts, and training developing state officials and lawmakers on trade agreement accession and "best practices" in financial management are all means of shaping class-relevant social struggles in developing and transition states and of expanding and maintaining informal imperialism via geoeconomic strategy.

The danger USAID faces in its role as site, strategy, and agent in these projects arises from the continual narrowing of its strategic selectivity. Neoliberal geoeconomics forms the basis for agency work, and further neoliberalization is the intended outcome. The benefit comes in the form of larger budgets, more and stronger institutional relations with more powerful agencies and actors, and even the reproduction of USAID itself. Because of its utility in strengthening USAID's position within state and hegemonic projects of neoliberalization, trade capacity building moved quickly up the list of agency priorities and

TABLE 2 U.S. Government TCB Funding, FY 1999–2010

Fiscal year	Total U.S. ($millions)	USAID ($millions)	Percent USAID
1999	380	249	65.5
2000	524	398	76.0
2001	624	423	67.8
2002	638	477	74.8
2003	760	554	72.9
2004	921	617	67.0
2005	1,345	695	51.7
2006	1,417	487	34.4
2007	1,409	337	23.9
2008	2,228	384	17.2
2009	1,817	479	26.4
2010	1,685	511	30.3

Adapted from USAID 2011c.

gained prominence as a guidepost for continued and intensified neoliberalization in strategic planning conducted between 2001 and 2004. It is important to note, however, that even as USAID funding for TCB projects steadily increased, the agency's proportional share of overall U.S. government spending on such activities decreased. This was due to the growth of TCB funding channeled into sector-specific trade facilitation activities, where agencies such as USTR may have more expertise, and because the State Department, the Millennium Challenge Corporation (MCC), and the U.S. military also increasingly handle a large amount of development programming and trade capacity building (GAO 2011; see table 2).

Geographically, and following the emphasis on developing state performance outlined toward the end of the 1990s, USAID concentrated TCB funding in states where acceptable neoliberalization was already underway, though a given state's strategic importance was not based solely on its trade policy or liberalization efforts. Major TCB recipients were clustered in the Middle East, Eastern Europe, and the former Soviet Union, while countries eager to engage in free trade agreements with the United States on a bilateral or regional basis also saw increased TCB assistance (USAID 2001b, 2003d). Between 2001 and 2004, TCB funding provided by USAID to countries engaged in free trade talks increased more than threefold, with much of this funding targeted at building institutions compatible with the requirements of WTO accession or specific features of bilateral and regional agreements with the United States (USAID 2004b).[4] In the period 2005 to 2010, funding for trade capacity building efforts increased to over $1.5 billion annually, though USAID's share of this amount decreased during this time, and a much greater emphasis was placed on aid for physical infrastructure due primarily to MCC's emergence as a TCB assistance provider (GAO 2011). Yet while USAID, the State Department, the U.S. Army, and MCC accounted for over 90 percent of all U.S. trade capacity building funding, only the former two made TCB a primary strategic priority for development assistance (GAO 2011).

The agency can now be counted on to center trade policy considerations in its development assistance strategies. Its strategic selectivity has effectively narrowed to permit a cartography of development consistent only with neoliberal globalization, in which the state's role is to institutionalize, manage, and facilitate the internationalization of capital. The agency's role hinges on knowledge production, legitimation, and diffusion; the articulation of strategies in line with the demands of neoliberal globalization; and the management of a dense nexus of development contracts. The agency's geostrategic basis and context would thus appear to have shifted almost entirely toward the geoeconomic and away from the geopolitical. Yet a significant geopolitical component remains entrenched in agency strategies and discourses, as national security discourses focusing on counterterrorism and state failure emerged in the late 1990s and gained traction after 9/11. The fears, tensions, and strategies associated with the geopolitics of networked terrorism and state failure had to be articulated with the geoeconomic emphasis embodied in trade capacity building, and USAID attempted to do so with a new development assistance rubric that could take into account the economic policy environment and commitment to liberalization in specific developing countries, as well as the threat of state failure, counterhegemonic disruption, and a commitment to security framed in terms of the global war on terror.

Security, State Weakness, and "the 3Ds" in the Foreign Assistance Framework

The second important change accompanying USAID's adoption of TCB rests on the altered relationship between development and security, as outlined in the 2002 and 2006 National Security Strategy documents. The core geopolitical and security concerns here are with state weakness and failure. Development bolsters "weak states" that might otherwise become havens for terrorist and criminal networks, which could then pose a threat to American interests abroad and domestic national security. This positioning of developing states as potential repositories and bases for international terrorist and criminal activity, or simply as chaotic gaps in the fabric of globalization, has led to the development of the so-called 3DS approach to foreign policy, in which USAID, the State Department, and the White House have identified development, defense, and diplomacy as the three pillars of American national security (USAID 2004b, 2004c; The White House 2002, 2006). This framing of state weakness focuses on states' inability or unwillingness to properly restructure and insinuate themselves into the networks, flows, and institutions of neoliberal globalization. Disconnection from such flows and networks is not only economically wrongheaded but also produces political and social weakness, which in turn results in geopolitical insecurity that threatens continued capitalist accumulation under the rubric of neoliberal globalization, as well as the smooth functioning of informal imperial relations. Roberts, Secor, and Sparke (2003, 889) lay out the contradictions of this "neoliberal geopolitics," in which "enforced reconnection" with circuits of internationalizing capital "is today mediated through a whole repertoire of neoliberal ideas and practices," backed and, if necessary, imposed through militarized violence. The agency's strategic articulation of geoeconomic with geopolitical discourses and strategies is predicated on such tangled configurations. Development should be centered on economic growth unrestrained by bureaucratic state institutions interfering with global market forces, and enforced by the global reach of the U.S. state's security apparatus, which faces numerous mutually reinforcing threats.

As discussed, USAID began to incorporate these kinds of assumptions into mechanisms of development policy and foreign aid allocation in the late 1990s, though the criteria and an appropriate rubric were only fully fleshed out over the next several years. The assertion of clear (or clearer, at least) geopolitical framings, functions, and objectives following the 9/11 terrorist attacks, and the launch of the U.S.-led global war on terror, sharpened the emphasis on state failure and provided a geopolitical, security-oriented rationale for state and hegemonic projects of neoliberal globalization that had been muddled and secondary since the end of the Cold War. This also provided USAID and other development-focused agencies and institutions a mandate for "promoting the right kind of state, or, better yet . . . promoting scope for governing capacity outside the state and market, in the realm of civil society" (Rankin 2004, 22).[5]

Trade capacity building, for example, offers a potential and enforceable technical fix for disconnection by building "the right kind of state" and for shaping relations between it and civil society. More generally, however, neoliberal geoeconomic discourses and strategies intertwined with geopolitical concerns regarding state failure and international terrorism resulted in a geostrategic framework that posits being outside the project of neoliberal globalization as being *against* this project and thus posing a security risk. Former USAID Administrator Andrew Natsios made this point in a May 2003 speech: "For countries that are marginalized, that are outside the international system, that are outside development, that are not developing, that are not growing economically, that are not democratizing, look at the different factors that lead to high risk in terms of conflict. Income level is one of the highest correlations between marginalized states and risks in terms of conflicts" (USAID 2003b).

The agency's 2004 white paper expanded on this sentiment to provide a more detailed strategic framework for development and aid programs, establishing a loose taxonomy of states according to the need for development assistance, the commitment to initiate or continue neoliberal policy reforms, and the degree to which states are capable and "fair" partners in the use of development resources (USAID 2004c). The reassertion of the geopolitical, and its focus on state weakness and failure, was not new, as concerns over the failure of developing and transition states to maintain social order and act responsibly in the context of the post–Cold War international system were expressed as early as the last stages of the Cold War itself. As noted, however, the global war on terror put state failure into new and sharper relief for American foreign policy elites. It meant that some states were of special interest in U.S. foreign policy and security strategies for reasons other than geoeconomic ones, although the agency's objective was to make sure these were complementary rather than oppositional or totally separate, as had often been the case during the Cold War. The agency (USAID 2004c, 21) recognized that the determination of which developing states were and are considered strategic is a matter for other U.S. state institutions, but it also noted that "[i]ncreasingly, the primary foreign policy rationale for assistance may be matched by or indistinguishable from the developmental or recovery objectives." Running across attempts to construct new taxonomies of aid recipient states and build appropriate mechanisms of aid selectivity and disbursement, then, has been consideration of "strategic states," a designation that depends less on USAID and development objectives than on the foreign policy and national security goals of other U.S. state institutions and associated class-relevant forces and blocs, reproducing USAID's position as a site for the displacement and (sometimes) resolution of tensions between capital, Congress, the White House, the State Department, and the Department of Defense.

Successful development under state and hegemonic projects of neoliberal globalization has come to mean, then, the integration of a state, its economy, and its sociopolitical structure into an internationalizing system of informal imperialism. In this system, each state treats foreign capital as it would domestic; trade and other economic relations are directed toward deeper and more intensive liberalization; and U.S. financial, political, and military power backs up and reproduces hegemonic and imperial relations between the United States and other states. Internationalizing market relations dominated by rampant financialization and speculation are fundamentally unstable and are completely insecure as a means of achieving either development or security, let alone both, outside the narrow concerns of capitalist accumulation. As Rankin (2004, 1) puts it in her examination of neoliberal development in Nepal, "market-led development will not necessarily expand opportunity, as the ideology of the 'free market' would have it; rather it may deepen existing injustice and inequality." Such tensions are not lost on USAID. Longstanding issues and contradictions within development assistance are reproduced in new forms, while more candid and off-the-record discussions with agency officials reveal that internal consensus on how new categorizations and geostrategic articulations can and should be put into practice remains fragile.

While the 2004 white paper identified many of these tensions, and a 2006 policy framework officially aligned the foreign aid program's core goals and objectives with the parameters set by the National Security Strategy (USAID 2006a), it was only with the creation of the Foreign Assistance Framework that the agency produced a mechanism aimed directly at resolving lingering conflicts between geoeconomic and geopolitical discourses and strategies by offering a new and comprehensive taxonomic categorization of developing states. The Foreign Assistance Framework, referred to hereafter as "the framework," represents the consolidation of a new cartography of development at USAID that favors a free market orientation and a narrowly defined conception of security, and which can guide programmatic decisions according to criteria based on the complementary interplay of geopolitical and geoeconomic discourses following the 9/11 terrorist attacks and the launch of the global war on terror (USAID 2006b). In this framework, the states most likely to be targeted for development assistance are those that are strategic relative to U.S. economic and security interests *and* that have demonstrated adequate commitment to acceptable neoliberal economic reform; these states thus deserve further assistance within the framework's parameters. On the other hand, those states that are not strategic or are unwilling to implement proper reforms are understood to pose investment and security risks, and they are less or not deserving of U.S. development assistance.

Despite the comprehensive and totalizing nature of the framework, perfect geostrategic complementarity and articulation remain elusive because of the problematic relationship between security and liberalization in official rhetoric and strategies and also due to changes in USAID's internal structures and external relations. While USAID was central to the framework's development and has been crucial to its implementation, the agency does not direct the process by which categories are defined or priorities set, reproducing organizational tensions in and around the agency and fomenting new ones with development partners and other state agencies. The increasing importance of development within the 3Ds approach to national security has meant a strengthening of USAID's position as a locus of expertise, but also a weakening relative to other agencies with development-related interests (especially the Departments of State and Defense) and those state agencies and private funders who control purse strings. The framework also emanates partly from concerns that foreign assistance funding has not been used effectively, along with a strong insistence on rationalizing budgeting and reporting processes. The State Department (2006, 1) noted, for example, that the foreign aid structure remained "stovepiped" and "fragmented across numerous bureaus and agencies," resulting in foreign assistance programs that "lack the coherence necessary for maximum impact" and making accountability "increasingly difficult."

Such statements indicate that a decade of intensive cuts and streamlining at USAID had not strengthened the agency's ability to fulfill its mandate, but instead exacerbated the fragmentary and ineffective character of its operation. While the framework asserted some self-control over continued reform efforts at the agency, this was conditioned and permitted as much by the particular configuration of institutional and class-relevant forces that took shape in the context of the global war on terror (especially the growing nexus of development contractors and NGOs, as well as the aggressive intervention of military institutions and agencies in programming and delivering American foreign assistance) as by internal innovation at the agency itself. The rapid proliferation of official U.S. development accounts outside of USAID's purview reflects "an organizational response to apparent dissatisfaction with USAID, which has been seen by many inside and outside the government . . . as slow, unresponsive, and difficult to reform" (Lancaster and Van Dusen 2005, 27).

The Millennium Challenge Corporation, a federal government agency formed in 2004 to target aid to countries far along the path to successful neoliberal economic reform, but deemed in need of specific kinds of infrastructural and other technical support, was one important result of this dissatisfaction. As Mawdsley (2007, 494) aptly demonstrates, the MCC also has its roots in the particularly neoliberal geostrategic emphasis on development articulated in the 2002 NSS, though its primary purpose has been "to pick winners" in allocating such aid. According to Mawdsley's (2007, 489) analysis, the MCC, echoing and enacting the vague but tightly linked development and security emphases outlined in the NSS, offers "a reductionist and facile construction of the relationships between neoliberal economic growth, poverty reduction and security" while actually "serv[ing] primarily the interests of U.S. and transnational capitalist elites." The MCC's aid selectivity criteria and categories were themselves adapted from and indexed to indicators, measures, and data provided or outlined by several international financial and development institutions, including the World Bank, as well as conservative think tanks such as the Heritage Foundation (Mawdsley 2007). The criteria and categories used by the MCC strongly influenced the development of USAID's 2006 Foreign Assistance Framework. The framework thus embodies an important expression of USAID's strategic and institutional place in current formations and practices of informal imperialism, positioning the agency as a vital mechanism of American foreign policy and a central node in managing multiple, diffuse development accounts and efforts.

The framework identifies those states deserving development assistance, as well as those in need of but *not* deserving aid because they lack proper governance or exhibit irresponsible behavior within the international state system. The relationship between need and deservedness thus remains contingent, with developing states placed into one of five categories based on economic and political performance criteria; a sixth "Global or Regional" category incorporates USAID programs that fulfill aid objectives but are not conducive to country-level programming (see table 3). The overarching goal of development assistance under the framework is "to build and sustain democratic, well-governed states that will respond to the needs of their people and conduct themselves responsibly in the international system" (USAID 2006b).[6] As a totalizing instrument, and unlike the MCC's narrower focus on investment-ready states completing or well on their way to appropriate neoliberal reforms, every developing state can be categorized within the USAID framework, though where different states fit in this schema is not necessarily public knowledge, and the categories must accurately and fully capture the full range of developing state types. Countries are meant to graduate from one category to the next, exhibiting adequate development progress according to specific economic, political, and security criteria,

TABLE 3 Foreign Assistance Framework, Developing Country Categories

Type of state	Category criteria	Goals of U.S. assistance
Sustaining Partnership Countries	Upper-middle income or greater; U.S. support provided to sustain partnerships, progress, and peace.	Continued partnership as strategically appropriate where U.S. support is necessary to maintain progress and peace.
Transforming Countries	Low or lower-middle income states; meet MCC performance and political rights criteria.	Government, civil society, and private-sector institutions capable of sustaining development progress.
Developing Countries	Low or lower-middle income states; not yet meeting MCC performance and political rights criteria.	Continued democratization, strengthening public and private institutions, and supporting policies that promote economic growth and poverty reduction.
Rebuilding Countries	States in or emerging from and rebuilding after internal or external conflict.	Stable environment for good governance, increased availability of essential social services, and initial progress to create policies and institutions for future progress.
Restrictive Countries	States of concern where there are significant governance issues.	Civil society empowered to demand more effective democracies and states respectful of human dignity, accountable to their citizens, and responsible toward their neighbors.
Global or Regional Programs	Activities that advance the five aid objectives, transcend a single country's borders, and are addressed outside country strategies.	Achievement of foreign assistance goals and objectives.

Adapted from USAID 2006b.

with aid dependent on whether the state deserves assistance to further push reforms and progress already made. Crucial to the agency's creation and deployment of the framework have been recent changes in mainstream development theory and official U.S. foreign policy strategies, especially foci on "smart power," "transformational development," and "fragile states." The framework emerged from new emphases on state fragility and weakness and the expanded use of American "soft power," those social, cultural, and intellectual resources relevant to diplomacy and development, alongside a more aggressive direct use of military "hard power."

Smart Power, Transformational Development, and Fragile States

The geostrategic emphases on liberalization, good governance, and securitization that have taken root at USAID and other development institutions, both official and private, have emerged from debates regarding the relationship between developing states, instability and terrorism, and national security. One influential understanding within this rests on the proposition that underdevelopment "breeds" terrorism and other networked, potentially global threats, presenting a security dilemma that must be addressed not only through traditional diplomacy and defense but also through development driven by capitalist growth. Finding an appropriate role for foreign aid in this paradigm has meant revisiting the functions of such assistance and, more specifically, USAID's role in managing aid and fostering development in a volatile global security environment. Official and other mainstream discussions of development have therefore emphasized making aid "play a direct role in the war on terror by supporting both frontline countries and weak states where terrorism might breed," while "allow[ing] the United States to project 'soft power' to accompany, and sometimes offset, its use of military power" (Radelet 2003, 109).[7] This instrumental understanding of development assistance relative to military power and strategy builds in part from concerns about the effectiveness and accountability of official development assistance in meeting security and geopolitical objectives and about domestic and foreign perceptions of American foreign aid programs generally.

These issues are also tied to the proliferation of private development assistance providers, especially as private donors' ability to offer and program aid outstrips that of the U.S. state and other official donors. Lancaster and Van Dusen (2005, 50), both of whom spent several years at USAID, argue that development policy and institutional reform must proceed with the recognition that the agency operates in "a world of multiple development actors where USAID programs may not be the most important or the best funded," but must remain flexible enough to "address diverse needs in recipient countries and serve a variety of purposes within the broader scope of U.S. foreign policy." The perception of effectiveness and of fulfilling promises made is equally important because it points to assumptions about the purposes of development assistance, and the risks of its failures, in the post-9/11 geopolitical context. Jeffrey Sachs (2005, 89), for example, has stressed the importance of foreign perceptions and support for the long-term success of USAID and American development assistance:

> The United States itself faces a widely unappreciated risk: the risk of business as usual, with the world wanting to discuss development while Washington focuses on the war on terrorism. The emotional, geopolitical, and operational divide between the United States and the rest of the international community could very well widen markedly, and dangerously. If their life-and-death needs are not met, impoverished countries may be much more reluctant to support Washington and its many security concerns.

This not only reiterates tensions and fears about aid gaps and global interdependence made since the late 1970s but also highlights significant potential contradictions in the melding of geopolitical and geoeconomic discourses and strategies within the project of neoliberal globalization as it confronts newly articulated foci of political disorder and waning hegemonic influence. A former State Department official expressed such fears clearly, stating that the "latest wave of globalization . . . has been of tremendous benefit to the United States, but there is the sense in the country that our economic dominance is eroding. . . . Economic issues are at the center of our most important international relationships" (quoted in Kopp and Gillespie 2011, 196). "Soft power," including those forms exercised and embodied in foreign assistance programs and institutionalized in agencies like USAID, thus forms an essential component of national security and American hegemony in a dangerous world of multiple competitor-partners and transnational networks of risks, threats, and counter-hegemonic forces.

The focus on soft power has since been folded into a broader conceptualization of "smart power," defined by then chair of the Senate Committee on Foreign Relations Joe Biden (D-Del.) as "the skillful use of all our resources, both nonmilitary as well as military, to promote our national interests" (U.S. Senate 2008, 2). Senator Richard Lugar (R-Ind.), a longtime proponent of foreign aid and a veteran of multiple congressional committees dealing with security, development, and foreign policy issues, added that the global war on terror brings new urgency to attempts at constructing a flexible foreign policy apparatus capable of wielding such smart power, though he sounded somewhat behind the curve when stating that the United States "must adjust our civilian foreign policy capabilities to deal with a dynamic world where national security threats are increasingly based on nonmilitary factors" (U.S. Senate 2008, 4). While I discuss what this has meant for the most recent restructuring of USAID, especially for its relationship to the Departments of State and Defense, in chapter 5, for now it suffices to say that such conceptual and official considerations of soft and smart power underlie USAID's white paper, the Foreign Assistance Framework, and an approach that melds military and civilian institutions, as well as geoeconomic and geopolitical framings and strategies of foreign assistance, national security, and informal imperialism (see also Hart 2009; Mohan and Mawdsley 2007).

This debate has given USAID new footing even as it has meant narrowing the agency's strategic selectivity. The agency noted in its fiscal year 2002 budget justification to Congress that "USAID as an institution must recognize its shortfalls and adjust rapidly to improve its effectiveness as a key foreign policy instrument," and it worked to codify priorities related to health and education, conflict prevention, and economic growth (USAID 2001a, 5). With the fiscal year 2003 budget, USAID found more stable ground on which to build a coherent vision of development policy and agency mission by linking development, economic liberalization, and national security. In doing so, USAID (2002a, 1) actually *anticipated* the Bush administration's 2002 National Security Strategy and staked its claim to relevance in a globalizing world imperiled by terrorism, arguing that U.S. national security depended "not only on [addressing] traditional security concerns, but also on maintaining a liberalized international economic system and democratic capitalism as the preferred model of governance."[8] According to the agency, this model promised a boon for development progress but made failures "more acute," as "states that fail to realize tangible benefits from globalization in trade could derail further economic openness in multilateral trade negotiations or face greater internal conflict domestically from those opposed to globalization" (USAID 2002a, 1). The agency went further in its fiscal year 2004 budget, stating that the threat from domestic "antiglobalization" forces in the Global South was not just a danger within and for developing states, but for the United States too, as the 9/11 terrorist attacks were understood as a product of underdevelopment that "breached the sense of security offered by geography" Americans hold so dear (USAID 2003a, 1).

The agency (USAID 2004c, 5) solidified this narrower strategic direction in the 2004 white paper, outlining "five core operational goals" for USAID and U.S. development assistance programs: "Promoting transformational development"; "Strengthening fragile states"; "Providing humanitarian relief"; "Supporting U.S. geostrategic interests"; and "Mitigating global and transnational ills." The latter three goals stem from the first two, with emphases on transformational development and strengthening fragile states most influential in the further elaboration of strategic priorities and structural changes, articulating a view of development as a total transformational process:

> "Transformational" development is development that does more than raise living standards and reduce poverty. It also transforms countries, through far-reaching, fundamental changes in institutions of governance, human capacity, and economic structure that enable a country to sustain further economic and social progress without depending on foreign aid. The primary determinant of progress in transformational development is political will and commitment to rule justly, promote economic freedom, and make sound investments in people. (USAID 2004c, 14)

Three aspects of this approach to development stand out. First, it is focused on institutions, a point the agency stressed in arguing elsewhere that "[i]nstitutions, not resources, matter most," and that "strengthening institutional capacity" must be emphasized to make U.S. development policy more coherent and effective (USAID 2004c, 6). Second, the focus on institutions is built on a state-centric view of development planning and aid allocation, highlighted by the idea that this approach to development transforms *countries*. Implicit is the idea that proper governance depends on strengthening state institutions in support of neoliberal globalization, even as, and perhaps because, this project encroaches upon state capacities to manage economic openness in moments of profound crisis. It is also a result of the elaboration of transformational development within the context of the State Department's focus on "transformational diplomacy" under Secretary of State Condoleezza Rice. Transformational diplomacy, outlined in the joint State Department/USAID 2007–2012 strategic plan, envisioned a wide-ranging approach to American diplomatic efforts designed to reinvigorate U.S. diplomatic capacities and relationships by "working with partners to help them build their own sustainable institutions of democratic governance" (U.S. Department of State and USAID 2007, 18). Finally, the success of transformational development hinges on "political will and commitment" within developing states, with the corollary that aid is most effectively allocated to those states already undertaking appropriate economic and political reforms. The political will to make necessary economic- and security-sector reforms is the major ideological building-block in the Foreign Assistance Framework constructed around and after these objectives and also used for measuring developing-country deservedness in aid allocation.

Past iterations of development assistance, progress, and success were likewise predicated on assumptions about the need to build appropriate institutions within developing, transition, and postconflict states, as well as the theoretical assertion that development was a totalizing process of modernization across the entire interconnected social, political, economic, cultural, and environmental-geospatial organization of a society. The recent turn toward "transformational development" achieved through soft or smart power adds new wrinkles based on the particular historical conjuncture in which the agency found itself following 9/11, namely, foci on helping states harness globalization and properly institute a specific project of neoliberal globalization as well as a geostrategic concern with "fragile states." The white paper provided a rough geographic rubric dividing the world of developing states into "relatively stable developing countries," where the basis for political will and development progress already exists and aid must work to maintain and expand this, and "fragile states," where basic governance and stability are perilous at best and it is questionable whether aid can adequately promote development progress (USAID 2004c, 13). In providing development assistance to fragile states, the agency argued that selectivity is paramount, with deservedness "based on criteria of need, commitment by the host government and/or nongovernmental actors to reform, feasibility of achieving results, and foreign policy importance" (USAID 2004c, 20). At the same time, the agency argued that due to the special nature of development and security concerns in fragile states, progress "should not be measured in standard development terms but rather in terms of progress toward stability and improvements in governance as a foundation for eventual efforts at transformational development" (USAID 2004c, 20). Development progress in fragile states implied first bolstering institutions of good governance, though this in turn is defined in relation to liberalization and security reforms, even if these do not produce immediately tangible development results and possibly even spur opposition.

The agency further elaborated the importance and difficulties posed by fragile states in its 2005 *Fragile States Strategy*, identifying three broad categories of fragile states (failing, failed, and recovering from conflict), while recognizing that the underlying causes of state fragility are not necessarily or only internal to individual states and that classification alone is inadequate for meeting security and development needs (USAID 2005a, 1). The agency therefore differentiates between vulnerable states and states already in crisis and emphasizes both selectivity in providing assistance to fragile states, particularly those in crisis, and the limits of agency programs, with "[t]he decision to engage . . . based upon a country's importance to U.S. foreign policy, as well as the ability of assistance to affect constructive change" (USAID 2005a, 5).[9] Under this view of state weakness and fragility, the agency sought engagement not only with fragile states themselves but also with other U.S. state agencies and private-sector assistance providers. This is due in part to limits on the agency's capacities, as USAID cannot effectively meet all development challenges in fragile states on its own, and to an institutional separation between the geoeconomic and the geopolitical, as the duty and ability to identify a state as strategic to American foreign policy remains elsewhere, fragmented across the White House, the Departments of State and Defense, and Congress. In order to make "many-to-many" donor coordination effective, however, USAID (2005a, 9) also laid out "a new Agency business model for fragile states response," proposing a number of internal reforms that repeated or expanded upon proposals discussed in the white paper, which itself had built on years of discussions and reforms that had moved in fits and starts (see USAID 2004c, 6).

By the same token, policy and structural reform efforts stressing both economic and security considerations did not remove the basis for criticisms leveled at USAID since the late 1980s, and which centered on the agency's inability to properly balance and meld geopolitical and geoeconomic functions, mandates, and visions. In fact, the post-9/11 geostrategic direction of American development policy has exacerbated such tensions and displaced their resolution more fully onto USAID. In particular, the agency has struggled with the fact that "in some [strategic] countries our programmatic goal is development progress, even if that is not the rationale for the assistance," noting that this convenient coupling of geopolitical and geoeconomic concerns "will likely become more frequent as development progress is increasingly seen as vital to achieving our strategic goals," and that the "overlap between strategic states and fragile states is more obvious," citing Iraq, Afghanistan, and Bosnia as examples (USAID 2004c, 30). This runs aground, however, when confronting "countries that are not making development progress, [where] strategic partnership and cooperation may be put at risk" by lack of political will and repeated failure to successfully facilitate neoliberal globalization (USAID 2004c, 30). The white paper posed these concerns as questions to consider in further reforms, while the geostrategic categories in the *Fragile States Strategy* quickly proved inadequate to resolve tensions between competing rationales and objectives for development assistance. These tensions crystallized in the 2006 Foreign Assistance Framework, which sought a more workable combination of the geoeconomic and geopolitical that was comprehensive in its consideration of aid selectivity criteria, even more so than in the MCC criteria. It also enabled the agency to assert its role as a nexus of strategic knowledge and capacity for the deployment of smart power in the service of transformational development and diplomacy, American hegemony, and informal imperialism amid a convoluted and competitive global system of aid donors, planners, and executors.

The determination of which states deserve assistance hinges on the particularity of the neoliberal state's forms and functions, at least as U.S. development and foreign policy dictate—formal multiparty democratic elections, liberalized economic governance that facilitates capital mobility, and security reforms that enhance the investment climate and promote law and order. Again, examining the complex and potentially contradictory character of new deservedness criteria requires critical attention to the framework's geostrategic and ideological components and how these are reflected in aid allocation processes and agency restructuring. Structurally, the framework is a reflection and product of the closer working relationship between USAID and the State Department, which has included new joint strategic planning and the State Department's creation of the Office of the Director of Foreign Assistance (DFA). The DFA serves concurrently as USAID administrator and deputy secretary of state. This arrangement creates the potential for disputes between the State Department and USAID on the purposes and allocation of aid, displacing tensions between each institution's mandate and objectives onto a single budgeting and strategy process (Kopp and Gillespie 2011). This, in turn, has become wedded to management and planning approaches borrowed heavily from the military, an aspect of State-USAID relations discussed in the next chapter with respect to the U.S. government response to recent global energy, financial, and food crises.

Yet in testament to the broad acceptance of a neoliberal emphasis on market-led development, and of securitization as a necessary component of this, there has so far been little disagreement between the State Department and USAID regarding the categorization of specific developing countries according to the new framework.[10] As an official with experience in USAID and the State Department put it, both institutions conform to the idea that development aid is not universally effective, and that criteria related to "good policies" must be paramount: "There is a huge emphasis on selectivity, [the idea] that aid will be most effective and productive in countries that are making a decent self-help effort, and this might have been an area where State and AID were at odds. State would say this country is important for foreign policy, and we'd say no. But State's on board with that too, that's a government-wide conviction" (Anonymous, 2006a). This reflects broader consensus about the importance of selectivity in aid allocation and, more specifically, that aid should be targeted at those countries displaying the most need and the most effective policies, informing "poverty-efficient" allocation strategies by donor nations and institutions and rewarding good policy behavior with aid (Burnside and Dollar 2000; Collier and Dollar 2001, 2002, 2004; for a critique, see Cogneau and Naudet 2007). Deservedness is understood as a function of institutional and policy quality, with good policies and institutions being those that spur poverty-reducing economic growth and embrace the opportunities offered by liberalized markets.

In practice, security and foreign policy considerations cut across this consensus on the basic criteria defining deservedness, as these are not necessarily or directly accounted for in the economic models and measures upon which the poverty-efficient paradigm of aid allocation is based. Yet such considerations are vital to understanding how development and humanitarian assistance are actually structured and allocated. While there has been little conflict over building selectivity into aid allocation, significant and potentially contradictory tensions and tendencies remain, most importantly between the ideological and geostrategic criteria that underpin different understandings of deservedness, and the difficulty of asserting USAID's political position around this framework. This becomes more acute as the Department of Defense expands its role in development policy and strategy. The U.S. military's increasing role in development strategy and policy, associated primarily with reconstruction efforts in Afghanistan and Iraq, has problematized USAID's strategic reforms, but it is linked closely to securitization concerns embedded in the framework. As Patrick and Brown (2007) argue, the military is more nimble than its civilian correlates in reconstruction and development efforts (due to the ability to force particular development projects with the threat or exercise of violence), but it remains overly concerned with narrow, short-term security interests rather than transformational development. These tensions are structured into the framework itself and rest on the construction and deployment of the categories constituting its geographical component; these are most clear when considering "restrictive countries," the difficulties in dealing with fragile states, and the reassertion of a state-centric cartography of development in programming.

With the concern that underdevelopment produces insecurity and translocal threats, it would seem that *all* developing states are strategically important and deserve assistance. When asked about this, the previously quoted agency official agreed that "it creates a dilemma, where only countries with reasonably good policies use aid effectively, but if every country matters, what do you do with foreign aid to countries that aren't using good policies?" (Anonymous, 2006a). This dilemma is perhaps most obvious in relation to restrictive countries, states where, my interviewee stated, "you can't have or it's hard to have a productive relationship [and] . . . there's at most a very limited role for foreign aid," as political will to undertake neoliberal economic and security reforms is not only lacking, but perhaps actively resisted (Anonymous, 2006a). Such states (Cuba, North Korea, Iran, and Venezuela were specifically named) are viewed as regional aggressors or supporters of terrorism, destabilizing the peace and order that come with economic interdependence and acceptance of the security umbrella associated with American hegemony. Despite the long-standing difficulty, or even impossibility, of effectively directing and using foreign aid in

TABLE 4 U.S. Development Assistance in "Restrictive Countries"

Aid objective area	Goals in restrictive countries
Peace and Security	Prevent the acquisition/proliferation of WMDs, support counterterrorism and counternarcotics
Governing Justly and Democratically	Foster effective democracy and responsible sovereignty, create local capacity for fortification of civil society and path to democratic governance
Investing in People	Address humanitarian needs
Economic Growth	Promote a market-based economy
Humanitarian Assistance	Address emergency needs on a short-term basis, as necessary

Adapted from USAID 2006b.

restrictive countries, the framework includes them as a category and delineates goals and objectives for aid allocation (see table 4). Yet how exactly USAID, or any aid donor, can achieve these specific goals remains unclear, as effective allocation, delivery, and use of development aid could not easily be aligned with U.S. foreign policy interests or political realities in such states (see Moss, Roodman, and Standley 2005).

Furthermore, the basis for deservedness among restrictive countries conflicts with that for other developing country categories, in that the "restrictiveness" of a given state does not necessarily imply fragility or weakness that would otherwise indicate a need for assistance. Instead, these states constitute a unique category due to foreign policy considerations separate from USAID's determination and capabilities; this is also true for countries deemed strategic for other than economic reasons. The strategic consequences of the framework's recognition of restrictive countries has proven difficult to manage, due to the difficulties of providing aid in restrictive environments, USAID's negligible role in determining this category's membership, and problems with adequately measuring development progress amid competing (if sometimes overlapping) rationales and a flurry of local, regional, and global crises. "Restrictive countries" pose perhaps the most direct threat to U.S. national security and would thereby seem to deserve aid the most in this framing, but the definition of such countries as restrictive according to the logic of foreign policy, as opposed to that of development progress, would likely prevent transformative development in these states, at least via any programmatic vehicle at USAID's disposal. Instead problems associated with isolation and nonengagement are reproduced, or "sub-imperial" relations with friendly but not necessarily progressive political and social groups are cultivated (Glassman 2005b).

The framework's underlying conceptualization of deservedness is likewise problematic in dealing with fragile states. Logically, if weak state governance is the root of underdevelopment, and this in turn promotes insecurity, then fragile states appear to deserve aid most. With concerns over accountability and effectiveness paramount in development policy and associated institutional reform, however, such states do not necessarily deserve assistance. While the agency has concrete measures of state fragility, and by extension deservedness, based on political, economic, social, and security criteria (USAID 2005b), it also must consider accountability when allocating aid to states where it may be ineffective due to waste, corruption, or incapacity. The Foreign Assistance Framework attempts to rationalize the increasingly sprawling structure of U.S. development assistance (with USAID as the central point in the tangled institutional and bureaucratic nexus) and thereby to increase the accountability of aid managers to aid funders. This means USAID itself must be more accountable in how it uses its funds, ensuring that aid does not work at cross-purposes with neoliberal globalization or the specific objectives of partner institutions. Defining, measuring, and demonstrating development progress and accountability in fragile states become prime responsibilities not only for states receiving U.S. development assistance but also for USAID.

Addressing the particular needs of fragile states, which could fall into the "rebuilding" or "developing country" categories depending on the presence of violent conflict, requires the agency to reassess foreign aid's place and transformational role within American smart power and also how the agency selectively allocates aid to those states where it will produce the most effective results. As one official explained it, aid can only accomplish so much in fragile states: "You don't make things happen with foreign aid, you just support the process. . . . One way to look at it is, we now have a strong national interest in *all* countries making development progress, because if they're not moving forward, there's every worry that they're moving backwards or downwards. And then the next statement is a *sine qua non* for development progress, is, it doesn't happen if you don't have stability, security, and order, and you can't have markets and economic growth" (Anonymous, 2006a). The framework thus incorporates the functional and ideological connection between market-led growth, security and order, and development progress, which taken together indeed constitute laudable objectives for societies torn apart by civil, ethnic, or sectarian violence. Whether these can be achieved through an aid allocation process that derives its criteria and categories from liberalization-first understandings of develop-ment, like those at work in the MCC, remains questionable. Another USAID offi-cial reiterated this point, arguing that many states simply do not register as de-serving aid under MCC criteria because they would not make good partners in terms of aid delivery and use. The solution is not to further refine this method of aid allocation but to measure aid effectiveness in new and different ways, confronting the diversity and complexity of contexts and problems under and through which development must occur (Anonymous, 2006b).

Looking especially at security concerns added to the framework's MCC-derived categories, a third agency official suggested that the timeframe for mea-suring development progress has been unduly shortened because short-term security goals are prioritized over long-term development strategies in fragile states. By focusing too heavily on security as understood by the Departments of Defense and State, economic, political, and social objectives that previously formed core components of USAID strategies are subordinated to or subsumed within short-term strategic and military concerns that only contingently sup-port development progress, and may even undermine it (Anonymous, 2006c). This echoes older critiques that argued allocating aid according to geopolitical considerations led to an ineffective and often instrumental use of development resources in support of narrow security goals and a disregard for other non-military objectives. In the current context, this criticism also points to concerns with the process that produced the framework and set strategic priorities, par-ticularly those related to fragile states and the agency's working relationship with other U.S. state institutions. While all such institutions dealing with devel-opment issues agree that peace, democracy, and economic growth are impor-tant, no consensus exists on what should be prioritized in any given instance. In this environment, every department and agency pushes its own agenda, and strategic decision-making and budgeting become a matter of exercising politi-cal and bureaucratic clout; USAID still possesses little of either, remaining an important but nonetheless junior partner in efforts to craft a smooth and coher-ent interagency budgeting and strategy process.

Tensions between different institutions over strategic and sectoral priori-ties belies the coherence of the neoliberal globalization project, insofar as it depends on competing geoeconomic and geopolitical criteria of deservedness underlying the framework, and the allocation of development aid to and within deserving fragile states. In this sense, relations between USAID and other U.S. state institutions highlight the domestic dynamics and politics of aid account-ability. As one agency policy analyst explained, the framework was designed with two objectives: to assist the agency in carrying out the State Department's foreign policy goals (themselves subordinated to geopolitical considerations tied to military strategies) and, as stated, to rationalize U.S. development assistance accounts (Anonymous, 2006d). As national security strategies incorporate development objectives and donors demand more frequent and detailed measures of accountability and effectiveness, the aid allocation process requires ever more specific and reportable outputs. The framework assists this by building on specific criteria and linking aid allocation to graduation between categories, with only deserving states receiving the aid deemed necessary to promote development that would allow such graduation. This creates the potential for development strategies and aid programs based on the framework to reproduce and exacerbate already existing tensions and contradictions in both USAID and fragile states, an issue taken up in the next chapter.

This points to the final geostrategic tension in the framework, namely, the reproduction of a statist cartography of development that achieves USAID's bureaucratic objectives but only contingently addresses underdevelopment. Deservedness and development remain properties of states, measured by yardsticks devised in line with political, economic, and social reforms, demanded as part of neoliberal globalization, and securitization objectives associated with the global war on terror and with the potential to suppress legitimate progressive social movements. In terms of agency structure, budgeting, and management, this presents a sharp contrast with the functional and issue-area focus of USAID development planning that had emerged in the 1990s, but returned the agency to its historical emphasis on country-level knowledge, planning, and programming. An agency official explained the new thinking:

> Until September 11th, the whole focus had shifted more to sectors and functions. You could make an argument for a country strategy, but it was just the sum of the different concerns, and the whole was less than the sum of its parts. . . . The goal of the white paper was to say no, we're back to the situation where countries matter. You can't turn your back on the Afghanistans of the world because of terrorism and all sorts of problems. So again there is a national security argument for foreign aid, as in the Cold War, and again that calls for a focus on countries, but the pendulum has been slow to shift. (Anonymous, 2006a)

The addition to the framework of the "Global or Regional" category reflects the difficulty of reorienting the functional basis of agency structure—institutionalized in units devoted to Democracy, Conflict, and Humanitarian Assistance (DCHA); Economic Growth, Agriculture, and Trade (EGAT); and Global Health (GH), as well as world regional bureaus—toward a focus on country-level planning. The above quote suggests, however, that planning primarily around thematic areas was a historical aberration. As discussed in chapters 2 and 3, country-level planning typically held sway because of Cold War geopolitics and the concentration of development resources in strategic allies. With budget, staff, and field presence reductions in the 1990s, functional rather than country-level planning allowed greater focus on specific problems of underdevelopment that were understood as global or regional rather than statist in character, and for which development strategies designed primarily to assist specific strategic allies would prove insufficient and costly. Despite the changes heralded by the 2002 and 2006 NSS documents, and growing concern with failed and failing states, USAID had already shifted toward planning around thematic areas, making the return to a statist approach difficult to manage.

This difficulty rests on persistent tensions between geoeconomic visions of a flat, borderless world of market-driven economic connection, in which the state is a facilitator and one among many partners in networked forms of multiscalar governance, and a geopolitical discourse that continues to emphasize the perils of openness, interdependence, and networked flows in a system of territorial nation-states operating according to neorealist assumptions and focused on security and survival. While the framework attempts to wed these two discourses through aid selection and development strategy processes, it emanates from bureaucratic needs pertinent to USAID's position within the U.S. state as much as from concerns with lasting and effective development progress in aid recipient states. Both geostrategic discourses inform and evolve from parallel and competing understandings of the state's role within an incomplete, contested, and variegated project of neoliberal globalization rife with security threats. The state's relative unity of purpose hinges on providing social cohesion and national security while also facilitating economic openness and capitalist internationalization, goals only contingently related to actual development progress, and just as likely to foment insecurity by exposing citizenry to economic shocks the neoliberal state can neither predict nor control. More directly centering security concerns in development programming reinforces the state's role as the guarantor of social cohesion, but only to the extent that countervailing forces unleashed by neoliberal globalization, and which may seek to undermine, threaten, or build alternatives to capitalist internationalization, are quashed.

This reaffirms the point that neoliberal development often reinforces and exacerbates existing social inequalities in developing societies (Mohan and Mawdsley 2007; Rankin 2004). It also demonstrates the lingering influence of the "territorial trap" within conventional approaches to and official understandings of foreign policy and development. These assumptions and the ways in which they are built into official planning, policy, and strategy, such as through the Foreign Assistance Framework, do not adequately address many of neoliberal globalization's on-the-ground realities, tensions, and contradictions. These include conceptual and practical conflicts between economic openness, national security, and development progress; the limitations public-sector austerity places on social and economic planning not directly conducive or counter to capitalist internationalization; and the emphasis on suppressing dissent in the name of security. The framework's statist underpinnings and vision reproduce neoliberal globalization's contradictory tendencies and, in the context of foreign aid and development policy, reinstitutionalize them in the relations between donor and recipient states and within USAID.

The question that routinely dogs such analyses is the dreaded *so what?* To this point, I have provided an account of how USAID has developed as a site, strategy, and agent of American foreign, development, and aid policies, focusing on the discursive and strategic articulation of geopolitics and geoeconomics as my structuring vehicle. This chapter has brought the analysis up to the period immediately following 9/11, when the agency had weathered many years of political criticism, downsizing, and intensive reform to emerge as a small but key part of the American foreign policy and national security apparatuses in an interdependent world of globalized threats and persistent underdevelopment. My critical focus has been on the interplay and articulation of various institutional, strategic, political, economic, and intellectual changes at the agency and in the U.S. state more generally as filtered through, framed by, and structured around broad discursive formations and strategic practices of geopolitics and geoeconomics. Documents such as the Foreign Assistance Framework stand as both artifacts of a particular geostrategic vision and configuration of forces within and around the agency and the tangible institutional means by which tensions, contradictions, and complementarities in these visions and configurations are resolved, displaced, or preserved in a dynamic political and economic context of neoliberal globalization.

Rather than asking *so what* here, a perhaps more useful if speculative question is, *how could it have been different?* Looking back over the cuts, critiques, and changes that have been the engine of change at USAID, would it have been better for the agency to be more nimble and massively funded, with immense political weight in the broader structure of U.S. foreign and development policy? How would the agency's development strategies and policies have been different, if the geostrategic views it promulgated and on which it based decisions were not bound to forms of developmentalism so tightly caught in the "territorial trap" mode of thinking? What if the agency had built stronger ties with social forces and movements more critical of neoliberal globalization's fundamental assumptions and components, but which had significant on-the-ground legitimacy and local presence in developing countries? These are difficult and perhaps impossible questions to answer, but they nonetheless point to dead ends and lost opportunities, either because they were available and not taken or because they were outside the range of viable, acceptable approaches to development given the agency's place in the structured coherence of the American state and its particular state and hegemonic projects.

These are, however, questions that must be asked continually and often, not only of analyses such as the one offered here but also of USAID as an entity, especially as the agency positions itself as an important node in a complex network of development organizations and institutions, what Ananya Roy (2010, 10) calls "a parallel apparatus of development." Many of these institutions are gigantic philanthropic associations tied to transnational corporations, while others are NGOs with strong international presence and expertise as well as heavy reliance on USAID and other official donors for funding. Still others are local organizations and movements decidedly unenthusiastic about advancing or protecting American national security interests in lockstep with local economic and social development. The agency's position and function within an informal American imperialism structured around state and hegemonic projects of neoliberal globalization, and facing serious challenges and tensions resulting from the uneasy marriage of geopolitics and geoeconomics under the rubric of neoliberalization, gives it considerable weight in shaping larger development agendas and legitimizing or alienating alternative visions and approaches.

Of course, and as repeatedly demonstrated, USAID's strategic selectivity, and indeed its long-term fate, does not rest necessarily or primarily in the agency's hands. While the 2006 Foreign Assistance Framework reinforces and extends state and hegemonic projects of neoliberal globalization, and USAID's place within these, the framework also exhibits a particularly diabolical moral calculus of deservedness for development and aid strategies. It enforces the idea that aid is best given to those who have already helped themselves according to the specific dictates of neoliberal globalization and American foreign policy, and it leaves others out of the necessarily unequal and narrowly limited moral community that these objectives produce and police. At the least, the framework advances a restricting influence on recipients' strategic selectivity, narrowing the potential uses of development aid, and reproducing the asymmetrical power relationships and ethical ambivalences that come with aid (Chatterjee 2004; Korf 2007). For USAID, it deepens the structural displacement of contradictory tendencies in the U.S. state's neoliberal project onto the agency, subordinating it more fully within foreign policy structures while demanding more in terms of accountability, effectiveness, and coordination with larger departments whose primary objective is not development. The final chapter takes up these issues by examining how such integration has proceeded in the context of deep global crises and a looming austerity phase in neoliberal globalization. In looking at USAID's attempts to manage such crises while working ever more closely with the Departments of State and Defense, I hope to answer the appeal Roberts, Secor, and Sparke (2003, 887) make to engage with neoliberalism's "inter-articulation with certain dangerous supplements, including . . . the violence of American military force."

CHAPTER FIVE

Development in Reverse

Crisis, Austerity, and the Future of USAID

IN HIS REMARKS TO A NOVEMBER 2011 student conference on the American role in global affairs held at the U.S. Military Academy in West Point, U.S. Agency for International Development (USAID) Administrator Rajiv Shah punctuated the agency's geostrategic tack in the wake of multiple intersecting global crises, growing doubts about the efficacy and costs of American-led military interventions associated with the global war on terror, and renewed political pressure on aid accounts in an era of severe budget cuts. Presenting development assistance, and USAID in particular, as the front line of American engagement with a developing world where "evil and suffering are inescapably linked," Shah (2011a) positioned the agency as the military's civilian counterpart in the American national security apparatus deployed abroad. "It is our responsibility," he said, "as members of the military, as development professionals, as students in a globalized world—to remind our country that . . . [every] dollar spent abroad is actually [an] investment in their national security and national values." Like the wall motif and informational plaque in USAID's Public Information Center with which I began, and which emphasize that development assistance represents a bargain for U.S. taxpayers, this statement highlights the agency's cost-effectiveness as a national security tool. Meeting the demands of global crisis and underdevelopment, Shah (2011a) stated, "will require serious investment in development cooperation, as fundamental to our national security and prosperity as the next piece of military hardware," *now*; missing this window of opportunity will require the United States "to spend far more blood and treasure securing a far more resource-constrained, insecure world" in the future. In his remarks to the West Point crowd, Shah (2011a) likewise stressed that the difficult security-oriented work carried out by both USAID and the military must ultimately serve geoeconomic ends, as "conflict is essentially development in reverse. It destroys capital, displaces people from productive activities and scares away investment." This echoed his earlier testimony in a Senate Foreign Relations Committee hearing on USAID's 2012 budget request. In addition to reiterating long-held arguments that today's aid-recipient nations are tomorrow's strongest trading partners, Shah (2011c) stated that "winning the future will depend on reaching the 2–3 billion people currently at the bottom of the pyramid who will come to represent a growing global middle class" and the future consumer base for American exports.

This underscores Cowen and Smith's (2009, 23) argument, first cited in chapter 1, that geopolitics is today "dead but dominant," a powerful but residual modality of sociospatial order and vision, eclipsed and absorbed by geoeconomics in practice, if not in the eyes of its practitioners. The logic and language of geopolitics, fixated on the strategic interactions among fixed territorial units, comparative military strength, and spatial control, has found a new home within the particular geoeconomic vision and strategies associated with neoliberal globalization and American informal imperialism, even as this form of geoeconomics aims to make a world in which such traditional geopolitical concerns no longer have much purchase. Concerns over how to identify and eliminate the relatively mobile networks of terrorist organizations that persist across Afghanistan and neighboring Pakistan, for example, work in service of a vision of Afghanistan as a regional trade, energy, agricultural, and transportation hub at the heart of what the State Department has dubbed the "New Silk Road." This initiative promises to build through liberalized economic integration "a web of economic and transit connections that will bind together a region too long torn apart by conflict and division" (Clinton 2011; see also Shah 2011a). It is important, then, not to see geopolitics and geoeconomics as either cleanly separated from one another in a neat strategic and discursive bifurcation or the same, the differences between them resolved by state institutions that have found a temporary balance between distinct geospatial and strategic framings. They remain, rather, bound together and cogenerative in complex ways that are at turns complementary and contradictory, with varying degrees of connection to the specific interests and strategies of class-relevant social forces. These forces are themselves intertwined with but distinct from those state apparatuses charged with policing, deploying, and articulating these discourses through active policy formation and implementation within a larger structured coherence of political, state, and hegemonic projects. The agency was and remains a crucial piece of this structured coherence as site, strategy, and agent.

As already discussed, USAID has since 9/11 reincorporated strong geopolitical elements into its strategic vision, development planning, and policy implementation, alongside a robust but narrowly neoliberal geoeconomic discourse that has moved to the center of development theory and practice since the early 1980s. This geopolitics focuses on the appropriate identification, measurement, and control of interlinked threats to American national security posed by underdevelopment, failed states, and terrorism. There is little recognition of how neoliberal globalization and its associated geoeconomic discourse creates the potential for rampant crisis; exacerbated social, political, and economic inequality; and a growing disconnect between the worlds perceived in these strategic visions and those made and inhabited by people in the Global South. In other words, USAID's current articulation and enactment of these geostrategic discourses position it as site, strategy, and agent for a form of development that fails to achieve many (if not most) of its own objectives. This articulation leaves the agency's strategic decision making increasingly subject to short-term foreign policy and security considerations emanating from more powerful state institutions, especially the Departments of State and Defense. It troubles relations with other development institutions not keen on participating in the defense or expansion of American informal imperialism. And it exposes developing country populations and state institutions ever more fully to the volatility of liberalized markets dominated by finance capital.

That the ups and downs of American development and foreign policy have made USAID's path winding and difficult is no surprise, as the agency is and has been inextricably shaped by and shaping of the broader system and structures of American informal imperialism, its geostrategic articulation, and its internal tensions and contradictions. The agency has been an important author of these processes and strategies, and it has served as site and strategy for resolving, displacing, and mitigating various tensions and contradictions. In this sense, USAID's geography is the geography of American informal imperialism, even as the projects through which this has been produced and reproduced have, at times, treated the agency as a sideshow, a politically convenient target, and even a countervailing influence. As Smith (2003, 456) puts it in his examination of American imperial geographies, "the very success of a liberal American internationalism in the twentieth century produced a globalism that threatens narrowly nationalist interests even in the United States itself." This inversion of the territorial nation-state's role in global systems of capitalist relations and accumulation, in which "[i]nternationalism now predicates nationalism rather than the other way around," embodies the modus operandi of USAID development programming, as the agency works "behind the border" in developing states to ensure a structured policy and institutional environment conducive to the geostrategic logic and foreign policy aims of the American state (Smith 2003, 456). Indeed, these aims are strongly shaped by the global interdependence and interlocking state institutional structures demanded and produced by exactly the kind of work USAID does. While the previously hegemonic project of liberal developmentalism has been superseded by one of neoliberal globalization,

USAID's role remains roughly the same—to stoke development progress in line with the objectives of American foreign policy, which in turn seeks a world of smooth capitalist internationalization. How exactly the agency views and carries out this mandate is the object of geostrategic discourse, as well as the historical geography I have sketched thus far.

Yet the current moment presents a potential turning point for USAID and other development institutions worldwide, as well as for development theory and practice generally. In the absence of a generalized systemic crisis, the agency has been able to navigate difficult political waters and indefinitely displace the resolution of neoliberal globalization's contradictory tendencies (both for itself and for aid partners and recipients) temporally and spatially through constant and ongoing processes of strategic, institutional, and programmatic reform. While USAID was forced to make some painful decisions and undertake stream-lining and cuts that severely threatened its institutional memory and clout prior to 9/11, critics could never muster support to replace or even overhaul its authorizing legislation, let alone kill the agency or development aid altogether. The agency retained enough political standing and strategic capability to weather the difficulties of the post–Cold War period and burgeoning critiques of neoliberal globalization as a development paradigm. The global financial, energy, and food crises that erupted in 2007–2008 changed this situation. Development organizations, including USAID, found their resources outmatched by the depth and complexity of intertwined crises that pushed millions more people into poverty and hunger as prices for fuel and food skyrocketed, credit evaporated, and leading financial and political institutions teetered on collapse.

Far from resolving these crises, the response of governments and major financial institutions has been to exacerbate them through a turn toward public-sector austerity. Foreign aid budgets are now prone to drastic, even lethal, reductions amid souring political and public opinion, placing USAID and many other development and aid institutions in a precarious position. While some observers have suggested the current crisis is neoliberal globalization's "Berlin Wall moment," Peck, Theodore, and Brenner (2009, 98) caution against this, arguing that such analyses "are primarily concerned with long-run geoeconomic and geopolitical dynamics, rather than with the particularities of neoliberalization as a political project, an ideological construct, or an institutional matrix." What I have tried to demonstrate in *this* account is that such long-term geopolitical and geoeconomic discourses and processes are not divorceable from neoliberalization's "particularities . . . as a political project." More specifically, and as Peck, Theodore, and Brenner (2009, 106) emphasize, crises can and do remake neoliberalization in a continuous fashion, such that neoliberal globalization should be understood as a project built on and "sustained by repeated regulatory failure," achieving "'progress' through a roiling dynamic of experimentation, overreach, and crisis-driven adjustment." This has given neoliberal globalization deep roots, engrained in the structures and relations of decision making; it is not to be undone by anything so straightforward as a global financial meltdown. In her own examination of neoliberal "D/development," Hart (2009) argues as well that political dynamics cannot be read cleanly or directly from economic crisis, and attention must instead be paid, following Gramsci, to the various "relations of force" that intersect across scales and political, social, and institutional boundaries, producing and reproducing tensions and contradictions such as those I have outlined in the strategies and structures of USAID. The primary challenge the current crisis presents, Hart (2009, 136) suggests, "is grasping how these tensions and contradictions are being produced in practice—and how they hold open the possibility for something different to emerge."

In what follows, I examine how USAID has responded to the recent crises in and of neoliberal globalization, and I consider the agency's present and future as site, strategy, and agent in articulating geostrategic discourses and in the possible emergence of "something different." The current struggle over strategic direction and institutional configuration is occurring amid what Roy (2010) calls "millennial development." The millennial moment for development theory and practice results from "the confluence of various forces" that have made poverty, inequality, and human development (as opposed to narrow conceptions of economic growth) highly visible, and it draws political and social strength from official institutions of aid and trade (largely located in the Global North), as well as complex global and translocal networks of social movements, NGOs, and private foundations (Roy 2010, 7). Millennial development is fraught with fractures, gaps, and compromises, and is driven by "the politics of knowledge" that defines and legitimates particular visions of poverty, development, and alternative approaches (Roy 2010, 15). This politics is one in which established and supposedly unassailable truths, such as those institutionalized by powerful knowledge creators and brokers deeply committed to neoliberal globalization (including USAID), have been thrown into question by the growing strength of alternative perspectives and practices and by the crises spawned by neoliberal globalization.

Millennial development also offers a crucible for the evolution of American informal imperialism, which increasingly centers the logic and objectives of national and international security in mainstream development theory and practice (Mitchell 2010, 2011). Roy (2010, 19) points out that millennial development conjures a geographical "imagination about places that work or fail," often interpreting neoliberalism's destructive path as progress while simultaneously provoking "imperial anxiety" (21) about the potential security threats posed by poverty and underdevelopment. Such anxieties are rooted in the hawkish neoliberal geopolitics that has driven wars and (sometimes) reconstruction in, most prominently, Iraq and Afghanistan, as well as hundreds of other smaller-scale sites of intervention. Roy (2010, 22) thus asks whether, in the uneasy proximity between development and war, "the end of poverty [is] the conscientious counterpoint to empire?" The prospect of such an outcome is nigh impossible given the securitized execution of imperial strategy under the rubric of neoliberal globalization and the specific turn toward "smart power" that formally and fully incorporates development as a modality of American national security (Hart 2009). I do not want to argue that the militarization or securitization of foreign development assistance is new. As I have demonstrated, the link between national security and development was present from the very establishment of American foreign aid programs, and ideals of security and social and geospatial order have long been fundamental to the geostrategic discourses framing development programs, policy, and strategy at USAID.

What I examine below are those aspects of USAID's geostrategic basis and actions that *are* novel in the current millennial moment, namely, new wrinkles in the institutional configuration of and strategic relation between geopolitics and geoeconomics that has drawn USAID, the State Department, the military, and internationalizing capital into a close working relationship amid numerous forms and spaces of crisis. A shared geostrategic vision of development, its alignment with diplomacy and defense in the pursuit and maintenance of American national security, and its place in a new phase of neoliberal globalization underlies and shapes the forms and practices of this configuration. I focus on two specific examples of political, institutional, and programmatic evolution—first, the development of a new agricultural development and food security strategy called "Feed the Future," and second, intensified ties between USAID, the State Department, the military, and multinational capital amid renewed calls for steep cuts to foreign aid.

Feeding the Future

Alongside the anxiety and concerns over contemporary geopolitical threats, there also exists hopefulness in the U.S. development and foreign policy community, evident in the almost-buoyant geoeconomic language of investment, renewal, and interdependence in many of USAID's public pronouncements, strategic documents, and initiatives. This is perhaps nowhere more so than in the Feed the Future (FTF) program, a large-scale agricultural development and food security initiative launched in 2010, which highlights the present status and articulation of several interrelated trends in official development assistance. The FTF program is a government-wide response to the 2007–2008 global food crisis that sent food prices skyrocketing and pushed millions of poor and vulnerable people into conditions of food insecurity and hunger. It aims to comprehensively address a set of persistent development challenges (rural poverty and low agricultural productivity, hunger and food insecurity, environmental degradation, and the inability of small farmers and poor countries to compete in liberalized markets) made worse by global economic and financial crises and their attendant political turmoil. Feed the Future builds from both the Obama administration's commitment at the July 2009 G8 meeting to provide $3.5 billion for development and food security programming and the Rome Principles of Sustainable Food Security, the result of the 2009 World Summit on Food Security. These principles include the usual calls for changes to development assistance to enhance food security and reduce or eliminate hunger, such as "country ownership" of development plans, more and better coordination between agencies and partner groups, comprehensiveness in program design, and emphasis on results, effectiveness, and accountability (FTF 2010a).

The agency comprises a principal institutional component of this program, but, as with so many other moments in the agency's history, FTF's formulation and implementation reveal lingering strategic and institutional tensions between geopolitical and geoeconomic approaches to development; the relative instability and precariousness of USAID's position in the American state and the global development industry; and the inability of neoliberal globalization to provide a stable, equitable, or just path to development. The geostrategic response to the global food crisis outlined through FTF rests on concerns over aid effectiveness that build from two intertwined sets of criteria, one based on the policy environment in recipient countries and long incorporated into USAID's aid selectivity mechanisms, the other on bureaucratic pressures to show measurable development progress in increasingly shortened time horizons. The net result is an agricultural development and food security strategy that programs and allocates assistance based on recipient countries' willingness and capacity to deepen liberalization of the agro-food sector and adopt biotechnology, while putting in place commitments to partner with civil society and the private sector (especially U.S. agribusiness and food retail giants) and ensure

TABLE 5 Feed the Future Focus/Partner Countries (May 2010)

Region	Countries
Africa	Ethiopia, Ghana, Kenya, Liberia, Mali, Malawi, Mozambique, Rwanda, Senegal, Tanzania, Uganda, Zambia
Asia	Bangladesh, Cambodia, Nepal, Tajikistan
Latin America and the Caribbean	Guatemala, Haiti, Honduras, Nicaragua

Adapted from Feed the Future 2010a, 15.

accountability in recipient governments and other stakeholders. Twenty developing countries in Sub-Saharan Africa, South Asia, and Latin America were initially targeted for FTF program aid (see table 5).

The FTF program represents an example of how the 3DS approach to national security, discussed in chapter 4, is being consolidated, combining development with traditional foci of defense and diplomacy. This has become a new orthodoxy in Washington over the past few years, and it "assumes that military, economic, political, and development goals are always mutually reinforcing and can be defined by and for U.S. security interests" (Essex 2010, 3365). It is in this context that aid effectiveness has taken on new importance, referring both to the effective use of aid to spur changes in the policy environment of recipient countries and to operational efficiency and the reproduction of institutions and programs themselves. In terms of the first of these, and specifically in relation to USAID and FTF, aid is meant to promote the adoption and harmonization of policies leading to further trade liberalization in the agro-food sector (where global efforts have largely stalled in the WTO), legislative and scientific approval of biotechnology and genetically modified organisms, and further agro-industrialization, which requires expensive imports and has increasingly demonstrable negative environmental impacts. The focus on operational effectiveness has taken on increased importance as well, as institutions like USAID and the State Department are under increasing pressure to report cost/benefit-style analyses to Congress and show development progress, so that further funding and aid can be determined along the lines of "bang for the buck" and on an annual basis. While neither of these trends is particularly new (the first is yet another expression of USAID's long-held goal of successfully changing developing state institutions according to U.S. strategic needs, while the second has been advanced through neoliberal reforms at the agency dating back to the 1990s), both embody an understanding of development that is primarily focused on effective *intervention* rather than effective *progress toward* qualitative and material improvement in daily life in aid recipient communities and states. The success and effectiveness of development assistance are gauged against donor-driven criteria rather than by the needs, interests, and desires of recipient communities and governments. This is an old story, retold through new configurations of development knowledge, institutions, and practices.

This is not to say, of course, that material improvements in aid recipients' daily lives or mitigation of poverty and structural vulnerability will not or cannot happen, but rather that an aid response such as FTF (meant to address both long-term underdevelopment and acute crisis) does not fundamentally alter the geostrategic discourses that guided and structured previous interventions and understandings of development, which were always defined in relation to the United States as an aid donor and global hegemon. Aid's effectiveness is measured less by the qualitative societal impact produced or imminent in recipient communities than by the extent to which the development intervention itself can be considered successful against a rubric generated by political and economic pressures unique to development funders, programmers, and knowledge brokers. This includes the shortened time horizon for reporting success to those holding the purse strings as well as the geoeconomic imperative to make aid lead not just to trade but also to a specific form of global economic and political integration that attempts the "enforced reconnection" necessary for neoliberal globalization's reproduction and expansion (Roberts, Secor, and Sparke 2003, 889). The emphasis in Feed the Future on further liberalization of global agricultural markets and the adoption of biotechnology, as well as the way in which country selection operates, indicates the extent to which the program is designed to meet geoeconomic and geopolitical goals by defining the effectiveness of development assistance in ways that not only have little chance of promoting development progress in targeted countries but also reinforce the neoliberal ideal of economic integration into volatile global commodities markets.

The FTF program highlights how broader geostrategic shifts have continued to find expression via institutional strategies and changes within the American state, and especially around USAID and development assistance. Consistent with changes to USAID and the State Department's strategic planning and vision introduced through the Foreign Assistance Framework, FTF emphasizes country-level programming and reporting development progress using donor-centered effectiveness criteria, and it serves as a model for a "whole-of-government" approach to development policy and planning. This solidifies an emerging practice around official development assistance, in which aid programming, implementation, and monitoring incorporate multiple other state actors (such as the State Department, MCC, USTR, and the Department of Defense) as well as the private sector, with a strong focus on comprehensive country implementation plans and alignment of resources, objectives, and strategies across all involved agencies. The whole-of-government approach is meant to overcome the piecemeal and fractured system of development assistance that had long existed, and which was itself a product of the multiple instrumental and strategic uses aid (and USAID) were meant to serve. This approach does not necessarily untangle the confusing web of objectives and actors swirling through and around U.S. development assistance, but it does put them all at the same table at the same time, establishing a forum for building coherence across different state institutions.

A recent Congressional Research Service report on FTF (Ho and Hanrahan 2011) catalogs the range of initiatives undertaken by the Obama administration to develop a whole-of-government approach to national security and development policy, including:

- an August 2009 Presidential Study Directive on Global Development Policy (PSD-7), which resulted in the September 2010 Presidential Policy Directive on Global Development (PPD-6), making the 3Ds approach official policy to be coordinated across agencies by national security staff starting in fiscal year 2012;
- the creation of a new USAID Bureau for Food Security in November 2010 to lead the whole-of-government effort to combat food insecurity outlined in FTF; and
- also in 2010, the first Quadrennial Diplomacy and Development Review (QDDR) in the State Department and USAID, adapting a mechanism for internal assessment and alignment used in the Departments of Defense and Homeland Security (U.S. Department of State and USAID 2010).

General trends related to the PPD-6 and the QDDR are discussed below, but the CRS report comprehensively details questions that remain regarding the actual implementation and impacts of Feed the Future as an important model for the whole-of-government approach. Budget and policy implications of this realignment and coordination remain unclear. The unpredictability of congressional interest in funding such initiatives makes the long-term viability of coordinating such cross-cutting programs unsure, and there is little to no consideration of how other USAID-administered food aid programs (especially the large PL 480 "Food for Peace" programs) will or should relate to FTF. In addition, details on temporal and institutional responsibility for monitoring Feed the Future's effectiveness are not fully elaborated, sparking concerns over waste, abuse, fraud, and general inefficiencies in program delivery (Ho and Hanrahan 2011; U.S. House of Representatives 2010). Yet this is precisely USAID's charge. While the agency's position here resembles one it has often held in the past (i.e., junior partner alongside bigger, more politically influential, and better-funded state institutions), its particular strength as a repository of development expertise, especially on rural development and agriculture, and its ability to act as an institutional gateway into the global aid architecture, means the agency is uniquely positioned to play a central coordinating role among multiple stakeholder agencies, from the State Department and the MCC to recipient country governments and partner NGOs. All of these must be aligned to meet the broader objectives of raising farmer incomes, integrating the poor and hungry into national, regional, and global markets, and sparking new rounds of agricultural investment, innovation, and productivity.

The first round of country and regional plans released as part of FTF's launch used the process of country selection as a first cut at ensuring effectiveness. The FTF partner countries are not only those where impacts may be most readily and quickly measured but also those "that have committed a substantial proportion of their own resources to provide the level of support necessary to catalyze growth and significantly contribute to accelerating progress toward the MDGS [Millennium Development Goals]" (FTF 2010a, 15–16). This is actually more difficult than it sounds, as partner countries, like USAID and other American state institutions involved in development policy and FTF, must also adopt a whole-of-government approach. Often poorly organized and weakly institutionalized, with problems of legitimacy, staffing, funding, and coherence, developing country institutions charged with promoting food security, poverty alleviation, and agricultural development face serious difficulties in coordinating activities and fulfilling the mandates of FTF or other similar development programs. While this can be alleviated somewhat by the efficient coordination of multiple donors and other partner agencies, Feed the Future operates in a political environment in which "prioritization and strategic choices are still required due to resource constraints" (FTF 2010a, 16).

Such proclamations about prioritizing aid selectivity amid limited or dwindling resources have been a common feature of USAID's operation and geostrategic framework, as discussed, especially under neoliberal globalization. A look at the Honduras FTF plan, and its subsequent strategic review, illustrates the extent to which geoeconomic and geopolitical discourses and strategies aimed at global market integration, regional political stability, and the maintenance of American informal imperialism through the project of neoliberal globalization are intertwined in FTF, and also shows how this initiative attempts to put old wine in new (institutional) bottles. Before I examine program strategy and implementation in Honduras, some general features of FTF in action can be highlighted, as well as the ways in which the program misses some important recent shifts in the geographies of food security and hunger in the Global South, despite its ostensibly comprehensive thematic and institutional approach.

First, FTF strongly emphasizes rural communities and rural food insecurity, agricultural development and modernization through industrialization of production, value chain enhancement and biotech adoption, and improved food availability and access for nutritional impacts, especially for mothers and children. There is very little within FTF on new challenges posed by urban hunger (a problem the agency identified at the height of the 2007–2008 food crisis; see USAID 2008), on appeals to political rights and food sovereignty articulated by growing peasants' rights movements (despite the growing power and prevalence of these movement groups; see Desmarais 2007), or on the dangers of market volatility amid rampant speculation in food markets and their interaction with other commodities and financial markets (see Clapp and Cohen 2009; Clapp and Fuchs 2009; Jarosz 2009). The geostrategic framing of food insecurity and appropriate agricultural development thus remains largely unchanged from dominant understandings that have held sway for thirty years, despite lessons supposedly learned in the global food crisis. Governments must facilitate capitalist internationalization and global integration along neoliberal lines, and food security can be enhanced through technical solutions, regional and global market integration, and behavioral changes among women and children. Again, this is not to suggest that FTF programs will not enhance food security or promote development at all. Rather, the Feed the Future initiative is a prime example of how aid effectiveness, food security, national security, and development remain enframed by geostrategic concerns articulated and enforced through the U.S. state's hegemonic position and power, working to expand and reproduce neoliberal globalization amid multiple potentially destabilizing crises.

A brief examination of the Honduras FTF implementation plan and its internal strategic review demonstrates this. The implementation plan notes that Honduras emerged from a 2009 coup with "70 percent of Hondurans expressing a desire for a greater voice in government decisions," providing "an ideal opportunity" for FTF programs to partner with the Honduran government "to directly assist the poor and address underlying causes of political instability" (FTF 2010b, 6). The link between national, regional, and global political stability, and government responsiveness to the aspirations and demands of the poor, are vital for framing not just FTF's necessity at this particular moment (following a global food crisis and the political crisis associated with the coup in Honduras) but also the means by which effectiveness can be measured and ensured in relation to the geostrategic goals associated with the project of neoliberal globalization. The implementation plan (FTF 2010b, 6) posits that "reduced public confidence in democracy and government institutions underscores the importance of partnering with the new government on poverty alleviation through FTF," simultaneously strengthening both the postcoup government of Honduras and FTF's geopolitical and geoeconomic utility as a strategically vital tool in the projection of American power in Latin America.

As the second-poorest state in the Western hemisphere (following only Haiti), with a strong economic and social reliance on agriculture and a relatively weak government facing significant legitimacy issues, Honduras presents a context in which rapid improvements in common measures of development progress are possible. In addition, FTF implementation can achieve significant short-term changes to the institutional and political-economic relations that manage Hondurans' engagement with local and international market forces, the complex array of donors and NGOs involved in food security and development work, and political decision-making bodies from local and national governments to the international state system. The FTF plan even envisions a "leadership" role for Honduras in terms of providing useful models for donor coordination in other FTF partner states. Most importantly, however, the implementation plan suggests that "through Feed the Future, *the United States will help define the new, post-crisis relationship between the international community and Honduras*" (FTF 2010b, 5, emphasis added). This, then, is Feed the Future's primary geostrategic purpose: it reinstitutionalizes American informal imperialism by reinforcing mechanisms through which the United States provides and manages development assistance, framing and directing a "new" development project of agricultural modernization toward well-established geopolitical and geoeconomic objectives. American hegemony is buttressed and expanded through technical training and resource transfers, a whole-of-government rather than a piecemeal approach to implementation and monitoring, and a strengthening of the idea that market-driven solutions are the best possible and only legitimate response to food, political, economic, and environmental crises and long-term development challenges.

More concretely, FTF has built not only on the long historical presence of U.S. assistance in Honduras but also on the prioritization of food security and agricultural development in the Honduran government's own national development strategy, released in January 2010, and that the postcoup government of President Porfirio Lobo "conceived as a tool for national reconciliation and for putting the country back on a constructive development trajectory" (FTF 2010b, 9). The U.S. government has provided aid to Honduras through both USAID and the MCC, and it "has been instrumental in diversifying the agricultural sector into value-added, export-oriented, nontraditional crops" (FTF 2010b, 10). This aid has been targeted at poor communities in the country's mountainous western region, and FTF builds on existing aid emphases to target agricultural development and improved farmer incomes in the same regions. According to the FTF plan, food insecurity in Honduras, and especially in the poorest western regions of the country, is the result of vulnerability to climate change and natural disasters, low incomes and purchasing power, and stagnant agricultural modernization, the latter itself a problem of access to credit, infrastructure, and technology. Income generated through off-farm employment is therefore vital to rural livelihoods, but is difficult to maintain and often poorly paid. Implementing FTF programs will therefore require market-driven solutions to build farm incomes and diversify the crop base toward high-value goods, as "[m]arket-based agricultural diversification has proven to be the most effective means of improving household incomes in rural areas" (FTF 2010b, 16). While a good deal of FTF-generated improvements to agricultural productivity in Honduras are aimed at crops for local or national markets (e.g., potatoes and plantains) and are achieved using methods adapted to soil and watershed management on smallholdings in highland areas, the plan also envisions moving toward cacao production for export and specialty coffee production and widening access to a range of financial and trade services in the countryside. As Roy (2010) details in her examination of microfinance, the entanglement of credit targeted at the rural poor, previously seen as too risky and "unbankable," with speculation-fueled and crisis-prone mechanisms of international finance, does not necessarily inspire confidence in such mechanisms of development for the poorest and most vulnerable. This is especially problematic when these credit systems are not "homegrown" but driven by the needs and interests of powerful Northern donors and development agencies, such as USAID.

Feed the Future's success in Honduras and elsewhere depends above all on effective institutional partnerships, with agencies coordinated via the U.S. embassy in Tegucigalpa working in concert with the government of Honduras, the private sector, international financial institutions, and a range of NGOs and civil society groups. Effectiveness is to be measured not just through impacts on agricultural productivity, nutritional standards and food access, or physical and economic infrastructure development but also through the capacity of relevant stakeholder agencies and organizations to participate in and reproduce partnerships on an ongoing basis, including developing mechanisms and measures of effective partnership itself. Indeed, the task of measuring and monitoring progress toward program goals takes up several pages of the FTF implementation plan, and it assigns various duties to different institutional partners. The Honduras FTF program as a whole is also measured against the economic goals laid out in the more general five-year Country Assistance Strategy for Honduras outlined by the U.S. embassy, which lists its primary objective as the establishment of "a market-based approach to food security as a [U.S. government] priority for assistance programming" (FTF 2010b, 33).

The December 2010 strategic review of the Honduras FTF plan provides more detail on the kinds of measurements and objectives required, and yet it also points out the difficulty and danger of specifying clear targets for development progress and effectiveness for the program.[1] Clarity, effectiveness, accountability, and budgeting are all of a piece. Such measurements are nonetheless necessities in a political environment increasingly marked by a turn toward public-sector austerity and the demand for quick political and economic returns to development aid. For example, the concentration of FTF efforts in Honduras, and especially the country's western regions, is in part designed to help Honduras meet development goals benchmarked in the MDGs. The review of FTF strategy and implementation in Honduras emphasizes that "[f]ocused investment in the [country's] West will have the greatest impact towards achieving MDG1," which aims to rid the world of extreme hunger and poverty, and that "[f]ocusing geographically in the West will reduce transaction costs and thereby increase results per dollar invested" (USAID 2010b, 17). The MCC and other donor funds have already been heavily invested in Honduras's western regions, and FTF seeks to build on these in part to produce institutional and infrastructural "synergies."

The review also highlights the alignment of FTF with the Honduran government's own development and food security targets, which are to be achieved by 2014, and emphasize measurable quantitative improvements to agricultural GDP and grains production, the incidence of extreme rural poverty, the amount and value of coffee and horticultural exports, and access to irrigation. The FTF program's efforts in aligning these goals "are in [the] Process of Being 'Costed' and [the] Funding Gap Determined with FAO [UN Food and Agriculture Organization] Support" (USAID 2010b, 11). A broader "results framework," setting out principles, timelines, and progress indicators, has been developed for the entire Feed the Future initiative and lists a wide variety of outcomes and outputs to be measured and assessed on a quarterly or annual basis, many of them in basic numerical accountings of tangible development artifacts such as loans granted, individuals trained, and number of farms applying new technology (FTF 2011). While such techniques for framing and measuring effectiveness assume rather than demonstrate aid's more complex and often ambivalent impacts and effectiveness, they emphasize returns on ODA dollars to a skeptical Congress, where legislators are eager to hear about numbers of farmers lifted out of poverty, economic opportunities for American capital, and development's security implications.

For USAID, Feed the Future represents a potential path toward greater political, bureaucratic, and budgetary clout, and it strengthens the agency's role as a knowledge creator, assessor, and broker because of its unique focus and expertise (among U.S. state institutions involved in FTF, at least) on capacity building and information and data management. The agency's position as the lead in-country coordinating agency in the whole-of-government approach developing through FTF centers the agency and its field staff relative to much larger partner institutions working out of the American embassy: in Honduras, these include the State Department, the Department of Defense, the Department of Agriculture, the Peace Corps, and the Millennium Challenge Corporation (USAID 2010b, 3). In the complex politics of development knowledge and interagency coordination, USAID's field presence (especially in rural areas) and claims on development program practice and assessment expertise bolster the agency's ability to participate in the making and execution of strategies designed to enhance and exercise "smart power" in the pursuit of both development and national security, but they also reproduce its political and budgetary vulnerability relative to other departments and institutions. Within FTF, USAID remains site, strategy, and agent for the articulation of geopolitics and geoeconomics and associated strategies, policies, and programs, but in new ways and with new partners.

Lean Times

The altered configuration of development and security partnerships evolving under Feed the Future represents a model for USAID's response to recent crises of and in neoliberal globalization. In important respects, these crises have not produced ruptures and disarticulations as one might expect, at least among elite policymakers and strategists, but have instead helped consolidate the official geostrategic framing of development in terms derived entirely from neoliberal globalization and American informal imperialism, and strengthened the security-oriented aspects of this framing and its associated institutional components. For a government that accounts for approximately half of the world's total military expenditures, USAID, development assistance, and the entire international diplomatic and development budget represent a bargain in the expansion, reproduction, and defense of the United States' hegemonic influence. Broad programs and initiatives like Feed the Future, with their insistence on interagency coordination, ostensibly embody a new institutional coherence and fiscal discipline. Yet bureaucratic inertia, turf disputes, and the contours of crisis itself confound internal harmony, as do the intricacies of interinstitutional relations in the global aid and development architecture, and various anti-imperial, counterhegemonic, and simply resistant and noncompliant places, people, and movements. The particular "relations of force" that have emerged for USAID have moved the agency closer to integration with the State Department, deepened links to internationalizing capital and the U.S. military, and placed it (once again) in the crosshairs of deficit hawks who have enthusiastically embraced calls for public-sector austerity. This threatens the agency's institutional viability and political future in significant ways, narrowing its strategic selectivity just as the emergence of "millennial development" has made a nuanced recognition of development's sociospatial complexity more necessary than ever.

It should be remembered that USAID has faced shortages of funding, staff, and support before, most recently and importantly in the interval between the Cold War's end and the strong reassertion of national security in agency strategies following the 9/11 terrorist attacks. The agency has been a target of fiscal and ideological conservatives since it came into being, and its muddled path through the transition between state and hegemonic projects made budget stagnation and slashing easier for those writing the checks. The current call for austerity and cuts, however, comes at a time of relative geostrategic clarity for the agency, and atop growth in funding and staff prompted by development's elevation to a central plank of official national security strategies. Public-sector austerity—especially when it means fatal cuts to programs and accounts portrayed as wasteful, unnecessary, and even dangerous, including international development assistance—has become the new mantra for crisis mitigation among plutocrats, technocrats, and pundits. Planned fiscal year 2012 cuts to American development assistance, and to the larger international affairs budget (which now includes the basic operating expenses of both USAID and the State Department, but still accounts for just around one percent of total U.S. government spending) do very little to ease the federal budget deficit. Such cuts do, however, according to observers in government, the development community, and foreign policy circles, threaten these institutions' ability to carry out their core missions.

The budgets for USAID and the State Department have, since fiscal year 2008, been rolled together into a single international affairs funding request, a key component of the closer strategic planning and institutional intersection that now exists between two of the 3DS (development and diplomacy) in the national security strategy. Recognizing the looming constraints on public-sector money, Secretary of State Hillary Clinton called the fiscal year 2012 funding proposal "a lean budget for lean times" (U.S. Department of State 2011a, 1). The so-called core budget for all international programs was proposed at $47 billion, only one percent more than the 2010 budget, with efficiencies coming in part from elimination or reduction of aid programs in over two dozen countries, and from a shift of "funds into programs that save money, such as stronger monitoring and evaluation systems, efforts to consolidate information technology, procurement reform at USAID, and targeted investment in innovative development programs" (U.S. Department of State 2011a, 3). The requested funding also includes, however, an additional $8.7 billion in an Overseas Contingency Operations (OCO) account for "extraordinary, temporary costs in Iraq, Afghanistan, and Pakistan" (U.S. Department of State 2011a, 2). The "OCO" reflects terminology and practice borrowed from the Department of Defense, and is deemed necessary by the increased presence of USAID and State Department employees and contracts in these three "frontline states." The OCO funds are contingent in that the State Department (2011a, 2) "expect[s] them to be phased out over time, as these countries rebuild and take responsibility for their own security." The OCO does not include the almost $5.3 billion in direct aid and support to Afghanistan ($2.3 billion), Pakistan ($1.9 billion), and Iraq ($1.0 billion) accounted for in the core budget (U.S. Department of State 2011b).

In response, an August 2011 appropriations bill put forward by the U.S. House of Representatives allotted $12 billion less than the executive request ($39 billion for the core budget and $7.6 for the OCO), which was on top of an $8 billion reduction to the State Department, the largest single cut to any department, resulting from a bipartisan budget agreement in April of that year to avert a federal government shutdown (Myers 2011). While the Senate version of the appropriations bill was not as austere, it nonetheless proposed an international affairs budget that was still approximately six billion dollars less than requested, and less than the amounts spent on development assistance and diplomacy in fiscal years 2010 and 2011 (Mungcal 2011a, 2011b; Myers 2011). With the failure of the so-called congressional super committee (officially known as the Joint Select Committee on Deficit Reduction) charged with finding more than one trillion dollars of savings in the federal budget, automatic cuts will reduce the budget lines of USAID and the State Department even more. In addition, the budget comes with strings attached, especially in relation to specific foreign policy and security concerns in frontline states of the war on terror. Representative Kay

Granger (R-Tex.), chairwoman of the House appropriations subcommittee that handles international affairs, for example, commented that the $250 million in flood relief the United States sent to Pakistan in 2010 was "bad policy and bad politics," depleting funds that could be used to assist domestic flood victims instead (quoted in Myers 2011). Republican proposals to radically cut the Federal Emergency Management Agency's budget in 2011, however, suggest that prioritizing domestic over international disaster relief is not the driving force behind concerns over aid to places such as Pakistan. Indeed, aid to Pakistan in particular has come under intense scrutiny, and an amendment to the Senate appropriations bill makes aid to Pakistan contingent on, among other conditions, that country's government "cooperating with the United States in efforts against the Haqqani Network, the Quetta Shura Taliban, Lashkar e-Tayyiba, Al Qaeda and other domestic and foreign terrorist organizations, including taking steps to end support for such groups and prevent them from operating in Pakistan and carrying out cross border attacks into neighboring countries" (U.S. Congress 2011, s7563). Meanwhile, approximately $3 billion of assistance to Israel remains politically untouchable as a seemingly permanent part of the U.S. foreign aid landscape (Myers 2011).

The response from the NGO sector, where numerous organizations depend on funding and contracts from USAID, has oscillated between grave concern about the overt militarization of American aid accounts and programs, or their evaporation altogether, and relief that proposed cuts will likely not be as deep as first expected (see Mungcal 2011a, 2011b). There is nevertheless a strong feeling that, as Anderson (2011) states, the current budget struggle is "another make-or-break moment for U.S. foreign policy and U.S. foreign assistance," with the impending cuts threatening not only to leave USAID's recent reforms "dead in the water" but also to put the agency in a position where it is "unlikely to survive as a significant and influential foreign assistance agency" over the long term. In this context, USAID and the State Department have more aggressively made the case that they play a vital national security role, and have worked to align their core strategies as well as accounting and other internal practices with those of the Department of Defense. This collective push in the face of budgetary pressure has strengthened and accelerated the long process of institutional, fiscal, and geostrategic integration among the development, diplomatic, and military apparatuses.

To accomplish this, USAID and the State Department have pursued several different initiatives that all flow from the broader directives and strategic reviews noted previously, and which have made the 3Ds, whole-of-government approach to national security the touchstone for agency action and reform.

Among the most important of these higher-level directives have been the most recent official National Security Strategy (NSS 2010), the Presidential Policy Directive on Global Development (PPD-6), and the Quadrennial Diplomacy and Development Review (QDDR). While the NSS laid out the broad contours and objectives of American national security, the PPD-6, the full text of which was not made publicly available, made the integration of development into national security decision-making an official policy and provided a set of principles for coordinating development efforts and funding across the national security apparatus (Ho and Hanrahan 2011; Kopp and Gillespie 2011). The QDDR, which has led to a new policy framework for USAID (2011d), set to a four-year cycle, provides a detailed overview of current development structures and practices across the State Department and USAID, and it lays out an ambitious program of reform to find efficiencies in the civilian complement of the 3Ds triad.

These strategy and policy documents all emphasize development's centrality to American national security, and they embody strong continuities between political administrations regarding the objectives and conduct of American foreign policy along with geostrategic visions of how development should proceed under American tutelage and support. All highlight the need for efficiency, thrift, and intrastate coordination in U.S. development assistance efforts, as well as the absolute necessity of development intervention for American national security and leadership amid intense global economic connectivity and competitiveness. This sounds a common refrain in high-level discussions of U.S. development policy dating to the late 1970s, as discussed in chapter 3. In fact, the 2010 NSS begins its articulation of national security with strengthening the domestic foundations of economic competitiveness, as this provides the basis both for financing national security and development efforts and for bolstering America's example of "moral leadership" in a globally connected world system of multiple powerful actors, including but not limited to national states (The White House 2010, 10). How official American development institutions engage one another and the larger global aid and development architecture provides the crucial difference from past moments of strategic reflection on development. The primary overarching objective is, as before, to preserve and expand American hegemony in a globalized world but to do so through a "smart power" strategy that leans heavily on the civilian components of the U.S. foreign policy and national security apparatus. The State Department has adopted the QDDR process in part, however, to emphasize "that civilian power in the world is not limited to [the Department of] State and USAID alone," and that "the savings and performance" promised by the deft exercise of American "smart power" depend on leveraging resources offered by other institutions, both within the formal limits of the U.S. government and beyond (U.S. Department of State and USAID 2010, ii).

As the goal of "[r]eestablishing our leadership in global development" by reasserting USAID's standing as both "the U.S. government's lead development agency" and "the world's premier development agency" collides with the budget cuts discussed above, the need for intensive engagement with a wide range of potential and existing partners makes economic sense in "lean times" (U.S. Department of State and USAID 2010, 76). As the agency contends with shrinking budgets, tepid political support from Congress and the American public, and the increasingly crowded institutional landscape for development assistance, it has seemingly embraced the strategic constraints that come with making national security, with both strong geoeconomic and geopolitical components, the alpha and omega of agency action. Many of the specific institutional and technical innovations at USAID that follow from this new strategic and government-wide coherence are only now underway, detailed in the new policy framework document released in September 2011 (USAID 2011d), and their full and successful implementation remains incomplete. While it is difficult to speculate on how exactly this round of agency reform will eventually unfold, some key elements can be sketched out.

First, the agency has identified seven core thematic areas for concentrating development resources: food security, global health, global climate change, broad-based economic growth driven by the private sector, advancing democratization, enhancing resilience and preparedness for humanitarian and natural disasters, and improving capacity and planning for development intervention in conflict and crisis situations. All are approached in similar fashion, with emphases on strategic partnerships; greater selectivity and focus in the use of limited resources; gender empowerment and sustainability; the application of advanced technology and scientific knowledge; and better integration, monitoring, and assessment of development approaches and programs. As the agency states, "these principles are not new," but they "will be applied more systematically and with greater discipline and analytical rigor across USAID" (USAID 2011d, iv). These strategic objectives and approaches are accompanied within the same policy framework by a program of internal reform called "USAID Forward," itself tied to the QDDR process and a planned expansion of USAID's staffing and planning capacity, to the point of bringing back in-house many aspects of development programming that were shed in the 1990s.

As Kopp and Gillespie (2011) note, this expansion promises extensive change for USAID's workforce, as a vast majority (upward of 90 percent) of senior agency officers become eligible for retirement and cohorts of new officers with different skills move up the ranks, filling the personnel vacuum left by retirements and staffing gaps created by streamlining in the 1990s. These changes are dependent not only on funding levels but also on the working relationship with the State Department. The new policy framework therefore stresses the need to attract and retain "talent" across the agency, and "will harmonize Department of State and USAID workforce planning models and catalogue the professional skills of our staff, which will inform a system to locate expertise more efficiently" (USAID 2011d, 35). Integration of workforce planning and expertise management, not to mention a variety of new cross-appointments (including at the highest levels of agency leadership), personnel exchanges, and combined training programs have drawn USAID closer to the State Department not just in terms of a shared geostrategic vision and budgeting procedures but also in both institutions' day-to-day operations. This has produced concern in some quarters, where critics contend that the agency and its development mission will be subordinated to the "short term outlook" prevailing at the State Department; others support such a move, hoping that the synergistic combination of perspectives, resources, and forms of expertise will strengthen both, especially as they are called on to develop and execute national security strategy alongside the military (quoted in Kopp and Gillespie 2011, 49). All current internal and strategic reform programs at USAID thus aim to make the agency, and the development process more generally, a primary component of American "smart power."

I have already discussed how a program such as Feed the Future attempts this integration of resources, expertise, and perspective, yet the roles played by two other important institutional components must also be addressed, namely, the U.S. military and internationalizing fractions of capital. The relationships USAID is forging with military and capitalist institutions (not just transnational firms but also philanthropic organizations tied to particular firms) strongly demonstrate the "relations of force" at work in the current moment of geostrategic alignment. These are, as with the other reforms discussed above, ongoing processes that are only now being instituted in concrete ways, and it is therefore difficult to predict their exact trajectory. The politics of development knowledge, and specifically USAID's role as a locus of relevant and legitimate development data, knowledge, and expertise, loom large in the relations the agency cultivates with the military and capital. The agency has, for example, revitalized its Office of Civilian-Military Cooperation, which facilitates USAID's interactions and planning with the military, and provided high-level staff as advisers to U.S. regional military commands around the world. Such cross-fertilization of development planning with military engagement in the field has prompted not only a new set of principles for development as an antidote to conflict and "violent extremism" (the first of its kind for USAID; see USAID 2011a) but also has led the agency to greatly increase its role and presence in conflict areas, especially the three "frontline states" noted above—Iraq, Afghanistan, and Pakistan. While some military commanders have argued that USAID has "focused too often on big development programs at the expense of quick-hit projects that would put large numbers of people to work," the agency has also expanded its field staff in remote areas of conflict zones, especially in Afghanistan (Jaffe 2011). It has also worked to support rapid funding of projects in "areas that have been stabilized by U.S. military forces," though this may not sit well with other selectivity and effectiveness criteria, and makes clear that two different visions of development are at work (Jaffe 2011).

In doing so, USAID has presented itself as the front line of premilitary humanitarian engagement with dangerous and underdeveloped societies torn by conflict, even though the showpieces of this engagement have come *alongside* rather than *prior to* military presence in places like Afghanistan and Iraq. Most recently, the agency has taken on a considerable role in the Horn of Africa, where its "FWD" (Famine, War, Drought) campaign has sought to provide both immediate relief and long-term development assistance in the context of famine, war, and drought, and has centered the agency's role as a coordinating institution and knowledge broker. Partnering with over three dozen large international NGOs and intergovernmental agencies, USAID has provided cash and commodity assistance to those suffering from acute hunger and famine in Somalia, Ethiopia, Kenya, and Djibouti, and it has begun implementation of Feed the Future agricultural development programs in Ethiopia and Kenya. The FWD website also encourages its audience to "do more than donate" and to "take action" instead; the site allows users to share USAID-provided information in a variety of ways, including social media and cross-linking, letters to the editor, and even materials for distribution at community events and public presentations (USAID 2011b). The agency also partnered with the Ad Council and the philanthropic social enterprise GOOD to host a competition for proposals on how to raise awareness of the Horn of Africa crisis in local communities in the United States, with the winning proposal chosen by online voters and granted $5,000 (Good Worldwide 2011).

The agency's interventions in the Horn of Africa are driven not just by humanitarian concerns but also by the "imperial anxiety" Roy (2010) identifies as a key part of millennial development, engendered by fears of state failure and the national security consequences of persistent underdevelopment, acute crisis conditions, and Islamist terrorism. Agency Administrator Shah's speech at

West Point, quoted at this chapter's outset, began with a story that highlighted the risks of nonintervention in places like Somalia. Recounting one American's generous presentation of emergency food aid to a refugee camp in southern Somalia, Shah ended with a twist: "[W]ritten on each sack of grain was a message: 'Charity relief for those affected by the drought. Al Qaeda campaign on behalf of the Martyr Bin Laden'" (Shah 2011a; see also Jaffe 2011). Since direct U.S.-led military intervention in Somalia remains strategically unviable and politically unpalatable at the moment, the aid and development work of USAID and its partner organizations becomes all the more necessary for enacting a vision of national security that depends on effective geospatial knowledge and administration of acute ecological, economic, and political crises in places like the Horn of Africa. Tales that emphasize Al Qaeda's provision of aid in the absence of American intervention bolster the agency's position as a vital and cost-effective component of "smart power," providing both boots on the ground and a platform for constructing, legitimating, and propagating accurate, real-time development knowledge.

The geopolitical is tied intimately with the geoeconomic here as well, as emphases on public-private partnerships and the embrace of "enlightened capitalism" have appeared in the agency's approach to development, as evinced by initiatives like FTF (where USAID and the Department of Agriculture are to bring the power of American agribusiness and biotechnology to agricultural development and spark a new Green Revolution); reform and streamlining of contracting, partnering, and reporting processes in the USAID Forward management overhaul; the agency's celebration of Public-Private Partnership Week in October 2011; and development programs more directly dependent on international capital for both funding and implementation. For example, USAID has partnered with PepsiCo and the World Food Programme (WFP) on the "Enterprise EthioPEA" initiative, in which PepsiCo will invest in expanded chickpea production in Ethiopia. In announcing the program's launch, the company stated that "chickpea-based products are an important part of [our] strategy to build a $30 billion global nutrition business by 2020" (PepsiCo 2011). Expanded production in Ethiopia is planned to increase farmer incomes without degrading soil or water supplies (like other legumes, chickpeas fix nitrogen in the soil and can improve soil quality with proper crop rotation) while also providing enough surplus for PepsiCo to produce a ready-to-eat paste for the WFP's use in emergency situations (PepsiCo 2011; see also Strom 2011; WFP 2011).

In a similar vein, USAID has also provided support to the public-private Haiti Hope Project, a $7.5 million development initiative launched by the Coca-Cola Company in 2010 that aims to "enabl[e] mango farmers to organize into small groups to increase production and improve supply linkages," and provides "[s]kill assessment and technical training . . . facilitated by experts on the ground in Haiti" (USAID 2010a). As a model of sustainable development, public-private partnership, and corporate responsibility and social investment, Haiti Hope also includes expertise and funding provided by the Gates Foundation, the Clinton Bush Haiti Fund, the Inter-American Development Bank, and the business-oriented NGO TechnoServe, and it allowed Coca-Cola's Odwalla brand to roll out the "Haiti Hope Mango Tango" smoothie line, with 10 cents of every bottle sold (up to $500,000 annually) donated to the mango project in Haiti (The Coca-Cola Company 2011). While Coca-Cola's operations in developing countries have long been targets of labor and environmental activism because of impacts on local water quality and access (BBC 2003; Shiva 2006) and antiunion efforts, including allegations of violence and murder in Colombia, Guatemala, and elsewhere (killercoke.org 2012), public-private partnerships like Haiti Hope, with the backing and support of USAID and other official and transnational development institutions, give the company a chance to promote itself as a responsible development partner and to seek new outlets for investment and accumulation through the aid and development intervention process.

For its part, USAID has enthusiastically taken on such projects and aggressively sought to include transnational capital in development efforts. As USAID Administrator Shah (2011b) stated in a speech to the USAID Public-Private Partnership Forum, which brought together agency officials and representatives of several large multinational firms: "Profit. Wealth. Development. Those words may sound like an odd combination. But at a time when businesses believe in the urgency of development, those words will define the future of our field." This conjures Reagan-era criticisms of USAID's neglect of the private sector and the agency's attempts then to more effectively and fundamentally engage with capital in development and aid work. In development's millennial moment, the belief in the essential link between responsible, effective, and socially just development and the interests of internationalizing capital goes even deeper, and Shah (2011b) called on his audience of development experts and business representatives to "embrace a new wave of creative, enlightened capitalism."

Such statements and associated efforts to engage capital across all stages of the development intervention process highlight the agency's coordinating role in the nexus of private and philanthropic organizations engaged in development financing, programming, and implementation as well as the balance of class-relevant social forces that define the geostrategic vision of development in the current configuration of discourses, institutions, and relations of force that make up neoliberal globalization and American informal imperialism.

While initiatives like Feed the Future, Enterprise EthioPEA, and Haiti Hope demonstrate the powerful and persuasive ideal of responsible capital engaging in development intervention in a series of win-win episodes that both expand opportunities for profit and alleviate poverty, they also produce and reproduce significant tensions and contradictions. Such forms of development intervention proceed, as Carr (2011) explains, on assumptions that development and globalization overlap directly, establishing much-needed connectivity to global markets and global systems of knowledge. By doing so, they ostensibly create unmitigated positive effects for their subjects and participants; cases where such measurable progress does not occur are set aside as outliers, irreconcilable with the discursive frameworks that have helped produce them and that express their appraisal in donor-defined terms and through donor-directed processes. Development under neoliberal globalization also creates strong potential not only for unintended and perhaps negative outcomes in the lives, relations, and fortunes of its subjects and agents but also for rampant legitimation crises if and when promises of social, economic, and political development go unfulfilled. A variety of development outcomes and responses to crisis are possible, but all are framed, at least in the official perspectives of the U.S. state, in terms of national security and regional and global order. Geoeconomic failure calls forth a geopolitical response, and vice versa; this is the internal discursive and strategic complementarity currently at work at USAID and across the U.S. state's entire development and national security structure.

Something Different?

As an institutional linchpin in American development and national security strategies, and a prime repository, producer, and disseminator of official development knowledge and its appropriate use, USAID today finds itself at a crucial juncture amid a confluence of social, strategic, and political economic forces. On the one hand, the agency now wields political and strategic clout in ways that seemed impossible just a decade ago, taking on a role as an agenda-setting, coordinating, and knowledge institution and helping to reassert structures and strategies of American informal imperialism in the global aid architecture, and in the broader system of capitalist governance, which includes states, corporations, international regulatory institutions, and numerous other kinds of actors. On the other hand, this confluence threatens to cut the agency's legs from under it as budgets are slashed in the response to systemic crises, development becomes a blunt instrument of "smart power" in the service of American military adventures abroad, and the agency's strategic selectivity is further eroded by closer relations with the Departments of State and Defense and transnational capital.

So does USAID retain any capacity for critical institutional self-reflection in a way that may open doors to something beyond or alternative to the liberalized market relations and securitized connectivity of neoliberal globalization? Does this all reduce the agency's role, now and into the foreseeable future, to coordinating and greasing the relations between other actors, and (if funds and personnel materialize in sufficient amounts) programming, implementing, and monitoring development interventions designed primarily to advance American informal imperialism and expanded capitalist accumulation? Can USAID adequately respond to (or find room for articulation with) the demands of people and movements in developing countries, and even at home, who have radically different views of development, justice, rights, and interdependence? The agency's strategic selectivity, narrow from its inception, has been steadily ceded to more powerful actors whose political and economic interests and geostrategic frames are decidedly narrow, locked into the maintenance of informal imperialism and capitalist accumulation. As an institution desperate to maintain its existence and permanently shed the critiques leveled against it since its establishment (as wasteful, too geopolitical, not geopolitical enough, too diffuse, inflexible, slow to respond, and so on), USAID has often eagerly taken up its part in this system. Its response to the crises of and in neoliberal globalization has been to double down on this project's critical assumptions. More broadly, neoliberal globalization has become more rather than less predatory through its recent crises, despite claims about the emergence of an "enlightened capitalism." Inequality and poverty are more prevalent and apparent than ever, and progress toward even the basic goals laid out in the MDGs is either far behind schedule or headed in reverse.

The stakes are thus also high for USAID's partners in the global aid architecture, from developing country governments and the many development-focused organizations in the UN system to new official donors like China and India and the vast global network of NGOs at work in the development sector. The current moment of geostrategic clarity within neoliberal globalization, sharpened by crisis, might mean increased flows of money, greater public awareness of development conditions and needs, more and better coordination between different aid donors and their various projects, and expanded opportunity to work with vulnerable and impoverished populations. It could also reduce such agents' abilities to manage their terms of engagement with transnational capital and the American national security apparatus or to include the voices of the diverse array of popular social movements across the Global South that may be opposed to particular state actions and policies, military ties with the United States, or the entreaties of capitalist investors. As recent reviews of critical development geography demonstrate, however, the diversity of popular social movements proposing and enacting alternative visions of globalization and development, and indeed the alternative and often radical new discourses and practices of geoeconomic and geopolitical articulation they express, is growing in complexity, visibility, and strength, as is the political space in which they operate (Glassman 2011; Silvey 2010; Silvey and Rankin 2011). In this context, the question raised at the end of chapter 4—*how could things be different?*—becomes even more pressing as a multitude of answers become more viable and difficult for official institutions like USAID to ignore or dismiss. If, as Hart (2009, 136) states, the contradictory tensions and tendencies produced and reproduced by the present set of crises "hold open the possibility for something different to emerge" in development theory and practice, we must ask what exactly this could be, and what might be USAID's role in it, if any.

Given the institutionalized power of and internal consensus on the geostrategic framing currently entrenched at and through the agency, it is hard to imagine how something different could sprout from the soil at USAID. If different and more just development approaches are to emerge, they will most likely not come from USAID but from class-relevant social struggles and movements working in other sites, via other strategies, and through other forms of geospatial connectivity than those championed by proponents of neoliberal globalization and informal imperialism. There are opportunities for a profound reconfiguration of the international development industry and global aid architecture through the action and coordination of well-organized social movement groups. Indeed, such groups and movements often work in and for precisely those spaces and populations marginalized (and often dominated) within and by the global aid architecture. The trajectory they follow does not depend on their integration or articulation into this system, though they must always work to define themselves in relation to it. The millennial moment for development practice and theory, however, means official actors and agents like USAID can no longer ignore or neglect such movements, their demands, or their perspectives, and that discursive articulation and strategy formation must become very much a two-way street. As a site, strategy, and agent of state internationalization, USAID remains in some ways open to such forces, interconnected as it is with civil society organizations and official development agencies of various stripes, including those that have begun to incorporate the views and voices of more radical social movement groups. While the constellation of geostrategic discourses and practices that now shape USAID's interaction with these organizations strongly constrains its choice of partners and approaches, there is no reason to think the current framing of and response to alternative visions of globalization and development, heavy on securitization and capitalist internationalization, can or will be indefinitely sustained.

I once interviewed someone at a large international NGO who asked me, at the end of our discussion and after the recorder was turned off, whether I planned to present the organization and its staff as "imperialists." Somewhat surprised by the question, I answered no. I knew quite well that the NGO did not enter into its work in the pursuit of American imperial power, but was instead part of a much larger interlocking system of institutions and practices that bent toward the reproduction of informal imperialism and capitalist internationalization. While this reassured my interviewee (somewhat), it occurred to me that no one with whom I had spoken at USAID had ever asked me this kind of question. The set of interviews cited in chapters 2 and 3 and my own formal and informal conversations with agency staff over the last several years indicate that those who work at USAID generally have not seen themselves as advancing a form of capitalist imperialism managed through and by the U.S. state, even if that is in the end what their work has accomplished. The current push to expand hiring at the agency, and to fold in new "talent" with new skills, knowledge, and experience, does present the possibility for something different to emerge within USAID itself, or at the very least for internal and perhaps fundamental challenges to the agency's geostrategic worldview and its institutional structures and relations. As development knowledge and geostrategic discourses do not exist in the abstract, but are dynamically embodied, institutionalized, produced, and reproduced as they are enacted, they remain always open to contestation, change, and new articulations. Whether and how this occurs, however, is a question that remains to be answered by those working in, with, alongside, and against the agency.

NOTES

CHAPTER 1 *"One-Half of 1%"*

1. According to the U.S. government's "Foreign Assistance Dashboard" website (http://www.foreignassistance.gov/AboutTheData.aspx), thirty-two billion dollars was budgeted for foreign aid of all types in fiscal year 2011, representing about one percent of annual government spending. This includes money for all foreign aid accounts directed through USAID and the State Department, as well as the Millennium Challenge Corporation (MCC). See chapter 5 for more on the relationship between USAID and the State Department.

2. In several dozen ADST interviews, recent agency retirees discuss the inner workings of USAID and its predecessors from World War II up to the 1990s. The transcripts can be found at Georgetown University's library in Washington, D.C., but are also downloadable as PDF files from USAID's Development Experience Clearinghouse (DEC) online archive. Citations of interviews used herein are listed by the last name of the interviewee, and are dated according to the transcript copyright date listed on the PDF versions of the transcripts.

CHAPTER 2 *"In the World for Keeps"*

1. This work is an attempt by USAID itself, through its internal research and development information unit (since reorganized and renamed), to outline its origins and purposes at a point in its history (1991) when the agency was under immense pressure to reform or be reorganized out of existence as the Cold War came to a close. It includes both the author's interpretation of the debate over USAID's establishment and a set of key contemporaneous documents related to U.S. foreign assistance programs. Its inclusion of snippets from various official sources in one document makes it useful, but difficult to cite. Though different pieces within the larger document come from many sources (e.g., the *Congressional Record*, government periodicals, presidential speeches), they are not always included in their entirety. I thus cite them here only by reference to the main document (Duffy 1991), but with descriptions of individual components in the text. I also rely on a more recent historical overview prepared by the agency (USAID 2002b). While parts of this source are replicated on the agency's "Our History" website (http://www.usaid.gov/about_usaid/usaidhist.html), I cite the more comprehensive and stable 2002 version here, available online as a downloadable PDF file, to avoid confusion.

2. The work cited here, an overview of the 1961 reorganization of U.S. foreign aid programs, was prepared by Edward Weidner, a frequent consultant on technical assistance programs for the government, and founder of the University of Wisconsin–Green

Bay. Weidner's examination of the political battles over aid reform and the FAA provides incredible detail on the various commissioned reports that underwrote reform efforts in the years leading up to the FAA as well as on debates within and surrounding the task force that helped prepare the final 1961 legislation. The version cited here is available online as a downloadable PDF file, but it remains marked as a "rough first draft" by the author, not for quotation. I therefore direct the reader to particular sections, but am reluctant to quote Weidner directly.

3. The initial five-year funding authorized under the act totaled approximately $9 billion (Duffy 1991, 10). The Chamber of Commerce did not absolutely oppose aid, but it felt funding should be substantially reduced.

4. Bruce Clubb and Verne Vance both worked in the Office of General Counsel for USAID shortly after the agency's establishment.

5. The Senate Committee was not entirely consistent on this point, reflecting some disagreement over the geopolitical rationale expressed here. For example, the committee stated that long-term funding to specific states (so-called supporting assistance, money designed not for discrete, time-limited development projects but rather to fill budget gaps for states carrying heavy military burdens or that seemed on the verge of total collapse) was no longer viable. Instead, individual states' aid deservedness must be weighed against both costs and development progress, since it "does not follow as the night the day that the vacuum created by the departure of some despotisms will be filled by communism," and "defending an essentially indefensible status quo would amount to injustice, political error, and waste of the taxpayer's money" (U.S. Senate 1961, 22).

6. Despite this, the agency maintained 64 percent of its staff in Washington in 1977; by comparison only 35 percent of USAID staff worked in the capital when the agency was established in 1961 (USAID 2007, 7).

CHAPTER 3 *Geoeconomics Ascendant*

1. Specifically, Nixon called for the creation of OPIC, the Overseas Private Investment Corporation (see chapter 2), which would help manage and channel foreign direct investment in developing countries and also expand an already existing system of government-funded guaranties and insurance for private investors as part of the U.S. development aid portfolio.

2. The IDCA, as USAID (2002b) and Auer (1998) point out, never really played the coordinating role envisioned by its creators. Understaffed with an unclear mandate and limited authority from its inception, it became an institutional backwater during the Reagan administrations and was finally dissolved in 1997.

3. Zaire, for example, had been a preferred recipient of aid within Sub-Saharan Africa during the Reagan years but fell out of favor once the USSR collapsed. An agency official who had worked for many years across Africa commented that "Mobutu played this Cold War card very well," paying lip service to market reforms but knowing well that the United States "really didn't push very hard, if they were on our side in the Cold

War" (Birnbaum 1996, 57). After the Cold War's end, Zaire was cut off from development funding targeted at Africa "because of a complete lack of performance" (Birnbaum 1996, 52).

4. The ten countries were Israel and Egypt (the two largest aid recipients, receiving 47 percent of all U.S. bilateral aid between 1977 and 1989), Turkey, Pakistan, Greece, El Salvador, the Philippines, Spain (which had received aid in exchange for military base agreements), India, and South Korea. Only in India was U.S. assistance predicated primarily on development rather than security considerations (U.S. House of Representatives 1989, 12).

5. The task force even highlighted a new "aid gap" facing the United States, reminiscent of that identified in the late 1950s and leading eventually to USAID's creation (see chapter 2). Pointing out that "U.S. foreign assistance is a declining world resource," it reported that Japan's bilateral assistance program would soon surpass that of the United States in size, and that total U.S. foreign aid represented less than 0.3 percent of American GNP, the lowest of any OECD member country and far below past levels (U.S. House of Representatives 1989, 25).

6. Not everything fell easily into the geostrategic discourses outlined here. Years of intense debate over the proper approach to population growth and family planning reached a crescendo with Reagan's election and the opportunity this provided for conservative religious groups to influence development policy. Such bitter struggles indicate the extent to which class-relevant social forces, such as staunch social conservatives who formed an important element of Ronald Reagan's electoral base, not to mention the Vatican and conservative Catholic groups in the United States and the developing world, also found American development policy a useful site and strategy for their own agendas. In any event, conditions that tied aid to changes in family planning and population policies in developing countries (i.e., aid money could not be used to fund abortions and would have to promote "natural" forms of contraception) followed the longstanding mantra that measured the success of U.S. development policy against fundamental changes to the internal workings, policies, and structures of recipient states (see USAID 1985, 50, and Sinding 2001 for more discussion).

CHAPTER 4 *Two Decades of Neoliberalization*

1. The General Accounting Office (GAO) changed its name but not its acronym in 2004, becoming the Government Accountability Office. In-text citations use the acronym only, though the appropriate full institutional name is used in the works cited list.

2. "U.S. direct hires" refers to American citizens hired directly into the Foreign Service. The agency categorizes its staff into several other categories, though it is difficult even for USAID to provide a thorough and accurate historical account of personnel numbers, as categorizations and hiring practices have shifted considerably over time.

3. The State Department, under the DRI and the direction of Secretary of State Colin Powell, began to follow standard U.S. military practice of overstaffing by approximately

15 percent, allowing for transitions, retirements, and other personnel moves without negatively impacting on administrative and functional capacity (Kopp and Gillespie 2011). While commitments in Afghanistan and Iraq pushed these expansions to their limit, the fact that the State Department received funding and support for such increases in staffing and training with relative ease and speed suggests the higher esteem and political necessity with which lawmakers and the White House viewed the diplomatic corps as compared to their counterparts in USAID. The link between management practices at State/USAID and the military are discussed in chapter 5.

4. Specifically, USAID mentioned three bilateral and regional FTAs the United States was pursuing or on which it had completed negotiations at the time. The Andean Pact includes Bolivia, Colombia, Ecuador, and Peru. The CAFTA-DR, the Central American Free Trade Agreement, includes Costa Rica, the Dominican Republic, El Salvador, Guatemala, Honduras, and Nicaragua. The SACU, the Southern African Customs Union, includes Botswana, Lesotho, Namibia, South Africa, and Swaziland.

5. Excavating the work of Hegel and Marx on civil society, Goonewardena and Rankin (2004, 138) point out that the distinctions between civil society, state, and market are not as fully complete as those advocating neoliberalism-as-development argue, emphasizing instead "the classical modern conception of civil society, [in which] the economy is endemic to it, not external."

6. The version of the Foreign Assistance Framework used here is dated October 12, 2006 (USAID Document PC-AAB-849), but it was updated in January and July 2007 as well (USAID Documents PC-AAB-575 and PC-AAB-699, respectively). These updates were minor, and did not alter any of the wording or strategic definitions and categorizations outlined in the original October 2006 version. The agency shuffled a handful of specific funding accounts between aid objectives in the January 2007 version, and it highlighted the desired concentration of aid resources according to specific objectives for different country categories (including areas of coordination with MCC) in the July 2007 version. These updates appear to be for clarification within the agency and its partner agencies in the U.S. government as the framework became a central resource for development aid planning following its release and subsequent inclusion in the 2007–2012 joint strategic plan of USAID and the State Department (U.S. Department of State and USAID 2007, 58).

7. Stephen Radelet (2003, 110), formerly deputy assistant secretary of the U.S. Treasury for Africa, the Middle East, and Asia, offers four reasons to make aid reform a priority for the Bush administration. Besides the two mentioned here are the more general recognition that poverty and inequality are threats to U.S. interests, and that the increasing extent and depth of poverty and inequality run counter to Americans' moral sensibilities.

8. The FY 2003 budget justification is dated February 26, 2002, while the White House released the National Security Strategy in September 2002.

9. Examples of failed, failing, and recovering states, as well as crisis states and vulnerable states, are provided in the strategy document, though the agency never provided a publicly available, comprehensive guide to explain how it classified developing

states under this framework. For example, El Salvador, Afghanistan, Sudan, and Sierra Leone were all identified in 2005 as states in crisis, while Indonesia, Macedonia, and Serbia-Montenegro (which has since split peaceably into the separate states of Serbia and Montenegro) were all considered vulnerable (USAID 2005a, 13–15). The diplomatically sensitive language of state failure was abandoned in favor of MCC-based categories in the Foreign Assistance Framework, which is more comprehensive in its attempts to categorize developing states.

10. One interviewee explained that, as with the categories used in the white paper and the *Fragile States Strategy*, specific information on which countries fit into which framework category was diplomatically sensitive and therefore not public (Anonymous, 2006a).

CHAPTER 5 *Development in Reverse*

1. The strategic review cited here is a preliminary assessment of Feed the Future implementation in Honduras. The review is dated December 17, 2010, only seven months after the public release of the larger FTF program guide. The document cited here as USAID (2010b), then, is less a review of a project or program already implemented than an assessment of the political, economic, and social terrain confronting FTF and its implementing agencies in Honduras. Importantly, USAID leads the charge on such reviews, settling into its role as knowledge broker, ground-truther, and assessment mechanism in the whole-of-government approach underlying Feed the Future.

WORKS CITED

A note on sources: USAID makes the vast majority of its reports, strategy and policy frameworks, congressional budgets and testimonies, and other documents available to the public for free through its online archive, the Development Experience Clearinghouse (DEC, accessible at http://dec.usaid.gov/index.cfm). Almost all official agency documents, as well as many other documents and reports that pertain to USAID programs or accounts, receive a unique eight- or nine-digit document identification or order code consisting of letters and numbers (i.e., xx-xxx-###). In the references to those documents below, I have included both the title of the document and the identification number/order code. Readers wishing to locate and download these documents would do well to use the DEC website's "advanced search" function and search by DOCID/order number rather than by title.

ARTICLES, BOOKS, AND OTHER NONOFFICIAL SOURCES

Agnew, John. 1994. "The Territorial Trap: The Geographical Assumptions of International Relations Theory." *Review of International Political Economy* 1:53–80.

———. 2005a. *Hegemony: The New Shape of Global Power*. Philadelphia: Temple University Press.

———. 2005b. "Sovereignty Regimes: Territoriality and State Authority in Contemporary World Politics." *Annals of the Association of American Geographers* 97:437–461.

Agnew, John, and Stuart Corbridge. 1995. *Mastering Space: Hegemony, Territory and International Political Economy*. London: Routledge.

Anderson, G. William. 2011. "A Make-or-Break Moment for U.S. Foreign Policy." Accessed March 15, 2012. http://www.devex.com/en/articles/a-make-or-break-moment-for-us-foreign-policy.

Arrighi, Giovanni. 1994. *The Long Twentieth Century: Money, Power, and the Origins of Our Times*. London: Verso.

Auer, Matthew R. 1998. "Agency Reform as Decision Process: The Reengineering of the Agency for International Development." *Policy Sciences* 31:81–105.

Barnett, Thomas P. M. 2004. *The Pentagon's New Map: War and Peace in the Twenty-First Century*. New York: Penguin.

———. 2006. *The Pentagon's New Map: Blueprint for Action*. New York: Penguin.

———. 2009. *Great Powers: America and the World after Bush*. New York: Penguin.

British Broadcasting Corporation (BBC). 2003. "Coca-Cola's 'Toxic' India Fertiliser." Accessed March 14, 2012. http://news.bbc.co.uk/2/hi/south_asia/3096893.stm.

Burnside, Craig, and David Dollar. 2000. "Aid, Policies, and Growth." *American Economic Review* 90:847–868.

Carr, Edward R. 2011. *Delivering Development: Globalization's Shoreline and the Road to a Sustainable Future*. New York: Palgrave Macmillan.

Castree, Noel. 2006. "From Neoliberalism to Neoliberalisation: Consolations, Confusions, and Necessary Illusions." *Environment and Planning A* 38:1–6.

Chatterjee, Deen K., ed. 2004. *The Ethics of Assistance: Morality and the Distant Needy*. Cambridge: Cambridge University Press.

Clapp, Jennifer, and Marc J. Cohen, eds. 2009. *The Global Food Crisis: Governance Challenges and Opportunities*. Waterloo, Ont.: Wilfrid Laurier University Press.

Clapp, Jennifer, and Doris Fuchs, eds. 2009. *Corporate Power in Global Agrifood Governance*. Cambridge, Mass.: MIT Press.

Clubb, Bruce E., and Verne W. Vance Jr. 1963. "Incentives to Private U.S. Investment Abroad under the Foreign Assistance Program." *Yale Law Journal* 72:475–504.

The Coca-Cola Company. 2011. "Odwalla's Mango Tango Smoothie Now Supporting Haiti Reconstruction." Accessed March 14, 2012. http://www.thecoca-colacompany.com/dynamic/press_center/2011/01/odwalla-smoothie-supports-haiti-reconstruction.html.

Cogneau, Denis, and Jean-David Naudet. 2007. "Who Deserves Aid? Equality of Opportunity, International Aid, and Poverty Reduction." *World Development* 35:104–120.

Collier, Paul, and David Dollar. 2001. "Can the World Cut Poverty in Half? How Policy Reform and Effective Aid Can Meet International Development Goals." *World Development* 29:1787–1802.

———. 2002. "Aid Allocation and Poverty Reduction." *European Economic Review* 46:1475–1500.

———. 2004. "Development Effectiveness: What Have We Learnt?" *Economic Journal* 114:F244–F271.

Cowen, Deborah, and Neil Smith. 2009. "After Geopolitics? From the Geopolitical Social to the Geoeconomic." *Antipode* 41:22–48.

Cox, Robert W., with Timothy J. Sinclair. 1996. *Approaches to World Order*. Cambridge: Cambridge University Press.

Dalby, Simon. 2008. "Imperialism, Domination, Culture: The Continued Relevance of Critical Geopolitics." *Geopolitics* 13:413–436.

Desmarais, Annette Aurelie. 2007. *La Vía Campesina: Globalization and the Power of Peasants*. Halifax: Fernwood.

Essex, Jamey. 2007. "Getting What You Pay For: Authoritarian Statism and the Geographies of U.S. Trade Liberalization Strategies." *Studies in Political Economy* 80:75–103.

———. 2010. "Sustainability, Food Security, and Development Aid after the Food Crisis: Assessing Aid Strategies across Donor Contexts." *Sustainability* 2:3354–3382. doi:10.3390/su2113354.

Farish, Matthew. 2010. *The Contours of America's Cold War*. Minneapolis: University of Minnesota Press.

Forgacs, David, ed. 2000. *The Antonio Gramsci Reader: Selected Writings, 1916–1935.* New York: NYU Press.

Friedmann, Harriet. 1993. "The Political Economy of Food: a Global Crisis." *New Left Review* I/197 (January–February):29–57.

———. 2005. "Feeding the Empire: Pathologies of Globalized Agriculture." In *Socialist Register 2005: The Empire Reloaded,* edited by Leo Panitch and Colin Leys, 124–143. Monmouth, U.K.: Merlin Press.

Garst, Rachel, and Tom Barry. 1990. *Feeding the Crisis: U.S. Food Aid and Farm Policy in Central America.* Lincoln: University of Nebraska Press.

Glassman, Jim. 1999. "State Power beyond the 'Territorial Trap': The Internationalization of the State." *Political Geography* 16:669–696.

———. 2005a. "The New Imperialism? On Continuity and Change in U.S. Foreign Policy." *Environment and Planning A* 37:1527–1544.

———. 2005b. "The 'War on Terrorism' comes to Southeast Asia." *Journal of Contemporary Asia* 35:3–28.

———. 2011. "Critical Geography III: Critical Development Geography." *Progress in Human Geography* 35:705–711.

Glassman, Jim, and Abdi Ismail Samatar. 1997. "Development Geography and the Third-World State." *Progress in Human Geography* 21:164–198.

Good Worldwide. 2011. "Do More Than Donate. FWD the Facts." Accessed March 15, 2012. http://fwd.maker.good.is/.

Goonewardena, Kanishka, and Katharine N. Rankin. 2004. "The Desire Called Civil Society: A Contribution to the Critique of a Bourgeois Category." *Planning Theory* 3:117–149.

Gregory, Derek. 2004. *The Colonial Present.* Malden, Mass.: Blackwell.

Hart, Gillian. 2001. "Development Critiques in the 1990s: Culs de Sac and Promising Paths." *Progress in Human Geography* 25:649–658.

———. 2002. "Geography and Development: Development/s beyond Neoliberalism? Power, Culture, Political Economy." *Progress in Human Geography* 26:812–822.

———. 2004. "Geography and Development: Critical Ethnographies." *Progress in Human Geography* 28:91–100.

———. 2009. "D/developments after the Meltdown." *Antipode* 41 S1:117–141.

Harvey, David. 2003. *The New Imperialism.* Oxford: Oxford University Press.

———. 2005. *A Brief History of Neoliberalism.* Oxford: Oxford University Press.

Ingram, Alan, and Klaus Dodds, eds. 2009. *Spaces of Security and Insecurity: Geographies of the War on Terror.* Farnham, U.K.: Ashgate.

Jackson, Peter, Neil Ward, and Polly Russell. 2008. "Moral Economies of "Food and Geographies of Responsibility." *Transactions of the Institute of British Geographers* 34:12–24.

Jaffe, Greg. 2011. "USAID Touts Role in Blunting Islamic Extremism." *Washington Post,* November 7. Accessed March 15, 2012. http://www.washingtonpost.com/blogs/

checkpoint-washington/post/usaid-casts-itself-as-key-to-national-security/2011/11/07/gIQAlCw8uM_blog.html.

Jarosz, Lucy. 2009. "Energy, Climate Change, Meat, and Markets: Mapping the Coordinates of the Current World Food Crisis." *Geography Compass* 3:2065–2083.

Jessop, Bob. 1990. *State Theory: Putting the Capitalist State in Its Place.* University Park: Pennsylvania State University Press.

———. 2000. "The Crisis of the National Spatio-Temporal Fix and the Tendential Ecological Dominance of Globalizing Capitalism." *International Journal of Urban and Regional Research* 24:323–360.

———. 2001a. "Institutional Re(turns) and the Strategic-Relational Approach." *Environment and Planning A* 33:1213–1235.

———. 2001b. "State Theory, Regulation, and Autopoiesis: Debates and Controversies." *Capital and Class* 75:83–92.

———. 2002a. *The Future of the Capitalist State.* Cambridge, U.K.: Polity Press.

———. 2002b. "Liberalism, Neoliberalism, and Urban Governance: A State-Theoretical Perspective." *Antipode* 34:452–472.

———. 2008. *State Power: A Strategic-Relational Approach.* Cambridge, U.K.: Polity Press.

Killercoke.org. 2012. "The Campaign to Stop Killer Coke." Accessed March 14, 2012. http://www.killercoke.org/index.php.

Kodras, Janet. 1993. "Shifting Global Strategies of U.S. Foreign Food Aid, 1955–1990." *Political Geography* 12:232–246.

Kopp, Harry W., and Charles A. Gillespie. 2011. *Career Diplomacy: Life and Work in the U.S. Foreign Service.* 2nd ed. Washington, D.C.: Georgetown University Press.

Korf, Benedikt. 2007. "Antinomies of Generosity: Moral Geographies and Post-Tsunami Aid in Southeast Asia." *Geoforum* 38:366–378.

Lancaster, Carol. 2000. *Transforming Foreign Aid: United States Assistance in the 21st Century.* Washington, D.C.: Institute for International Economics.

Lancaster, Carol, and Ann Van Dusen. 2005. *Organizing U.S. Foreign Aid: Confronting the Challenges of the Twenty-First Century.* Washington, D.C.: Global Economy and Development Center, Brookings Institution.

Lawson, Victoria. 2007. *Making Development Geography.* London: Hodder Arnold.

Lederer, William J., and Eugene Burdick. 1958. *The Ugly American.* New York: W. W. Norton.

Lovett, William A., Alfred E. Eckes Jr., and Richard L. Brinkman. 1999. *U.S. Trade Policy: History, Theory and the WTO.* Armonk, N.Y.: M. E. Sharpe.

Luttwak, Edward. 1990. "From Geopolitics to Geo-Economics: Logic of Conflict, Grammar of Commerce." *National Interest* 20:17–23.

Massey, Doreen. 2004. "Geographies of Responsibility." *Geografiska Annaler, Series B, Human Geography* 86:5–18.

Mawdsley, Emma. 2007. "The Millennium Challenge Account: Neo-Liberalism, Poverty and Security." *Review of International Political Economy* 14:487–509.

Mayer, Martin. 1983. *The Diplomats*. Garden City, N.Y.: Doubleday.

McMichael, Philip. 2000. "Global Food Politics." In *Hungry for Profit: The Agribusiness Threat to Farmers, Food, and the Environment*, edited by Fred Magdoff, John Bellamy Foster, and Frederick H. Buttel, 125–143. New York: Monthly Review Press.

———. 2008. *Development and Social Change: A Global Perspective*. 4th ed. Thousand Oaks, Calif.: Pine Forge Press.

———. 2009. "A Food Regime Analysis of the 'World Food Crisis.'" *Agriculture and Human Values* 26:281–295.

Mitchell, Katharyne. 2010. "Ungoverned Space: Global Security and the Geopolitics of Broken Windows." *Political Geography* 29:289–297.

———. 2011. "Zero Tolerance, Imperialism, Dispossession." *ACME* 10:293–312.

Mohan, Giles, and Emma Mawdsley. 2007. "The War on Terror, American Hegemony and International Development." *Review of International Political Economy* 14:439–443.

Moss, Todd, David Roodman, and Scott Standley. 2005. *The Global War on Terror and U.S. Development Assistance: USAID Allocation by Country, 1998–2005*. Working Paper no. 62, July 2005. Washington, D.C.: Center for Global Development.

Mungcal, Ivy. 2011a. "The Lesser Evil: U.S. Aid Community Rallies behind $6B Cuts." Accessed March 15, 2012. http://www.devex.com/en/blogs/development-assistance-under-obama/us-aid-groups-commend-senate-state-foreign-appropriations-bill-but-make-case-against-further-aid-cuts.

———. 2011b. "U.S. Aid Cuts for FY2012 Approved by Senate Panel." Accessed March 15, 2012. http://www.devex.com/en/articles/senate-committee-approves-fy2012-state-foreign-operations-appropriations-bill.

Murphy, Sophia, and Kathy McAfee. 2005. *U.S. Food Aid: Time to Get It Right*. Minneapolis: Institute for Agriculture and Trade Policy.

Mustard, Allan. 2003. "An Unauthorized History of FAS." *Foreign Service Journal* 80:36–43.

Myers, Steven Lee. 2011. "Foreign Aid Set to Take a Hit in U.S. Budget Crisis." *New York Times*, October 3. Accessed March 15, 2012. http://www.nytimes.com/2011/10/04/us/politics/foreign-aid-set-to-take-hit-in-united-states-budget-crisis.html.

Obey, David R., and Carol Lancaster. 1988. "Funding Foreign Aid." *Foreign Policy* 71:141–155.

Ó Tuathail, Gearóid. 1986. "The Language and Nature of the 'New Geopolitics': The Case of U.S.–El Salvador Relations." *Political Geography Quarterly* 5:73–85.

———. 1993. "The Effacement of Place? U.S. Foreign Policy and the Spatiality of the Gulf Crisis." *Antipode* 25:4–31.

———. 1996. *Critical Geopolitics: The Politics of Writing Global Space*. Minneapolis: University of Minnesota Press.

———. 2000. "The Postmodern Geopolitical Condition: States, Statecraft, and Security at the Millennium." *Annals of the Association of American Geographers* 90:166–178.

Panitch, Leo. 1994. "Globalisation and the State." In *Socialist Register 1994: Between*

Globalism and Nationalism, edited by Ralph Miliband and Leo Panitch, 60–93. London: Merlin Press.

Panitch, Leo, and Sam Gindin. 2004. *Global Capitalism and American Empire*. London: Merlin Press.

Patrick, Stewart, and Kaysie Brown. 2007. *The Pentagon and Global Development: Making Sense of the DoD's Expanding Role. Working Paper no. 131, November 2007.* Washington, D.C.: Center for Global Development.

Peck, Jamie. 2001. "Neoliberalizing States: Thin Policies/Hard Outcomes." *Progress in Human Geography* 25:445–455.

Peck, Jamie, Nik Theodore, and Neil Brenner. 2009. "Postneoliberalism and Its Malcontents." *Antipode* 41 S1:94–116.

Peck, Jamie, and Adam Tickell. 2002. "Neoliberalizing Space." *Antipode* 34:380–404.

Peet, Richard, and Elaine Hartwick. 2009. *Theories of Development: Contentions, Arguments, Alternatives.* 2nd ed. New York: Guilford Press.

Peet, Richard, and Michael Watts. 1993. "Introduction: Development Theory and Environment in an Age of Market Triumphalism." *Economic Geography* 69:227–253.

PepsiCo Inc. 2011. "PepsiCo, World Food Programme and USAID Partner to Increase Food Production and Address Malnutrition in Ethiopia." Accessed March 15, 2012. http://www.pepsico.com/PressRelease/PepsiCo-World-Food-Programme-and -USAID-Partner-to-Increase-Food-Production-and-A09212011.html.

Phillips, Lynne, and Suzan Ilcan. 2004. "Capacity-Building: The Neoliberal Governance of Development." *Canadian Journal of Development Studies* 25:393–409.

Power, Marcus. 2003. *Rethinking Development Geographies*. London: Routledge.

Radelet, Stephen. 2003. "Bush and Foreign Aid." *Foreign Affairs* 82:104–117.

Rankin, Katharine N. 2004. *The Cultural Politics of Markets: Economic Liberalization and Social Change in Nepal.* Toronto: University of Toronto Press.

Roberts, Susan, Anna Secor, and Matthew Sparke. 2003. "Neoliberal Geopolitics." *Antipode* 35:886–897.

Robinson, William I. 2004. *A Theory of Global Capitalism: Production, Class, and State in a Transnational World.* Baltimore: Johns Hopkins University Press.

Rostow, Walt W. 1990. *The Stages of Economic Growth: A Non-Communist Manifesto.* 3rd ed. Cambridge: Cambridge University Press.

Roy, Ananya. 2010. *Poverty Capital: Microfinance and the Making of Development.* London: Routledge.

Sachs, Jeffrey D. 2005. "The Development Challenge." *Foreign Affairs* 84:78–90.

Shiva, Vandana. 2006. *Earth Democracy: Justice, Sustainability, and Peace.* London: Zed Books.

Silvey, Rachel. 2010. "Development Geography: Politics and 'the State' under Crisis." *Progress in Human Geography* 34:828–834.

Silvey, Rachel, and Katharine Rankin. 2011. "Development Geography: Critical Development Studies and Political Geographic Imaginaries." *Progress in Human Geography* 35:696–704.

Sklair, Leslie. 2001. *The Transnational Capitalist Class*. Malden, Mass.: Blackwell.

Slater, David. 1993. "The Geopolitical Imagination and the Enframing of Development Theory." *Transactions of the Institute of British Geographers* NS18:419–437.

———. 2004. *Geopolitics and the Post-Colonial: Rethinking North-South Relations*. Malden, Mass.: Blackwell.

Smith, Neil. 2003. *American Empire: Roosevelt's Geographer and the Prelude to Globalization*. Berkeley: University of California Press.

Sparke, Matthew. 2005. *In the Space of Theory: Postfoundational Geographies of the Nation State*. Minneapolis: University of Minnesota Press.

———. 2007a. "Acknowledging Responsibility for Space." *Progress in Human Geography* 31:7–15.

———. 2007b. "Geopolitical Fears, Geoeconomic Hopes, and the Responsibilities of Geography." *Annals of the Association of American Geographers* 97:338–349.

Sparke, Matthew, and Victoria Lawson. 2007. "Entrepreneurial Geographies of Global-Local Governance." In *A Companion to Political Geography*, edited by John Agnew, Katharine Mitchell, and Gerard Toal, 315–334. Malden, Mass.: Blackwell.

Strom, Stephanie. 2011. "PepsiCo to Foster Chickpeas in Ethiopia." *New York Times*, September 20. Accessed March 15, 2012. http://www.nytimes.com/2011/09/21/business/pepsicos-chick-pea-plan-includes-taking-on-famine.html.

Taylor, Peter J. 1999. "Locating the American Century: A World-Systems Analysis." In *The American Century: Consensus and Coercion in the Projection of American Power*, edited by David Slater and Peter J. Taylor, 1–16. Malden, Mass.: Blackwell.

Toner, Joseph S. 1962. "Organization of Our Foreign Aid Program." *Proceedings of the Academy of Political Science* 27:2–7.

Truman, David B. 1962. "The Domestic Politics of Foreign Aid." *Proceedings of the Academy of Political Science* 27:62–72.

Walker, Margath, Susan M. Roberts, John Paul Jones III, and Oliver Fröhling. 2008. "Neoliberal Development through Technical Assistance: Constructing Communities of Entrepreneurial Subjects in Oaxaca, Mexico." *Geoforum* 39:527–542.

Williamson, John. 2008. "A Short History of the Washington Consensus." In *The Washington Consensus Reconsidered: Towards a New Global Governance*, edited by Narcis Serra and Joseph E. Stiglitz, 14–30. Oxford: Oxford University Press.

Wisner, Ben. 1989. *Power and Need in Africa*. Trenton, N.J.: Africa World Press.

World Food Programme [WFP]. 2011. "WFP, PepsiCo and USAID Fight Child Malnutrition in Ethiopia." Accessed March 15, 2012. http://www.wfp.org/stories/wfp-pepsico-and-usaid-fight-child-malnutrition-ethiopia.

OFFICIAL GOVERNMENT SOURCES

Clinton, Hillary Rodham. 2011. "Remarks at the New Silk Road Ministerial Meeting, New York City, New York, September 22, 2011." Accessed March 15, 2012. http://www.state.gov/secretary/rm/2011/09/173807.htm.

Congressional Budget Office [CBO]. 1997. *The Role of Foreign Aid in Development.* Washington, D.C.: Congressional Budget Office.

Duffy, Sean P. 1991. *The Origins of the Agency for International Development: Foreign Assistance Reorganization in 1961* [USAID Document PN-ABL-500]. Washington, D.C.: USAID.

Ehrlich, Thomas. 1980. *Statement of Thomas Ehrlich, Director, United States International Development Cooperation Agency before the Committee on Foreign Affairs, House of Representatives, Tuesday, February 5, 1980* [USAID Document PN-AAU-174]. Washington, D.C.: IDCA.

Feed the Future [FTF]. 2010a. *Feed the Future Guide, May 2010.* Washington, D.C.: Feed the Future.

———. 2010b. *Honduras: FY 2010 Implementation Plan.* Washington, D.C.: Feed the Future.

———. 2011. "Progress." Accessed March 14, 2012. http://www.feedthefuture.gov/progress.

Ferris, George M., Jr. 1992. *The President's Commission on the Management of AID Programs: Report to the President: An Action Plan* [USAID Document PC-AAA-222]. Washington, D.C.: President's Commission on the Management of AID Programs.

Foreign Agricultural Service [FAS]. 1973. *Agricultural Trade and the Proposed Round of Multilateral Negotiations: Report Prepared at the Request of Peter Flanigan, Assistant to the President for International Economic Affairs, for the Council on International Economic Policy.* Washington, D.C.: Government Printing Office.

General Accounting Office [GAO]. 1993. *Foreign Assistance: AID Strategic Direction and Continued Management Improvements Needed [GAO/NSIAD-93-106].* Washington, D.C.: General Accounting Office.

———. 1998. "USAID's Reengineering at Overseas Missions, GAO/NSIAD-97-194." *International Journal of Technical Cooperation* 4:133–149.

———. 2003a. *Financial Management: Sustained Effort Needed to Resolve Long-Standing Problems at U.S. Agency for International Development [GAO-03-1170t].* Washington, D.C.: General Accounting Office.

———. 2003b. *Foreign Assistance: Strategic Workforce Planning Can Help USAID Address Current and Future Challenges [GAO-03-946].* Washington, D.C.: General Accounting Office.

———. 2003c. *Major Management Challenges and Program Risks: U.S. Agency for International Development [GAO-03-111].* Washington, D.C.: General Accounting Office.

Government Accountability Office [GAO]. 2011. *Foreign Assistance: The United States Provides Wide-Ranging Trade Capacity Building Assistance, but Better Reporting and Evaluation Are Needed [GAO-11-727].* Washington, D.C.: Government Accountability Office.

Ho, Melissa D., and Charles E. Hanrahan. 2011. *The Obama Administration's Feed the Future Initiative.* Washington, D.C.: Congressional Research Service.

Morss, Elliott R. 1980. *New Directions and Beyond: A Review of Accomplishments and*

an Agenda for the Future [USAID Document PD-AAM-506]. Washington, D.C.:
Congressional Research Service.

Nixon, Richard M. 1969. *New Directions in Foreign Aid: President Nixon's Message to the Congress* [USAID Document PC-AAA-593]. Washington, D.C.: The White House.

Pillsbury, Michael. 1993. AID *and Economic Policy Reform: Origins and Case Studies* [USAID Document PN-ABR-851]. Vienna, Va.: Policy Analysis International.

Shah, Rajiv. 2011a. "The Best Gesture of Partnership: Remarks to the Student Conference on U.S. Affairs, West Point, New York, November 4, 2011." Accessed March 15, 2012. http://www.usaid.gov/press/speeches/2011/sp111104.html.

———. 2011b. "Embracing Enlightened Capitalism: Remarks at the USAID Public-Private Partnership Forum, Washington, D.C., October 20, 2011." Accessed March 15, 2012. http://www.usaid.gov/press/speeches/2011/sp111020.html.

———. 2011c. "Statement by Dr. Rajiv Shah, Administrator, United States Agency for International Development Before the Senate Foreign Relations Committee, Wednesday, April 13, 2011." Accessed March 15, 2012. http://www.usaid.gov/press/speeches/2011/ty110413_1.html.

Udall, Morris K. 1961. "The Foreign Assistance Act of 1961: A Special Report by Congressman Morris K. Udall." Accessed March 15, 2012. http://www.library.arizona.edu/exhibits/udall/special/foreign.html.

United States Agency for International Development [USAID]. 1962. *Training for Development: AID Participant Training for Social and Economic Development of Cooperating Countries.* Washington, D.C.: USAID.

———. 1963. *Food for Peace: The Creative Use of America's Abundance in International Development.* Washington, D.C.: USAID.

———. 1964. *The* AID *Program* [USAID Document PN-ABT-248]. Washington, D.C.: USAID.

———. 1966. *The* AID *Story* [USAID Document PN-ABT-249]. Washington, D.C.: USAID.

———. 1975. *Implementation of "New Directions" in Development Assistance: Report to the Committee on International Relations on Implementation of Legislative Reforms in the Foreign Assistance Act of 1973* [USAID Document PN-ABT-558]. Washington, D.C.: Government Printing Office.

———. 1978. *Agency for International Development: Congressional Presentation, Fiscal Year 1979, Main Volume* [USAID Document PN-AAT-499]. Washington, D.C.: USAID.

———. 1980. *Agency for International Development: Congressional Presentation, Fiscal Year 1980, Main Volume* [USAID Document PD-AAP-858A]. Washington, D.C.: USAID.

———. 1981. *Agency for International Development: Congressional Presentation, Fiscal Year 1982, Main Volume (Amended Version)* [USAID Document PN-AAL-945]. Washington, D.C.: USAID.

———. 1982. *Agency for International Development: Congressional Presentation, Fiscal Year 1983, Main Volume* [USAID Document PD-ACE-292]. Washington, D.C.: USAID.

———. 1983. Video Recording No. 286.266, "Bureau for Private Enterprise AID." Records of the Agency for International Development, Record Group 286, National Archives and Record Administration (NARA) at College Park, Md.

———. 1984. *Agency for International Development: Congressional Presentation, Fiscal Year 1985, Main Volume* [USAID Document PD-AAP-154]. Washington, D.C.: USAID.

———. 1985. *Blueprint for Development: The Strategic Plan of the Agency for International Development* [USAID Document PN-AAS-485]. Washington, D.C.: USAID.

———. 1988. *Agency for International Development: Congressional Presentation, Fiscal Year 1989, Main Volume* [USAID Document PN-AAZ-241A]. Washington, D.C.: USAID.

———. 1992. *Agency for International Development: Congressional Presentation, Fiscal Year 1993* [USAID Document PN-ABK-398A]. Washington, D.C.: USAID.

———. 1993. *Agency for International Development: Congressional Presentation, Fiscal Year 1994* [USAID Document PN-ABN-978]. Washington, D.C.: USAID.

———. 1995. *Agency for International Development: Congressional Presentation, Fiscal Year 1996* [USAID Document PN-ABU-070]. Washington, D.C.: USAID.

———. 1997. *Agency for International Development: Congressional Presentation, Fiscal Year 1998* [USAID Document PN-ACA-130]. Washington, D.C.: USAID.

———. 2001a. *Budget Justification to the Congress, Fiscal Year 2002* [USAID Document PD-ABU-802]. Washington, D.C.: USAID.

———. 2001b. *United States Government Initiatives to Build Trade Related Capacity in Developing and Transition Countries: Main Report* [USAID Document PN-ACN-110]. Washington, D.C.: USAID.

———. 2002a. *Budget Justification to the Congress, Fiscal Year 2003* [USAID Document PD-ABZ-984]. Washington, D.C.: USAID.

———. 2002b. *A History of Foreign Assistance* [USAID Document PN-ACP-064]. Washington, D.C.: USAID.

———. 2003a. *Budget Justification to the Congress, Fiscal Year 2004* [USAID Document PD-ACE-110]. Washington, D.C.: USAID.

———. 2003b. "Remarks by Andrew S. Natsios, Administrator, U.S. Agency for International Development, Advisory Committee on Voluntary Foreign Assistance, Washington, D.C., May 14, 2003." Accessed March 15, 2012. http://www.usaid.gov/press/speeches/2003/sp030514.html.

———. 2003c. USAID *Strategy: Building Trade Capacity in the Developing World* [USAID Document PD-ABX-241]. Washington, D.C.: USAID.

———. 2003d. *U.S. Contributions to Trade Capacity Building: Improving Lives through Trade and Aid* [USAID Document PD-ABY-500]. Washington, D.C.: USAID.

———. 2004a. *Human Capital Strategic Plan, 2004–2008: Building a New Generation* [USAID Document PD-ACA-455]. Washington, D.C.: USAID.

———. 2004b. "Testimony of Administrator Andrew S. Natsios, United States Agency for International Development, before the Subcommittee on Foreign Operations, Committee on Appropriations, U.S. House of Representatives, April 1, 2004." Accessed March 15, 2012. http://www.usaid.gov/press/speeches/2004/ty040401.html.

———. 2004c. *U.S. Foreign Aid: Meeting the Challenges of the Twenty-First Century* [USAID Document PD-ABZ-322]. Washington, D.C.: USAID.

———. 2005a. *Fragile States Strategy* [USAID Document PD-ACA-999]. Washington, D.C.: USAID.

———. 2005b. *Measuring Fragility: Indicators and Methods for Rating State Performance* [USAID Document PN-ADD-462]. Washington, D.C.: USAID.

———. 2006a. *Policy Framework for Bilateral Foreign Aid* [USAID Document PD-ACG-244]. Washington, D.C.: USAID.

———. 2006b. *Foreign Assistance Framework (as of October 12, 2006)* [USAID Document PC-AAB-849]. Washington, D.C.: USAID.

———. 2007. *Supporting the USAID Mission: Staffing and Activities from Inception to Present Day* [USAID Document PN-ADM-027]. Washington, D.C.: USAID.

———. 2008. "Special Report: Global Food Crisis." *FrontLines* (June):7–10.

———. 2010a. "The Coca-Cola Company's Haiti Hope Project Momentum Continues with Investment from United States Government." Accessed March 14, 2012. http://www.usaid.gov/press/releases/2010/pr100818.html.

———. 2010b. *Honduras: Strategic Review, Feed the Future, December 17, 2010* [USAID Document PD-ACR-809]. Washington, D.C.: USAID.

———. 2011a. *The Development Response to Violent Extremism: Putting Principles into Practice* [USAID Document PD-ACS-400]. Washington, D.C.: USAID.

———. 2011b. "FWD: Famine War Drought Relief." Accessed March 14, 2012. http://action.usaid.gov/home.php.

———. 2011c. "Trade Capacity Building Database." Accessed March 15, 2012. http://tcb.eads.usaidallnet.gov/.

———. 2011d. USAID *Policy Framework 2011–15* [USAID Document PD-ACS-333]. Washington, D.C.: USAID.

U.S. Congress. 1973. "The Flanigan Report on Agriculture Trade Policy [Statements by Senator Hubert H. Humphrey]." *Congressional Record—Senate* 199, April 12:S12029-S12042.

———. 2011. "SA 956 [Reid Amendment]" *Congressional Record—Senate* 157, November 15, Part 1:S7457-S7513.

U.S. Department of State. 2006. *Fact Sheet [June 22, 2006]: U.S. Foreign Assistance Reform: Achieving Results & Sustainability in Support of Transformational Diplomacy* [USAID Document PC-AAB-574]. Washington, D.C.: Department of State.

———. 2011a. *Executive Budget Summary—Function 150 and Other International Programs, Fiscal Year 2012* [USAID Document PC-AAC-201]. Washington, D.C.: Department of State.

———. 2011b. "FY 2012 State and USAID—Core Budget." Accessed March 15, 2012. http://www.state.gov/s/d/rm/rls/fs/2011/156553.htm.

U.S. Department of State and USAID. 2007. *Strategic Plan, Fiscal Years 2007–2012* [USAID Document PD-ACJ-333]. Washington, D.C.: U.S. Department of State and USAID.

———. 2010. *Leading through Civilian Power: The First Quadrennial Diplomacy and Development Review* [USAID Document PD-ACQ-604]. Washington, D.C.: U.S. Department of State and USAID.

U.S. House of Representatives. 1973. *Mutual Development and Cooperation Act of 1973: Report of the Committee on Foreign Affairs Together with Minority and Additional Views on H.R. 9360 to Amend the Foreign Assistance Act of 1961, and for Other Purposes, Together with Minority Views.* Washington, D.C.: Government Printing Office.

———. 1976. *New Directions in Development Aid: Excerpts from the Legislation.* Washington, D.C.: Government Printing Office.

———. 1989. *Report of the Task Force on Foreign Assistance to the Committee on Foreign Affairs, U.S. House of Representatives.* Washington, D.C.: Government Printing Office.

———. 1994. *Mission of Foreign Agricultural Service, U.S. Department of Agriculture: Joint Hearings before the Subcommittee on Foreign Agriculture and Hunger of the Committee on Agriculture and the Subcommittee on Information, Justice, Transportation, and Agriculture of the Committee on Government Operations, House of Representatives, 103rd Congress, 1st Session, November 10 and 16, 1993.* Washington, D.C.: Government Printing Office.

———. 2010. *Oversight of the Feed the Future Initiative, Joint Hearing before the Subcommittee on International Organizations, Human, Rights and Oversight and the Subcommittee on Africa and Global Health of the Committee on Foreign Affairs, House of Representatives, 111th Congress, 2nd Session, July 20, 2010.* Washington, D.C.: Government Printing Office.

U.S. Senate. 1961. *Foreign Assistance Act of 1961: Report of the Committee on Foreign Relations, United States Senate on S. 1983.* Washington, D.C.: Government Printing Office.

———. 1995. *Foreign Aid Reduction Act of 1995: Report Together with Additional and Minority Views (to Accompany S. 961).* Washington, D.C.: Government Printing Office.

———. 2008. *Implementing Smart Power: Setting an Agenda for National Security Reform, Hearing before the Committee on Foreign Relations, United States Senate, 110th Congress, 2nd Session, April 24, 2008.* Washington, D.C.: Government Printing Office.

Weidner, Edward W. 1961. *The Reorganization of Foreign Aid of 1961: Part I* [USAID Document PN-AAY-198]. Washington, D.C.: USAID.

The White House. 2002. *The National Security Strategy of the United States of America.* Washington, D.C.: The White House.

———. 2006. *The National Security Strategy of the United States of America*. Washington, D.C.: The White House.

———. 2010. *The National Security Strategy of the United States of America*. Washington, D.C.: The White House.

PERSONAL INTERVIEWS

Anonymous. 2004. Interview with author, conducted December 14, 2004.

———. 2006a. Interview with author, conducted July 10, 2006.

———. 2006b. Interview with author, conducted July 12, 2006.

———. 2006c. Interview with author, conducted July 11, 2006.

———. 2006d. Interview with author, conducted December 15, 2006.

USAID ORAL HISTORY INTERVIEWS

Behoteguy, Scott. 1999. Oral History Interview, Foreign Affairs Oral History Collection. Georgetown University Library, August 11, 1997 [USAID Document PN-ACF-123].

Bernbaum, Marcia. 1999. Oral History Interview, Foreign Affairs Oral History Collection. Georgetown University Library, April 21, 1999 [USAID Document PN-ACH-621].

Birnbaum, Philip. 1996. Oral History Interview, Foreign Affairs Oral History Collection. Georgetown University Library, February 22, 1996 [USAID Document PN-ACA-039].

Church, Phillip Ely. 2001. Oral History Interview, Foreign Affairs Oral History Collection. Georgetown University Library, May 7, 1997 [USAID Document PN-ACM-897].

Herrick, Allison B. 1996. Oral History Interview, Foreign Affairs Oral History Collection. Georgetown University Library, April 1, 1996 [USAID Document PN-ABZ-153].

Kean, John H. 1995. Oral History Interview, Foreign Affairs Oral History Collection. Georgetown University Library, August 1, 1994 [USAID Document PN-ABZ-250].

Kleine, Herman. 1996. Oral History Interview, Foreign Affairs Oral History Collection. Georgetown University Library, February 14, 1996 [USAID Document PN-ABZ-778].

Love, Alexander Ray. 1998. Oral History Interview, Foreign Affairs Oral History Collection. Georgetown University Library, February 10, 1998 [USAID Document PN-ACF-333].

Lowenthal, William. 1996. Oral History Interview, Foreign Affairs Oral History Collection. Georgetown University Library, July 10, 1989 [USAID Document PN-ABZ-295].

North, W. Haven. 1995. Oral History Interview, Foreign Affairs Oral History Collection. Georgetown University Library, February 18, 1993 [USAID Document PN-ABZ-252].

Sinding, Steven W. 2001. Oral History Interview, Foreign Affairs Oral History Collection. Georgetown University Library, February 27, 2001 [USAID Document PN-ACN-391].

Venezia, Ronald F. 1996. Oral History Interview, Foreign Affairs Oral History Collection. Georgetown University Library, January 31, 1996 [USAID Document PN-ABZ-150].

Vreeland, Nena. 1998. Oral History Interview, Foreign Affairs Oral History Collection. Georgetown University Library, April 28, 1998 [USAID Document PN-ACD-984].

Wedeman, Miles. 1995. Oral History Interview, Foreign Affairs Oral History Collection. Georgetown University Library, September 12, 1995 [USAID Document PN-ABZ-151].

INDEX

Afghanistan, 45–46, 124, 130, 162n3; as fragile state, 118, 163n9; in global war on terror, 146, 151; reconstruction in, 120, 134

aid selectivity, 57–58, 108, 135, 139, 149, 151; deservedness and, 15, 89, 111, 116–124, 127, 160n5. *See also* Foreign Assistance Framework

Alliance for Progress, 46–47

austerity, 16, 126, 128, 132, 143; funding for USAID and, 145–147

basic needs approach, 52, 54–59, 61, 64, 72–73, 76, 77. *See also* poor majority

Burdick, Eugene, 31

Bush, George H. W., 52, 79, 82, 91

Bush, George W., 12, 18–19, 89, 103, 115, 162n7

Carter, Jimmy, 64

Chile, 47

civil society, 8, 23, 27, 54, 59, 135, 142, 156, 162n5; neoliberalism and, 75, 96; trade capacity building and, 97, 99, 107–108. *See also* global aid architecture; nongovernmental organizations

Clinton, Bill, 82, 92

Clinton, Hillary, 12, 146

Cold War, 5, 6, 14; American foreign aid as strategy in, 35–37, 43, 45, 48, 50, 65, 124–125, 160n3; development and, 9, 11, 26–27, 40; neoliberalization and end of, 52–53, 82–83, 107–108; post-Cold War political and economic environment, 3, 15, 84, 86–87,

89–92, 97, 132, 159n1. *See also under* geoeconomics; geopolitics; national security

development: expertise, 18, 44–45, 55–60, 70–71, 78, 96, 139–144, 150; informal imperialism and, 133, 154–157; as intervention, 9–11, 22–23, 25, 134, 136–137, 148, 152, 154; as process, 10–11, 51, 56, 59, 73, 153–154; strategic selectivity and, 26–27; theory, 4, 9–14, 26, 55, 58, 132, 156; transformational, 16, 112, 115–118, 120; women and, 57–58, 140. *See also* neoliberalism: globalization and, in uneven development; *and under* Cold War; geoeconomics; geopolitics; global war on terror; hegemony; national security; 9/11; smart power; terrorism

Development Experience Clearinghouse (DEC), 159n2, 165

Development Loan Fund (DLF), 43, 44

Diplomatic Readiness Initiative (DRI), 95, 161n3

Director of Foreign Assistance, 119

Economic Cooperation Agency (ECA), 28, 30

Economic Support Funds (ESF), 79–81

Ehrlich, Thomas, 61–62

Ethiopia, 136, 151, 152

Europe, 30, 36, 76; American aid to, 9, 27, 41, 102, 105; European states as aid donors, 33, 54, 92; European states as economic competitors and partners, 64–67, 71; Marshall Plan in, 28–29, 34 failed state. *See* state failure

Feed the Future (FTF), 16, 134–145, 150, 151, 154, 163n1; Food for Peace and, 43, 138; green power and, 42, 65; in Honduras, 136, 139, 140–144; informal imperialism and, 139, 141. *See also* food aid; food security

food aid, 31, 41–42, 65, 79, 92, 152; Food for Peace and, 43, 138; green power and, 42, 65. *See also* Feed the Future; food security

Food for Peace, 43, 138

food security, 135, 138–143, 149

Foreign Aid Reduction Act of 1995, 96

Foreign Assistance Act of 1961 (FAA), 28, 31, 38, 39, 41, 42, 80, 160n2; amendment to, in 1973, 53–54, 61; congressional debate about and passage of, 32–37; failed amendment to, in 1991, 91–92; failed replacement of, in 1994, 92; Hamilton-Gilman task force and, 80–82, 91. *See also* military aid

Foreign Assistance Framework, 16, 89, 109–113, 115–116, 118–127, 137, 162n6, 163n9; fragile states and, 115, 117–118, 120, 122–123, 163n10; informal imperialism and, 111, 118; restrictive states and, 120–122

fragile state. *See* Foreign Assistance Framework

free trade. *See* trade liberalization

General Accounting Office (GAO), 161n1

General Agreement on Tariffs and Trade (GATT), 65–67, 71, 85

geoeconomics: in Cold War, 20–21, 26, 29–30, 61; development and, 9–10, 55, 82–83, 129; "geoeconomic social," 5, 38, 55, 63–64; as geostrategic discourse, 2–8, 42, 130, 156; humanitarianism and, 64; post-9/11 articulation of, with geopolitics, 12, 13–16, 107–109,

113–118, 125–127, 134, 149–154; as secondary to geopolitics in U.S. strategies, 14, 17, 21–22, 38, 42, 45, 47. *See also* geopolitics

—neoliberalism and, 51–53, 68–70; as basis for USAID strategies, 76–77, 82–83, 85–88, 99, 130–132

geopolitics: in Cold War, 14, 17, 20–22, 27–30, 34–40, 45–50; critical, 3, 6, 17–20, 22; development and, 9–10, 42–43, 52–53, 68, 106; "geopolitical social," 5, 38; as geostrategic discourse, 2–8, 42; "neoliberal," 6, 107, 134; neoliberalism and, 77–79, 81–83, 86–90, 106, 132; post-9/11 articulation of, with geoeconomics, 12, 13–16, 107–109, 113–118, 125–127, 149, 152, 154; tensions between geoeconomics and, in late Cold War, 63, 69, 78–79; U.S. foreign aid programs and, 55, 61, 123–124, 135, 155, 160n5. *See also* geoeconomics

global aid architecture, 4, 7, 16, 101, 139, 154, 156

global war on terror, 6, 18, 86, 87, 110; development and, 4, 113–114, 129; state failure and, 107–109. *See also* national security; 9/11; terrorism

globalization, 12, 24, 82, 83, 84–86; American hegemony and, 6, 62; antiglobalization movements, 115, 125; 9/11 and, 6, 89. *See also* neoliberalism: globalization and, in fragile and failed states

Government Accountability Office (General Accounting Office), 161n1

Gramsci, Antonio, 10, 23, 133

green power, 42, 65

Haiti, 1, 136, 141, 152–153

Hamilton, Fowler, 44, 59

Hamilton-Gilman task force, 80–82, 91

Hart, Gillian, 10–11, 25, 133, 156

GEOGRAPHIES OF JUSTICE AND SOCIAL TRANSFORMATION